THE CATHOLIC UNIVERSITY OF AMERICA
CANON LAW STUDIES
No. 288

The Rogatory Commission

A HISTORICAL SYNOPSIS AND A COMMENTARY

BY

REVEREND MARION J. REINHARDT, S.T.B., J.C.L.
Priest of the Diocese of Brooklyn

A DISSERTATION

Submitted to the Faculty of the School of Canon Law of the Catholic University of America in Partial Fulfillment of the Requirements for the Degree of Doctor of Canon Law

THE CATHOLIC UNIVERSITY OF AMERICA PRESS
WASHINGTON, D. C.
1949

Nihil Obstat:

LUDOVICUS MOTRY, S.T.D., J.C.D.,
Censor Deputatus.

Washingtoni, die XIII Maii 1949.

Imprimatur:

✠ THOMAS EDMUNDUS MOLLOY, S.T.D.,
Episcopus Brooklyniensis.

Brooklyni, die XVI Maii 1949.

Printed by
THE PAULIST PRESS
401 WEST 59TH STREET
NEW YORK 19, N. Y.

51

TABLE OF CONTENTS

FOREWORD

It will be the purpose of this dissertion to examine the juridical institute of the rogatory commission according to the legislation of the Code of Canon Law and to describe its use by the tribunals of local ordinaries of the Latin rite. It would be impossible to pursue this end without, at times, making mention of other ecclesiastical tribunals. Throughout the treatise, however, it should be presumed that the word tribunal refers to the ecclesiastical courts of local ordinaries. Where other tribunals are intended, express mention of that fact will be made.

In the treatment of formal cases, the discussion of the nature of the power used in the execution of a rogatory commission has been brought forward considerably from the place where one would naturally expect to find it. This was thought advisable because the position that is taken on this fundamental point will influence very many of the opinions that are taken on other points throughout the commentary.

The writer takes this occasion to express his gratitude to His Excellency, the Most Reverend Thomas Edmund Molloy, S. T. D., Bishop of Brooklyn, for the opportunity of advanced study in Canon Law and for his generosity in making possible this publication. The writer likewise wishes to express his gratitude to the Most Reverend Raymond A. Kearney, S.T.D., J.C.D., Auxiliary Bishop of Brooklyn, and to the members of the Faculty of the School of Canon Law, The Catholic University of America, Washington, D. C., for their kind encouragement, learned guidance and valuable assistance in the preparation of this dissertation.

Part One

Historical Synopsis

CHAPTER I

THE DEVELOPMENT OF THE ROGATORY COMMISSION UP TO THE ENACTMENT OF THE CODE OF CANON LAW (1918)

Article 1. The Judicial Principles Necessitating the Rogatory Commission

Section 1. Jurisdiction can be Exercised Only Over Subjects

During their lifetime after the establishment of the Church the Apostles both collectively and individually enjoyed universality of jurisdiction. All Christians were subjects of the Apostles both as a group and as individuals. Before their death, however, the Apostles had already provided for the division of the Universal Church into distinct territorial units. There is also ample evidence that during the lifetime of St. John, the Apostle, there were individual bishops at the head of local communities.[1]

With the death of the last of the Apostles and the passing of his universal jurisdiction, the power of the successors of the Apostles was definitely limited to their respective territories and to the Christian souls who inhabited those territories. As one might expect from its importance, this principle of the limitation of the power of the local bishop to his own territory was early enunciated in ecclesiasti-

[1] Ryan, *Principles of Episcopal Jurisdiction,* The Catholic University of America Canon Law Studies, n. 120 (Washington, D. C.: The Catholic University of America Press, 1939), p. 38.

cal legislation. It was found in the Council of Antioch (341?),[2] in the I General Council of Constantinople (381),[3] in the III Council of Carthage (397),[4] and in the III Council of Orleans (538).[5] The various canons which these councils enacted in reference to the restriction of the power of the local bishop to his own subjects were finally received by Gratian into his *Concordia Canonum Discordantium* or *Decretum* as it is more commonly known today.[6]

[2] Capit. 22; cf. Turner, *Ecclesiae Occidentalis Monumenta Iuris Antiquissima: Canonum et Conciliorum Graecorum Interpretationes Latinae* (2 vols. in 7 parts, Oxonii: E Typographeo Clarendoniano, 1899-1939), II, 2, 296-298 (hereafter cited as Turner); Mansi, *Sacrorum Conciliorum Nova et Amplissima Collectio* (53 vols. in 60, Parisiis, 1901-1927), II, 1326 (hereafter cited as Mansi); Hardouin, *Acta Conciliorum et Epistolae Decretales ac Constitutiones Summorum Pontificum* (12 vols., Parisiis, 1714-1715), I, 604 (hereafter cited as Hardouin).

[3] Canons 2, 3; cf. Mansi, III, 566, 567; Hardouin, I, 809.

[4] Canon 20; cf. Mansi, III, 883; Hardouin, I, 963; Bruns, *Canones Apostolorum et Conciliorum Saeculorum IV-VII* (2 vols., Berolini, 1839), I, 126 (hereafter cited as Bruns). By all three of these authors an Isidorian redaction of the ninth century of the canons of the III Council of Carthage was used; cf. Mansi, III, 876, nota 1; Hardouin, I, 963; Bruns, I, 122, nota 8; Hinschius, *Decretales Pseudo-Isidorianae et Capitula Angilramni* (Lipsiae, 1863), p. 298 (hereafter cited as Hinschius).

[5] Canon 15; cf. Mansi, IX, 16; Hardouin, II, 1426; Bruns, II, 196-197.

[6] C. 7, 8, 9, C. IX, q. 2; c. 27, 28, C. VII, q. 1. According to the *Versio Hispana* and consequently also according to Isidor Mercator and Gratian, c. 9, C. IX, q. 2 is the third canon of the I General Council of Constantinople; according to the version of Dionysius Exiguus, it is a continuation of the second canon; according to the *Versio Prisca*, it is a continuation of the third canon of that Council; cf. Turner, II, 3, 414-416; Mansi, III, 567, 573; Hardouin, I, 809-810. Compare the text in Gratian of c. 7, C. IX, q. 2 with the Pseudo-Isidorian version found in Mansi, II, 1334; Hardouin, I, 603; Hinschius, p. 272. Compare the text in Gratian of c. 8, 9, C. IX, q. 2 with the Pseudo-Isidorian version of the second and third canons of the I General Council of Constantinople found in Mansi, III, 572-573; Hardouin, I, 810; Hinschius, p. 276. Also the text of c. 27, C. VII, q. 1 with the Pseudo-Isidorian version of the 20th canon of the III Council of Carthage in Mansi, III, 883; Hardouin, I, 963; Hinschius, p. 298. Apparently Gratian had used Pseudo-Isidorian sources for his version of these canons. The Pseudo-Isidorian collection was made from the *Collectio Hispana* seu *Isidoriana;* cf. Van Hove, *Commentarium Lovaniense in Codicem Iuris Canonici,* Vol. I, tom. 1, *Prolegomena ad Codicem Iuris Canonici* (2. ed., Mechliniae-Romae: H. Dessain, 1945), p. 306 (here-

Just as jurisdiction in general so too judicial power in particular was declared capable of being exercised only over subjects. This principle was enunciated by St. Paul [7] and was found later in the *Decretum Gratiani* [8] and in the Decretals of Gregory IX.[9] According to Bartholomew of Brescia (d. 1258) and Bernard of Parma (d. 1266) it was also had in the Code of Justinian.[10] In the Council of Trent the limitation of judicial power was considered as springing from the very nature of that power.[11]

In 1193 Pope Coelestine III (1191-1198) stated that a law putting a penalty on stealing obliged only the subjects of the lawgiver unless greater power had been delegated to him by a superior authority.[12] The usual interpretation given this decretal was that

after cited as *Prolegomena*); Cicognani, *Canon Law* (2. ed., authorized English version by J. O'Hara and F. Brennan, Philadelphia: Dolphin Press, 1935), p. 239. The *Collectio Hispana* seu *Isidoriana* had its origin in the *Versio Hispana* seu *Isidoriana* of the fifth century; cf. Cicognani, *op. cit.*, pp. 212, 218. For canon 22 of the Council of Antioch and canons 2 and 3 of the I General Council of Constantinople as they were in the *Versio Hispana*, cf. Turner, II, 2, 296; II, 3, 410-416. Gratian erroneously ascribed c. 28, C. VII, q. 1 to Pope Anacletus (Cletus?) instead of the III Council of Orleans; cf. Jaffé, *Regesta Pontificum Romanorum ab condita Ecclesia ad annum MCXCVIII* (2. ed. [by F. Kaltenbrunner (to the year 590), P. Ewald (from 590 to 882), and S. Loewenfeld (from 882 to 1198), and so referred to as JK, JE, and JL], 2 vols. in 1, Lipsiae, 1885-1888), JK, n. 6 (hereafter cited as Jaffé).

7 "Tu quis es, qui iudicas alienum servum? Domino suo stat, aut cadit."—St. Paul to the Romans, XIV, 4.

8 ". . . sententia non a suo iudice dicta, nichil firmitatis obtineat."—c. 7, C. II, q. 1. This was from a letter of Pope Gregory the Great, of the year 603; cf. Jaffé, JE, n. 1912.

9 "Sicut enim sentenita a non suo iudice lata non tenet, ita nec facta confessio coram ipso."—c. 4, X, *de iudiciis*, II, 1. This was a decretal of Alexander III (1159-1181) to the Archbishop of Salerno; cf. Jaffé, JL, n. 14091. Similarly in c. 3, X, *de consuetudine*, I, 4, and c. 3, X, *de parochiis, et alienis parochianis*, III, 29.

10 Cf. *Glossa Ordinaria* s. v. *a suo iudice*, ad c. 7, C. II, q. 1 and s. v. *non tenet*, ad c. 4, X, *de iudiciis*, II, 1. They both refer to C. 7 (48, 4).

11 "Quoniam igitur natura et ratio judicii illud exposcit, ut sententia in subditos dumtaxat feratur . . ."—Sess. XIV, *de poenitentia*, c. 7; cf. Schroeder, *Canons and Decrees of the Council of Trent: Original Text with English Translation* (St. Louis and London: B. Herder Book Co., 1941), p. 371.

12 C. 21, X, *de sententia excommunicationis*, V, 39; cf. Jaffé, JL, n. 17053.

the law could not oblige others than subjects because the lawgiver had no power to go beyond the limits of his jurisdiction.[13] In the period from the Council of Trent (1545-1563) to the enactment of the Code of Canon Law it was explicitly taught by some and unanimously presupposed by the remaining authors that laws could bind only the subjects of the lawgiver. Those who stopped to explain gave the reason that the making of a law was an act of jurisdiction and as such could be exercised only over subjects.[14]

Section 2. Contentious Jurisdiction Cannot be Exercised Outside the Territory

In the year 1200 Pope Innocent III (1198-1216), answering a letter of the French king, Philip Augustus (1180-1223), who had charged that an interdict published by the apostolic legate was of no force since the publication was executed by the latter outside the

[13] Cf. *Glossa Ordinaria* s. v. *non nisi subditi,* ad c. 21, X, *de sententia excommunicationis,* V, 39; also Hostiensis, *Commentaria in Quinque Decretalium Libros* (5 vols. in 3, Venetiis, 1581), Lib. V, tit. 39, c. 21, s. v. *subditos;* Boich, *In Quinque Decretalium Libros Commentaria* (Venetiis, 1576), Lib. V, tit. 39, c. 21, n. 15; Panormitanus, *Commentaria In Quinque Libros Decretalium* (5 vols. in 7, Venetiis, 1588), Lib. V, tit. 39, c. 21, n. 4. These works are hereafter cited as *Commentaria.* In these and similar commentaries on the decretals and the *Decretum Gratiani* which were written before the Council of Trent, the enumeration of the titles and chapters is made as they appear in the *Corpus Iuris Canonici;* consequently there may be at times a slight variation from the enumeration of the individual author.

[14] Reiffenstuel, *Ius Canonicum Universum* (5 vols. in 6, Romae, 1831-1834), Lib. I, tit. 2, n. 264 (hereafter cited as Reiffenstuel); Schmalzgrueber, *Ius Ecclesiasticum Universum* (5 vols. in 12, Romae, 1843-1845), Lib. I, tit. 2, n. 35 (hereafter cited as Schmalzgrueber); Pichler, *Ius Canonicum secundum Quinque Decretalium Titulos Explicatum* (2 vols., Venetiis-Ravennae, 1741), Lib. I, tit. 2, n. 46 (hereafter cited as Pichler); De Angelis, *Praelectiones Iuris Canonici* (5 vols. in 9, Romae, 1877-1891), Lib. I, tit. 2, n. 13; Santi, *Praelectiones Juris Canonici* (5 vols., Ratisbonae, Neo-Eboraci et Cincinnati, 1886), Lib. I, tit. 2, n. 30; Sanguineti, *Iuris Ecclesiastici Institutiones* (3. ed., Romae, 1896), n. 98; Grandclaude, *Jus Canonicum iuxta Ordinem Decretalium* (3 vols., Parisiis, 1882-1883), I, 141-142; Lombardi, *Iuris Canonici Privati Institutiones* (2. ed., 3 vols., Romae, 1901), I, 27; Aichner, *Compendium Juris Ecclesiastici* (6. ed., Brixinae, 1887), p. 698.

realm of the Franks,[15] responded that, even if the legate had gone beyond the borders of the Frankish realm, he didn't thereby exceed the limits of his delegation, for his mandate had also included the provinces of Vienne, Lyons and Besançon.[16] It was implied that, if the legate had gone beyond the territorial limits of his legation, he would not have been able to exercise there the powers of his office. The usual interpretation given to this decretal, which was known as *Novit,* was that the legate outside of his territory could not issue an interdict, since that required a judicial decision, and that neither a legate nor any other ordinary judge could sit in judgment outside of his territory.[17]

While it was the common interpretation of the decretal *Novit* that the interdict of the legate would not have been binding on account of the territorial limitation on the use of judicial power, it must be admitted that this reason was not expressed by Innocent III in the decretal itself. Clearer mention of this principle of the limitation of the use of judicial power to one's own territory was given by Pope Clement V (1305-1314) in a constitution he issued at the Council of Vienne (1311-1312). Admitting that it was generally forbidden by canon law that bishops use their jurisdiction in the diocese of another, Clement V made the exception that bishops who were forcibly and unjustly expelled from their sees could proceed judicially against those who expelled them, even though they themselves were outside their dioeceses.[18] This constitution stated that in general the canons had forbidden that one who was outside his territory should use his jurisdiction there in the diocese of another.[19] Jurisdiction was understood in the specific sense of con-

15 *Casus* ad c. 7, X, *de officio legati,* I, 30.

16 C. 7, X, *de officio legati,* I, 30; cf. Potthast, *Regesta Pontificum Romanorum inde ab anno post Christum natum MCXCVIII ad annum MCCCIV* (2 vols., Berolini, 1874-1875), n. 1074 (hereafter cited Potthast).

17 *Glossa Ordinaria* s. v. *terminos,* ad c. 7, X, *de officio legati,* I, 30.

18 C. un., *de foro competenti,* II, 2, in Clem.

19 The determination of the meaning of the word jurisdiction as it was used in medieval canon law is not easy. In classical Roman Law jurisdiction was a public power of judging about the rights of parties according to the norms prescribed by law. Justinian however began the extension of the term *ius dicere* to include the whole power of ruling subjects. In this sense it was

tentious jurisdiction, such as is exercised in the settling of disputes and disagreements or when there is opposition to the exercise of jurisdiction itself.[20] Thus the exercise of contentious jurisdiction

used by Gregory the Great. Cf. Kerckhove, "De Notione Iurisdictionis in Iure Romano," *Jus Pontificium,* XVI (1936), 49-65 (hereafter cited as *Jus Pont.*). In canon law in the period from Gratian to Sicard of Cremona (1140-1180) the word *iurisdictio* was practically equal to *lex dioecesana.* Under the effect of the Romanists, the term was narrowed in the period from Huguccio to Ioannes Teutonicus to cover not only administrative power that was solely spiritual but also acts that depended on the power of Orders. In the period from the IV Lateran Council (1215) to Bernard of Parma (1250), the notion of jurisdiction simply meant a public power of ruling a perfect society, including legislative, judiciary and coercive efficacy. At this time it excluded the power of Orders and the administration of ecclesiastical temporal matters. Cf. Van de Kerckhove, "De Notione Iurisdictionis apud Decretistas et priores Decretalistas," *Jus Pont.,* XVIII (1938), 10-14; also Hilling, "Über den Gebrauch des Ausdrucks *Iurisdictio* im Recht während der ersten Hälfte des Mittelalters," *Archiv für katholisches Kirchenrecht,* CXVIII (1938), 165-170.

20 *Glossa Ordinaria* s. v. *iurisdictionem,* ad c. un., *de foro competenti,* II, 2; cf. also Zabarella, *Commentaria in Clementinarum Volumen* (Venetiis, 1504), Lib. II, tit. 2, cap. 1. The term contentious jurisdiction was common in Roman Law and was considered the use of jurisdiction *inter invitos;* cf. *Glossa Ordinaria* s. v. *contentiosam,* ad D. (1, 16) 2. Which particular acts belonged to contentious jurisdiction was not clear, at least in the minds of the earlier decretalists. Ioannes Andreae held that contentious power included the power to excommunicate, absolve, confer benefices and to delegate tribunals; cf. *Glossa Ordinaria* s. v. *iurisdictionem,* ad c. un., *de foro competenti,* II, 2, in Clem. Ioannes Teutonicus conceded that under certain conditions tribunals could be delegated by one outside his territory, i. e., if the delegation did not require a judicial hearing and it was willingly accepted; cf. *Glossa Ordinaria* s. v. *terminos,* ad c. 7, X, *de officio legati,* I, 30. Hostiensis held that benefices could be conferred outside the territory; cf. *Commentaria,* Lib. I, tit. 30, c. 7, n. 6. They all agreed that a judge could not adjudicate a trial outside the territory, and that when any act of jurisdiction required a court session it could not be done outside the territory. In Panormitanus is had the doctrine that contentious jurisdiction embraced all things which required a judicial hearing by a tribunal; cf. *Commentaria,* Lib. I, tit. 30, c. 7, n. 3. This eventually became the accepted doctrine; cf. Pirhing, *Jus Canonicum in V Libros Decretalium* (5 vols. in 4, Dilingiae, 1722), Lib. I, tit. 31, n. 2 (hereafter cited as Pirhing); Reiffenstuel, Lib. I, tit. 29, n. 8; Ferraris, *Prompta Bibliotheca Canonica, Iuridica, Moralis, Theologica, necnon Ascetica, Polemica, Rubricistica, Historica* (ed. noviss., 8 vols., Parisiis, 1852-1857), s. v. *Jurisdictio,* n. 4 (hereafter cited as *Prompta Bibliotheca*); Leurenius, *Forum Ecclesiasti-*

was limited to one's proper territory. A judge was not permitted to use his jurisdiction outside his territory with the exception of the case stated by Pope Clement V. This limitation of contentious jurisdiction was still an accepted principle in the early twentieth century before the publication of the Code of Canon Law.[21]

The territorial limitation on the exercise of contentious jurisdiction was closely connected with the conception of a diocese in Decretal Law. A diocese was a territory in which a bishop had ordinary jurisdiction. In any place within its boundaries he was able to bring force to bear and also set up a tribunal for the hearing of cases.[22] Only within the diocese did the bishop have contentious jurisdiction.[23] Leaving his diocese he was stripped of it: [24] he was no longer a judge but had the status of a private person.[25] Apparently,

cum . . . Jus Canonicum Universum (5 vols. in 4, Venetiis, 1729), Lib. I, tit. 29, quaes. 671, n. 2; Mocchegiani, *Jurisprudentia Ecclesiastica* (3 vols., Friburgi Brisgoviae, 1904-1905), I, n. 819.

[21] Cf. Wernz, *Ius Decretalium* (2. ed., 6 vols., Romae et Prati, 1906-1913), V, n. 314; Lega, *Praelectiones in Textum Iuris Canonici: De Iudiciis Ecclesiasticis* (4 vols., Romae, 1896-1901), I, n. 365 (hereafter cited as *De Iudiciis Ecclesiasticis*); Sebastianelli, *De Iudiciis Ecclesiasticis*, Pars Prima, *De Iudiciis Civilibus* (2. ed., Ratisbonae, Neo-Eboraci et Cincinnati, 1906), n. 126 (hereafter cited as *De Iudiciis Civilibus*).

[22] *Glossa Ordinaria*, s. v. *dioecesim* et *territorium*, ad c. 2, *de constitutionibus*, I, 2, in VI°.

[23] *Glossa Ordinaria* s. v. *terminos*, ad c. 7, X, *de officio legati*, I, 30. To this gloss which he took from Ioannes Teutonicus, Bernard of Parma added that by going out of his territory a judge was deprived of his authority and his jurisdiction immediately expired. Later glossators admitted that this was true if a judge in the manner of a legate left the territory after he had completely terminated his mission. If only temporarily he crossed the borders, he was deprived of his contentious jurisdiction for the time being but he still maintained his voluntary jurisdiction; cf. Guido de Bayso, *In Decretorum Volumen Commentaria* (Venetiis, 1577), C. IX, q. 2, c. 2, n. 2; also Ioannes Andreae, *Commentaria Novella* (5 vols. in 4, Venetiis, 1505), Lib. I, tit. 30, c. 7.

[24] *Summarium*, c. un., *de foro competenti*, II, 2, in Clem.; cf. Guido de Bayso, *In Decretorum Volumen Commentaria*, C. XI, q. 1, c. 16, n. 2.

[25] Cf. the marginal note to the *Glossa Ordinaria* s. v. *iurisdictionem*, ad c.

for this reason, acts placed outside the territory were invalid.[26]

In the period after the glossators the authors continued to regard the bishop as deprived of his power when outside the diocese, with the consequent effect that any judicial act he performed would not be binding.[27]

In the eighteenth century F. Schmier (d. 1728) [28] and Pichler (d. 1736) [29] explicitly taught that the exercise of contentious jurisdiction outside the territory was invalid. Other authors stated that voluntary and contentious jurisdiction differed in this that the former could be validly and sometimes licitly exercised outside the territory, while the latter could not be exercised outside the territory. Apparently they meant to say that the use of contentious jurisdiction outside the territory was invalid.[30] Up to the publication of the Code canonical writers continued to teach that a judge

un., de foro competenti, II, 2, in Clem.; also Panormitanus, Commentaria, Lib. I, tit. 30, c. 7, n. 3.

[26] "Citatio non valet."—*Casus* ad c. un., *de foro competenti,* II, 2, in Clem.

[27] Tuschus, *Practicae Conclusiones Iuris in Omni Foro Frequentiores* (8 vols., Lugduni, 1634; *Additiones,* Vol. IX, Lugduni, 1670), Littera I, concl. 546, n. 23; Begnudelli Basso, *Bibliotheca Juris Canonico-Civilis Practica* (ed. novissima, 4 vols., Mutinae, 1757-1758), s. v. *Episcopus,* n. 82. Cf. also Paulus Piasecus, *Praxis Episcopalis* (Coloniae Agrippinae, 1620), p. 253; Erasmus a Chokier, *Tractatus de Jurisdictione Ordinarii in Exemptos* (2 vols. in 1, Coloniae Agrippinae, 1629) I, 192-193; G. Ubertus, *De Citationibus* (Romae, 1680), Cap. 11, n. 26; Blasius Altimarus, *Tractatus de Nullitatibus* (2 vols., Neapoli, 1678-1682), I, p. 467; Ioannes Baptista Ventriglia, *Praxis Rerum Notabilium* (2 vols. in 1, Venetiis, 1694), I, 193.

[28] *Jurisprudentia Canonico-Civilis* seu *Jus Canonicum Universum* (2 vols., Venetiis, 1754), Lib. I, tract. 5, c. 8, n. 12 (hereafter cited as Schmier).

[29] *Ius Canonicum secundum Quinque Decretalium Titulos Explicatum,* Lib. II, tit. 2, n. 7.

[30] Pirhing, Lib. I, tit. 31, n. 2; Schmalzgrueber, Lib. I, tit. 32, n. 5; Ferraris, *Prompta Bibliotheca,* s. v. *Jurisdictio,* n. 5; Reiffenstuel, Lib. I, tit. 29, n. 9. Reiffenstuel's doctrine can also be deduced from his statements that one was not required to obey a judge who was outside of his territory. If such a decree were illicit but valid, it would give rise to an obligation; cf. *Regulae Juris,* XXIV, n. 8, and LX, n. 6.

acted invalidly outside his territory.[31] No one can be found who taught otherwise.

From the period of Decretal Law, therefore, to the publication of the Code of Canon Law it was a firmly established principle that contentious jurisdiction could not be exercised outside one's proper territory. The origin of this principle before Decretal Law is not known with certitude. In his commentary on the decretal *Novit,* Ioannes Teutonicus (d. 1245) made reference to c. 7, C. IX, q. 2, to prove that a judge could not hear a trial in the territory of another.[32] This canon was chapter 22 of the Council of Antioch.[33] It does not however prove what Ioannes Teutonicus intended. The most useful phrase, *ad aliquid ordinandum,* is not authentic: in the version of Dionysius Exiguus the reading *super ordinatione cuiusquam* is found; in the *Versio Hispana* seu *Isidoriana, ad aliquem ordinandum.*[34] Evidently this referred to the elevation of an individual into the hierarchy of Orders rather than to the exercise of judicial power.

The phrase that followed in the text of Gratian, *nullatenus ad alios pertinentes iudicare praesumat,* did not exclude a bishop from judging his own subjects while he was outside of his territory. But here a more general reading occurred in the version of Dionysius Exiguus, namely: *nam si ordinare non potuerit, nullatenus iudicare.* This text could possibly have implied that a bishop was prohibited from judging his own subjects as well as the subjects of others. However, one does not expect that a conclusion go beyond the reason that substantiates it. Here a bishop was forbidden to judge, and that was a conclusion from his being forbidden to ordain. But even according to the version of Dionysius Exiguus a bishop was forbidden by this chapter of the Council of Antioch to ordain those who were subject to others, but not necessarily his own subjects.

[31] Lega, *De Iudiciis Ecclesiasticis,* I, n. 365; Icard, *Praelectiones Juris Canonici* (3 vols., Lutetiae Parisiorum, 1859), I, n. 249; Craisson, *Manuale Totius Juris Canonici* (5. ed., 4 vols., Pictavii, 1877), I, n. 281.

[32] *Glossa Ordinaria* s. v. *terminos,* ad c. 7, X, *de officio legati,* I, 30.

[33] Cf. *supra,* p. 2, footnote 2.

[34] Cf. Turner, II, 2, 296-297. The *Collectio Hispana* seu *Isidoriana* had already contained the reading *ad aliquid ordinandum;* cf. Turner, II, 2, 296, note to line 5 of the *Versio Isidori.*

Thus the appeal of Ioannes Teutonicus to previous ecclesiastical legislation for the restriction of the use of contentious jurisdiction to one's proper territory does not seem efficacious.[35] Ioannes Teutonicus seemed to realize this himself as in the *Glossa Ordinaria* to the *Decretum Gratiani* he appealed to the decretal *Novit* for ecclesiastical legislation forbidding the use of contentious jurisdiction outside of the territory.[36] He seems not to have known any ecclesiastical legislation either in Gratian or before Gratian which would substantiate this principle.

Gratian also seems to indicate that up to his time there was no ecclesiastical legislation which prohibited the use of contentious jurisdiction in the territory of another. He gave the general principle that, if a bishop was outside of his territory, he was not to mingle in the affairs of the bishop in whose territory he was a visitor. He explained that a bishop outside of his territory was neither to ordain to Orders nor to administer things which did not pertain to him.[37] This did not necessarily bar a bishop outside of his diocese from handling ecclesiastical affairs even in a judicial manner, as long as they were matters of his own concern.

To prove his statement that a judge could not conduct trials in the territory of another, Ioannes Teutonicus, in addition to the

[35] Ioannes Andreae (*Glossa Ordinaria* s. v. *canonibus,* ad c. un., *de foro competenti,* II, 2, in Clem.) appealed also to c. 8, 9, C. IX, q. 2, and c. 27, 28, C. VII, q. 1, which were respectively the second and third canons of the I General Council of Constantinople, the twentieth canon of the III Council of Carthage and the fifteenth canon of the III Council of Orleans; cf. *supra,* p. 2, footnotes 2-5. Certainly none of these canons explicitly and clearly forbid the use of contentious jurisdiction in the territory of another with one's own subjects. This is even more manifest after a study of the early versions of these canons. The canons referred to by Ioannes Andreae very definitely forbid a bishop to mingle in the affairs of another bishop both as regards the use of jurisdiction and as regards the use of Orders. But more than this they do not prove.

[36] *Glossa Ordinaria* s. v. *ordinandum,* ad c. 7, Q. IX, q. 2. The very wording of this gloss seems to indicate that Ioannes Teutonicus did not regard the canon as referring to the use of contentious jurisdiction over one's own subjects. The gloss seems to offer an additional case not covered by the canon.

[37] *Dictum Gratiani* ante c. 7, C. IX, q. 2.

decretal *Novit* and the legislation from the Council of Antioch as had in Gratian, called upon the three following laws from the *Digest* of Justinian: [38]

> Praeses provinciae in suae provinciae homines tantum imperium habet, et hoc dum in provincia est; nam si excesserit, privatus est.[39]
>
> Extra territorium ius dicenti impune non paretur. Idem est et si supra iurisdictionem suam velit ius dicere.[40]
>
> Omnes proconsules statim quam urbem egressi fuerint habent iurisdictionem, sed non contentiosam, sed voluntariam.[41]

These excerpts from Roman Law clearly seem to contain the principle found in the decretals and the decretalists as regards the use of contentious jurisdiction outside of the proper territory of the judge. In view of the lack of evidence for ecclesiastical legislation before and at the time of Gratian on the use of judicial power outside of the territory, one may conclude that Roman Law exercised an influence in the formulation of the decretal legislation of Popes Innocent III and Clement V, and in clarifying the minds of the glossators in this regard.

Article 2. The Use of the Rogatory Commission in Citation

Section 1. Before the Council of Trent

In the period before the Council of Trent there seems not to have been any explicit ecclesiastical legislation regarding the citation of a party or of a witness who was outside of the territory wherein the prosecution of the trial proceeded. A certain amount of judicial speculation with regard to the citing of such persons

[38] *Glossa Ordinaria* s. v. *ordinandum,* ad c. 7, Q. IX, q. 2.

[39] D. (1, 18) 3. This law was ascribed by the compilers of the *Digest* to Paul (d. 228).

[40] D. (2, 1) 20. This law likewise was attributed by the compilers of the *Digest* to Paul.

[41] D. (1, 16) 2. This law was ascribed to the jurist Marcian, a younger contemporary of Paul.

was aroused by the decretal *Romana* of Innocent IV (1243-1254). This decretal in the part which is of interest here reads as follows:

> Contrahentes vero aliarum dioecesum super contractibus, initis in Remensi dioecesi ab eisdem, nisi inveniantur ibidem, trahere coram se non debent invitos, licet in possessionem bonorum, quae ibi habent, etiam quum alibi copiam sui faciant, si eorum auctoritate citati comparere contemnant, possint missionem facere contra eos, vel, si forte malitiose se ipsos occultent, ne citatio perveniat ad eosdem, decernere faciendam in possessionem bonorum, quae in alia etiam dioecesi obtinere noscuntur; sed tunc loci dioecesanus ad denunciationem ipsorum faciet huismodi missionem.[42]

In commenting on the words *"si eorum auctoritate,"* Hostiensis (d. 1271) declared that they were to be understood in the sense that the contracting party was to be cited if he was found in the territory wherein the trial was held.[43] If the party did not make an appearance within the judge's territory, the judge was not able to cite him. Apparently this meant, according to Hostiensis, that the judge's power of citing someone before the court was restricted within his own territory. The judge could, however, intimate by a letter to the person that his presence was desired at the seat of the trial. In addition the person could be cited outside of the territory in accordance with the decretal *Romana*. What Hostiensis meant by this is difficult to say. Possibly he contemplated the aid which could be furnished by the tribunal of the place where the person actually was found. If this assumption is correct, then it was possible also that Hostiensis did not consider the judge obliged to make the citation.[44]

[42] C. 1, § 3, de foro competenti, II, 2, in VI°.

[43] *Commentaria, Liber Sextus,* Lib. II, tit. 2, c. 2, n. 11. The *Liber Sextus* of Hostiensis as mentioned here was not a commentary on the *Liber Sextus* of Boniface VIII, who actually lived after Hostiensis, but a commentary on the decretals of Innocent IV which was added to certain editions of Hostiensis' work. Cf. Van Hove, *Prolegomena,* p. 480, footnote 7. The *missio in bona* mentioned in the decretal *Contrahentes* pointed to a temporary sequestration granted in consequence of existing contumacy. For this see *infra,* p. 40.

[44] *Commentaria,* Lib. III, tit. 4, c. 11, n. 6.

Durantis (d. 1296) clearly held that a judge could not cite a party who was outside of his territory. This, he claimed, followed from the doctrine of the civilist, Ubertus de Bobio (d. circa 1245), and was based on the principle of the *Digest* of Justinian, namely, that outside of his territory a judge had no jurisdiction. In order that the person who was outside of the judge's territory might be cited, the judge of the trial had to petition the judge of the place to cite the person who was found in his territory.[45]

In his commentary on the decretal *Romana* Ioannes Andreae (d. 1348) felt that it was clear from the wording itself that the assistance of the other tribunal was not required if there was a question merely of citing a person outside of the judge's territory.[46] In this matter he followed the doctrine of the canonist Goffredus de Trano (d. 1245).[47] The same doctrine was taught by the civilists Cynus Pistoriensis (d. 1336 or 1337) and Iacobus de Arena. Ioannes Monachus (wrote ca. 1300) also regarded this view as tenable, but held that it was safer to use the instrumentality of the other tribunal.[48]

Against the objection that a judge could not adjudicate an issue outside of his territory, Ioannes Andreae answered that to cite a party was not the equivalent of adjudicating his cause, but simply implied a search after judicial testimony. Following a distinction supposedly made by Ioannes Monachus, he pointed out that in a citation there are two component elements, namely, the interlocutory decree, which by some was called a sentence, and the act of inviting a person to appear in court. The interlocutory decree, which determined that a person was to be cited, was an act of jurisdiction, and, therefore, could not be executed outside of the territory. But the second component element did not connote an act of jurisdiction, for it could be accomplished through a simple announcement.

[45] *Speculum Iuris* (4 vols. in 3, Venetiis, 1577), Lib. II, Partic. I, *De Citatione*, 4, § *Sequitur*, n. 18; also *ibidem*, *De compententis iudicis aditione*, 1, § *Generaliter*, n. 5.

[46] *Commentaria Novella* (6 vols., Venetiis, 1505), *Liber Sextus*, Lib. II, tit. 2, c. 4, n. 4.

[47] *Ibidem*, n. 2; cf. also Durantis, *Speculum Iuris*, Lib. II, Partic. I, *De competentis iudicis aditione*, 1, § *Generaliter*, n. 5.

[48] All three according to Ioannes Andreae, *ibidem*, n. 4.

The act by which the announcement of his desired presence in court was made to a person could be executed outside of the territory of the judge of the trial. It could be undertaken simply at the judge's behest. Since the act was concerned primarily with the conduct of the trial within the proper territory, and thus affected the cited party only indirectly, the question of the rightful jurisdiction was not at stake. If the cited party did not respond, he could be declared contumacious for his lack of interest in contesting the judicial issue at court, and the judge could then permit the plaintiff to take possession of the property of the one who had proved contumacious. This was the procedure that could be followed in civil suits concerning contracts or property. But in criminal trials, wherein the penalty for the spurned citation would have affected the party directly, it was necessary for the execution of the citation to enlist the assistance of the court within whose jurisdiction the party was resident.[49]

Thus, according to Ioannes Andreae, a rogatory commission was not essential for the citing of a party outside of the territory of the judge in the event of a civil suit about property or a contract. In criminal trials, however, wherein the act of citation directly affected the cited person, the judge of the trial had to seek recourse with and enlist the help of the tribunal of the place where the person was resident. This recourse was designated with the word *"rogamus."*[50] It will be seen, however, that in criminal trials, at least when they involved serious crimes, the ordinary procedure was that of extradition, which evidently, even in the measure in which the citation played a part, directly affected the person.

Panormitanus (d. 1453) agreed with Ioannes Andreae on the point that the party outside of the territory could be cited by the judge of the trial even apart from any aid given by a second tribunal. But in addition he adopted the more liberal view in accordance with which the judge of the trial could also inflict a penalty upon the absent subject for his contumacy in the event that the citation had been spurned by him.[51]

[49] *Commentaria Novella, Liber Sextus,* Lib. II, tit. 2, c. 1, nn. 4-5.
[50] *Casus* ad § *Contrahentes,* c. 1, *de foro competenti,* II, 2, in VI°.
[51] *Commentaria,* Lib. II, tit. 2, c. 20, nn. 41-42.

Section 2. From the Council of Trent to the Code

In the period before the Council of Trent there were two main attitudes toward the use of the rogatory commission with reference to the citing of a person who was outside of the territory of the judge who was conducting the trial. Durantis on the one hand had held the view that the use of the rogatory commission was a matter of necessity in such a case, and he based this on the principle that outside of his territory the judge had no jurisdiction. Ioannes Andreae represented the opposite view, namely, that while the rogatory commission was an instrument of utility, it was not a matter of necessity. Admitting the principle that a judge has no jurisdiction outside of his territory, he denied that the delivery of a decree of citation by the court beadle *(cursor)* to the desired party implied any act of jurisdiction.

Such was the dispute before the Council of Trent, and such it remained until the time of the present Code of Canon Law.[52] This problem, however, was definitely settled by the Code when it took effect on May 19, 1918. The Code provided that the copy of the citation had to be delivered to the desired party wherever he might be found, and to this effect the beadle could enter even another diocese, provided that the judge of the case considered it expedient, and ordered him to do so.[53] Corroborating evidence that previous to the present Code there was no legislation which permitted the beadle to enter the diocese of another bishop is had from the fact that Cardinal Gasparri (d. 1934) did not provide any annotations in revelation of any source-material for this particular provision in the Code. Thus the Code ruled out the absolute necessity of the rogatory commission for the summoning of persons outside of the territory of the judge presiding over the case. This held true for the parties in the trial and at least for such witnesses who were subject to that particular judge.

Among those who contended for the necessity of the rogatory commission in the summoning of a person outside of the territory

52 "Non convenit inter DD. an citationis decretum in alieno territorio per apparitorem denunciari possit."—Lega, *De Iudiciis Ecclesiasticis*, I, n. 408.

53 Canon 1717, §§ 1-2.

of the court one may mention Nicolaus Fermosinus (d. 1669), who based his opinion on that of Durantis and Felinus Sandaeus (d. 1503).[54] This doctrine still received support even in the beginning of the twentieth century, for it was accepted by Wernz (d. 1914), who mentioned Maranta (d. 1530) and Leurenius (d. 1723) as having held the same doctrine.[55]

The opinion, however, which thought of the rogatory commission as an expedient possibility rather than as an imperative necessity for the summoning of a person outside of the territory of the court seems to have had a larger number of adherents. Schmalzgrueber (d. 1735) mentioned three ways for making such a citation: first, the citation could be delivered outside of the territory by the beadle who was sent by the judge of the trial; secondly, it could be done by means of a request to the judge of the place to the effect that he actually cite the person and have the citation executed by his own beadle; and, lastly, it could be accomplished by means of an edict, which, he added, could be issued only if the other two possibilities were lacking. Schmalzgrueber indicated that in his opinion either of the first two methods could be used. Under the particular circumstances of the individual case the one might be more expedient than the other, but the choice between the two depended on expediency rather than on necessity.[56] This had also been the doctrine of Fagnanus (d. 1678) [57] and De Luca (d. 1683). The latter, however, felt that the citation as made through a rogatory commission proved more expedient, especially when the danger of physical harm loomed for the beadle in the event that he tried to

[54] *Opera Omnia* (2. ed., 14 vols., Coloniae Allobrogum, 1741), tit. *De foro competenti*, c. 19, q. 29, nn. 5-7. According to Fermosinus the judge had to use the rogatory commission to cite his own subjects who were outside of his territory. In this case the judge of the trial appealed to the judge of the place where the desired person actually was. This judge then issued the decree of citation. According to Fermosinus this was the general practice of ecclesiastical tribunals of the time.

[55] *Ius Decretalium*, V, n. 402.

[56] *Ius Ecclesiasticum Universum*, Lib. II, tit. 3, n. 23.

[57] *Commentaria in V Libros Decretalium* (5 vols., Romae, 1661), Lib. II, tit. *de foro competenti*, c. 20, n. 12.

deliver a citation outside of his territory.[58] More modern authors who followed this opinion were Bouix (d. 1870)[59] Sebastianelli (d. 1920) [60] and Lega (d. 1935).[61]

ARTICLE 3. EXTRADITION

Section 1. Before the Council of Trent

Before the Council of Trent decretalists and glossators already held that a traveler was not bound by the laws of his own territory while he was outside of that territory.[62] There quite naturally arose the further question whether the traveler was bound by the particular laws of the territory in which he was traveling. The *Decree* of Gratian could have been interpreted to imply that he was, and the early decretists did consider it in that light.

The later decretists and the decretalists finally took the stand that the traveler was not directly bound by the laws of the territory he was visiting, but that he could become indirectly bound if he committed a delict there, if he entered into a contract, if he gained possession of property, or if there was question of any law in regulation of the solemnity or legality of an act.[63] These later views were embodied in the decretals of various popes.[64] There seemed to be no question about one's being bound by the particular laws of a territory in which one held domicile, but there was some discussion regarding the requisite time for the acquisition of a domicile.[65]

[58] *Theatrum Veritatis et Justitiae* (16 vols. in 9, Coloniae, 1706), Lib. III, Pars I, disc. 20, n. 16.

[59] *Tractatus de Judiciis Ecclesiasticis* (3. ed., 2 vols., Parisiis, 1883), II, 161.

[60] *De Iudiciis Civilibus,* n. 98.

[61] *De Iudiciis Ecclesiasticis,* I, n. 408.

[62] Hammill, *The Obligations of the Traveler according to Canon 14,* The Catholic University of America Canon Law Studies, n. 160 (Washington, D. C.: The Catholic University of America Press, 1942), p. 37.

[63] Hammill, *op. cit.,* pp. 26-35.

[64] Cf. C. 21, X, *de sententia excommunicationis,* V, 39; c. 1, X, *de raptoribus, incendiariis et violatoribus ecclesiarum,* V, 17; c. 14, X, *de foro competenti,* II, 2; and c. 20, X, *de foro competenti,* II, 2.

[65] Hammill, *op. cit.,* p. 32.

The question of extradition arises when a person has obligations to meet in a certain territory in consequence of having committed a crime, of having entered a contract, or of holding real property, but, at the time, is actually outside of that territory. In extradition the tribunal of the place where the person actually resides is called upon to assist in effecting the return of the person to the former territory where he is to meet his obligations or to answer in court with regard to them.

According to Hostiensis, the civilist Azo (d. 1230), as well as Ioannes Teutonicus (d. 1271), held that the violator of a contract who had absconded had to be returned to the place of the contract, but his own teacher, Iacobus Balduinus (d. 1235), held the opposite view, namely, that the one who had entered the contract in a certain territory could not be forced to return there even if he had purposely left there to elude the trial. If he did not return to answer in court, and thus impeded the prosecution of the case, the judge of the trial could deprive him of the goods he had in that territory.[66]

Innocent IV in the decretal *Romana* followed the doctrine of Balduinus to the extent that in the case of a contract a party could not be forced to return to the territory where the contract was entered into. He went further, however, than Balduinus; if the party hindered the conduct of the trial by not coming, the judge of the trial could not only sequester the goods which the person had in his own territory, but he could also sequester the goods which the person had in the territory where at the time he was resident or also elsewhere; this latter sequestration, however, was to be accomplished through the tribunal of the place where the goods were found.[67] Thus the necessity of the rogatory commission was ruled out for extradition in the case of suits regarding contracts, and probably in all civil suits unless the public good demanded that commission.[68]

66 Hostiensis, *Commentaria, Liber Sextus,* Lib. II, tit. 2, c. 1, nn. 9-10; cf. also *Glossa Ordinaria* s. v. *invitos,* ad c. 1, *de foro competenti,* II, 2, in VI°.

67 C. 1, *de foro competenti,* II, 2, in VI°; cf. *supra,* p. 12; also Hostiensis, *Commentaria, Liber Sextus,* Lib. II, tit. 2, c. 1, n. 12.

68 Boich, *Commentaria,* Lib. V, tit. 17, c. 1, n. 7.

With criminal trials the situation was quite different. In the *Decree* of Gratian the competency of a tribunal in whose territory a delict had been committed was fully recognized.[69] The accused had to be summoned.[70] Judgment could not be given in his absence.[71] The accuser wasn't even to be heard unless the accused was present in the court.[72] If the sentence was passed in contravention of these canons it was invalid.[73]

Although an exception to these requirements was apparently made in the case of contumacy, and possibly also in the case of notorious crimes,[74] it is evident that much emphasis was placed on the securing of the actual presence of the accused at the trial. It was a matter of importance that the accused had to return from another territory to face trial, and that the assistance of the tribunal of that territory was required to secure his return. Accursius (d. ca. 1260) held that the tribunal of the place where the accused was found would provide for his return by reason of courtesy, but that it was not obliged to do so. A strict obligation arose only when the accused had left the territory of his crime with the intention of absconding, or when some special reason of public utility demanded it, as in shipwreck.[75] Innocent IV seemed to espouse the same opinion as Accursius.[76]

But even among the civilists there was no uniform agreement to the opinion of Accursius, for the French jurists, Jacques de Revigny (d. 1296) and Pierre de Belleperche (d. 1308) held that a tribunal

[69] C. 1, C. III, q. 6; c. 4, C. 6, q. 3.

[70] C. 6, C. XXIV, q. 3.

[71] C. 2, 5, 6, 7, 8, 9, 11, 13, 14, C. III, q. 9.

[72] C. 1, 3, 11, 18, C. III, q. 9; cf. *Glossa Ordinaria* s. v. *de accusatoribus,* ad *Summarium* ante c. 1, C. III, q. 9.

[73] C. 4, C. III, q. 9.

[74] *Dictum Gratiani* post c. 13, C. III, q. 9. Huguccio (d. 1210) permitted a criminal trial to proceed in notorious cases even if the accused was absent. Ioannes Teutonicus permitted the action to proceed in notorious cases only if the joining of issues had already taken place; cf. *Glossa Ordinaria* s. v. *de accusatoribus,* ad *Summarium* ante c. 1, C. III, q. 9.

[75] *Glossa Ordinaria* s. v. *remitteret,* ad D. (48, 2) 7.

[76] *Glossa Ordinaria* s. v. *de more,* ad c. 2, *de sententia et re iudicata,* II, 11, in Clem.; cf. also Boich, *Commentaria,* Lib. V, tit. 17, c. 1, n. 10.

was obliged to assist in returning an accused person to the territory where the crime had been committed.[77] In opposition to the opinion of Innocent IV, and as subscribing to the opinion that a tribunal had an obligation to assist in returning the accused person to the territory where the crime had been committed, were Hostiensis (d. 1271),[78] Boich (d. circa 1350),[79] Ioannes Andreae, (d. 1348) [80] and Panormitanus, (d. 1543).[81] They held this opinion at least for a case that involved a serious crime. In order to prove the necessity of returning the accused to the territory where the crime had been committed, they appealed to a Novel of Justinian, known as "*Si vero quis comprehensorum*" of the year 556.[82]

In this constitution of Justinian, the word "*iubemus*" led to a consideration of what could be done if the tribunal, which was requested in such a matter, refused to cooperate. According to Ioannes Andreae, the two civilists, Jacques de Revigny and Pierre de Belleperche, were of the opinion that, if the tribunal refused to surrender the accused, the tribunal where the delict was committed could bring force to bear, for, although they were equal, yet in consequence of this neglect of duty the one became the superior of the other.[83]

Huguccio (d. 1210), although not considering the case at hand, seemed to admit this principle, which was denied, however, by Ioannes Teutonicus.[84] Boich and Ioannes Andreae, accepting the opinion of Ioannes Teutonicus, applied it to the present matter. According to them, the one tribunal could not force the other in the case of

[77] According to Boich, *loc. cit.*

[78] *Commentaria,* Lib. II, tit. 2, c. 14, n. 4.

[79] *Commentaria,* Lib. V, tit. 17, c. 1, n. 10.

[80] *Glossa Ordinaria* s. v. *de more,* ad c. 2, *de sententia et re iudicata,* II, 11, in Clem.

[81] *Commentaria,* Lib. II, tit. 2, c. 20, n. 15. Panormitanus added, however, that the accused had to be sent back if the judge where the delict had been committed called for him; otherwise the judge of the actual residence could try him.

[82] Auth. 9, 9, 5 (Nov. 134, 5).

[83] *Glossa Ordinaria* s. v. *de more,* ad c. 2, *de sententia et re iudicata,* II, 11, in Clem.

[84] *Glossa Ordinaria* s. v. *convocet,* ad c. 9, D. LXV.

negligence, but had to seek recourse with a superior. They drew an argument from the decretal *Romana,* wherein Innocent IV had stated that a judge of the place wherein a contumacious party of a contract had his goods was to turn over the goods to the adversary of the contumacious one.[85] This was to be done according to the declaration of the judge of the trial; Innocent did not state that it was to be done according to the judge's command or order. In explanation of the word *"iubemus,"* they stated that, although Emperor Justinian (527-565) ordered that the accused be returned to the place of the crime, he gave no power of ordering or commanding to anyone else.[86]

It was the doctrine of the decretalists after Innocent IV that the accused had to be returned to the place of his alleged crime. Bernard of Parma (d. 1266) did not make any special mention of the reason of the necessity for the return of the accused, but he did say that he was to be returned when he was accused of serious crimes. Lighter crimes could be tried in the place where the accused held actual residence.[87] This distinction between more and less serious crimes, as Bernard himself pointed out, was based on a law of the *Digest* of Justinian known as *"Desertorem,"* [88] and it was accepted by Hostiensis,[89] Boich,[90] Ioannes Andreae,[91] and Panormitanus.[92]

Panormitanus added, however, that this returning of the accused to the place of his alleged crime was falling into disuse in his day. He agreed that a tribunal had to co-operate if called upon, but said that frequently this request was not forthcoming. In this case

[85] Cf. *supra,* p. 12. This sequestration was solely for reasons of custody; cf. *infra,* p. 40.

[86] *Glossa Ordinaria* s. v. *de more,* ad c. 2, *de sententia et re iudicata,* II, 11, in Clem.; cf. also Boich, *Commentaria,* Lib. V, tit. 17, c. 1, n. 10.

[87] *Glossa Ordinaria* s. v. *excommunicentur,* ad c. 1, *de raptoribus, incendiariis et violatoribus ecclesiarum,* V, 17.

[88] D. (49, 16) 3.

[89] *Commentaria,* Lib. II, tit. 2, c. 14, n. 4.

[90] *Commentaria,* Lib. V, tit. 17, c. 1, nn. 9-10.

[91] *Glossa Ordinaria* s. v. *de more,* ad c. 2, *de sententia et re iudicata,* II, 11, in Clem.

[92] *Commentaria,* Lib. II, tit. 2, c. 20, n. 15.

he reported and accepted the doctrine of Ioannes Calderinus (d. 1365) to the effect that the competency of one tribunal by reason of the perpetration of a delict did not exclude the competency of another tribunal especially by reason of domicile. When a request was not forthcoming for the return of the accused, the tribunal under which he had his domicile could prosecute him. Panormitanus could not agree with Calderinus that the judge of the domicile could refuse the request if he preferred to conduct the trial himself, or that he was obliged to fulfill the request merely out of courtesy.[93]

Finally, regarding the point of returning the accused to the tribunal of the alleged crime, Ioannes Andreae reported that Jacques de Revigny and Pierre de Belleperche held that the extradition was to be effected merely on the word of the judge requesting it, apart from all need of investigation into the matter on the part of the judge of whom it was requested. The argument was that the judge of the domicile was in such a case a mere executor, and that the judge requesting the extradition had to be presumed to be acting justly. On the other hand, according to Ioannes Andreae, a certain Bartholomaeus de Pratis held that a tribunal had to protect its own people from defamation and, to do so, it had to study, in some summary fashion, the justification of the request made to it.[94] Neither Ioannes Andreae nor Henricus Boich took any clear stand on this point, but Boich felt that Ioannes Andreae leaned toward the opinion of Bartholomaeus de Pratis; for reasons of equity rather than for reasons of law, he found this doctrine acceptable to himself.[95] The same point of view found acceptance with Panormitanus.[96]

Section 2. From the Council of Trent to the Code

Though in the period after the Council of Trent the juridical institute of extradition was maintained, it sustained a number of

[93] *Commentaria,* Lib. II, tit. 2, c. 20, nn. 15-16.

[94] *Glossa Ordinaria* s. v. *de more,* ad. c. 2, *de sententia et re iudicata,* II, 11, in Clem. Concerning Bartholomaeus de Pratis no information was available from the bibliographies on hand.

[95] Boich, *Commentaria,* Lib. V, tit. 17, c. 1, n. 11.

[96] *Commentaria,* Lib. II, tit. 2, c. 20, n. 18.

adaptations and changes. Its continuance responded to the very purpose of the *forum delicti,* namely, that the juridical order might be re-established in the place where the crime had been committed and that others might be deterred from violations and infringements of the law. This of itself, however, probably would not have made extradition necessary apart from the extant requirement of the presence of the accused at the trial. From the time of Gratian the presence of the accused at the trial was essential for all criminal court procedure.[97]

After the Council of Trent the authors almost universally agreed that a tribunal, if competent solely for the reason that the crime had been committed in its territory, could not proceed in a criminal trial against the accused if the accused had already left that territory, unless before his departure he had been properly summoned. Unless he had been legitimately summoned before his departure, the accused could not be tried *in absentia.* Citation made by means of an edict or through a beadle sent by the judge of the trial to the accused who at the time resided in alien territory did not serve to evince the accused's contumaciousness if he refused to heed the citation.[98]

In order then to make the competency of the tribunal effective when a crime had been committed, all the authors appealed to the process of extradition. The tribunal of the place where the accused was found was to co-operate in returning the accused to the tribunal where he was to face trial for the alleged crime.[99] Through the

[97] Cf. *supra,* p. 19.

[98] Cf. Scaccia, *De Iudiciis* (2 vols., Venetiis, 1663), I, c. 40, n. 10; Barbosa, *Collectanea Doctorum tam Veterum quam Recentiorum* (5 vols., Lugduni, 1656), Lib. II, tit. 2, c. 14, n. 2; Oliva e Souza, *Tractatus de Foro Ecclesiae* (3 vols. in 1, Coloniae Allobrogum, 1733), III, q. 20, n. 29; Schmalzgrueber, Lib. II, tit. 2, n. 61; Engel, *Collegium Universi Iuris Canonici* (Beneventi, 1760), Lib. II, tit. 2, n. 37 (hereafter cited Engel); Reiffenstuel, Lib. II, tit. 2, nn. 56-58; Ferraris, *Prompta Bibliotheca,* s. v. *forum,* n. 12; Bouix, *Tractatus de Judiciis Ecclesiasticis,* I, 298; Sebastianelli, *De Iudiciis Civilibus,* n. 46; Wernz, *Ius Decretalium,* V, n. 290; Lega, *De Iudiciis Ecclesiasticis,* IV, n. 166.

[99] Scaccia, *De Iudiciis,* I, c. 40, n. 10; Barbosa, *Collectanea Doctorum tam Veterum quam Recentiorum,* Lib. II, tit. 2, c. 14, n. 2; Oliva e Souza, *Tractatus de Foro Ecclesiae,* III, q. 20, n. 16; Schmalzgrueber, Lib. II, tit. 2,

famous canonists of the seventeenth century the conditions for the practical working of the process of extradition were clearly outlined. They agreed that five conditions were postulated before a judge was required to force an accused person to appear elsewhere in order to be tried before the tribunal of the place where it was alleged that he committed the crime: (1) the tribunal claiming competence for the reason that the crime had been committed within the borders of its territory had to make a formal request of the judge of the place where the accused was in actual residence; (2) the crime had to be of a serious nature and actually committed within the territory of the tribunal which requested the extradition; (3) no other competent tribunal must, as yet, have cited the accused in order to try him for the same crime, as could have happened in the territory where the accused had his domicile, for that tribunal was considered competent to try its subjects even for crimes committed elsewhere; (4) before the request for the extradition could be made, the tribunal which proposed to make the request had to conduct a summary process by means of proofs and witnesses, so that the danger of an unjust and unfounded defamation of character would be duly eliminated; and (5) both the judge requesting the extradition and the judge of whom it was requested had to be of a territory that was subordinate to the same sovereign authority, otherwise no effective purpose could have been served in the attempt to bring about the extradition, since there would have been no authority which could have compelled the one to assist the other.[100]

Because of the abstract nature of legal speculation, it is difficult to say exactly how this process of extradition was actually carried out. It seems that at the time of the later decretalists the Church could rely on the physical force which the civil authority would supply for enforcing the appearance of the accused before the tribunal before which he was accused. This deduction is based on the fact

n. 64; Engel, Lib. II, tit. 2, n. 28; Reiffenstuel, Lib. II, tit. 2, nn. 62-74; Devoti, *Ius Canonicum Universum Publicum et Privatum* (3 vols., Romae, 1837), Lib. II, tit. 2, c. 26 (hereafter cited *Ius Canonicum Universum*); Bouix, *Tractatus de Judiciis Ecclesiasticis,* I, 298; Wernz, *Ius Decretalium,* V, n. 290.

[100] Engel, Lib. II, tit. 2, n. 28; Reiffenstuel, Lib. II, tit. 2, nn. 62-74; Schmalzgrueber, Lib. II, tit. 2, n. 64.

that Ioannes Andreae, Henricus Boich, and Abbas Panormitanus together with others mentioned by them spoke of the accused as being "*ligatus*" when he was being returned to the place where he was to be tried.[101] This seems also to have been the opinion of such men as Engel (d. 1674), Reiffenstuel (d. 1703), and Schmalzgrueber (d. 1735) when they required as a condition for the extradition proceedings that the two tribunals concerned be located in a territory that was subordinate to the same sovereign authority, that is, the same supreme civil authority. When the Roman Empire of the Middle Ages began to break up into smaller principalities, extradition began to disappear.[102]

While it is not clear from these authors how exactly the civil authority intervened, it seems that they felt the intervention of the civil authority to be a matter of necessity. Writers of the present age have a completely different concept regarding extradition proceedings. With the separation of Church and State accomplished to a great extent in most of the countries, the Church could not look to the civil authorities for help in the return of the accused to the scene of their alleged crimes. Extradition has become a purely ecclesiastical measure, whereby a local tribunal constrains an accused person by means of penal measures and censures to report to the tribunal of the place where the alleged crime was perpetrated.[103]

Already in the time of Panormitanus there seemed to exist strong customs against the use of extradition proceedings.[104] Reiffenstuel confirmed the fact that extradition was falling into disuse, but he also pointed to the continued practice in Germany and in some other places, especially with reference to the more serious crimes.[105] In the beginning of the twentieth century, however, this institute seemed to have disappeared, not from the point of view of law, but from the practice of the Church, as Lega bore witness.[106]

[101] Cf. *supra*, p. 22, footnotes 94-96.

[102] Reiffenstuel, Lib. II, tit. 2, n. 70; Schmalzgrueber, Lib. II, tit. 2, n. 63.

[103] Lega, *De Iudiciis Ecclesiasticis*, IV, n. 166; Bouix, *Tractatus de Judiciis Ecclesiasticis*, I, 298.

[104] Panormitanus, *Commentaria*, Lib. V, tit. 17, c. 1, n. 9.

[105] *Ius Canonicum Universum*, Lib. II, tit. 2, n. 70.

[106] *De Iudiciis Ecclesiasticis*, IV, n. 166.

The necessity for extradition was precluded by the Code of Canon Law in 1918 through the provision that a judge is able to cite anyone who is accused of having committed a crime within the territory, even though the accused has already left the territory, and is able also to issue a sentence against him in his absence.[107]

Article 4. The Taking of Testimony on Commission

Section 1. Before the Council of Trent

The decretal law on the assistance granted one tribunal by another in the taking of testimony is given in a decretal entitled *Constitutus,* issued by Pope Lucius III (1181-1184), and sent to the Archbishop of Canterbury. At the time of the III General Council of the Lateran (1179), Peter of Blois, chancellor to the Archbishop of Canterbury, had borrowed a sum of money at Bologna, and Stephen, a professor at Bologna, had given security for the loan. Peter of Blois did not repay the money, and the creditors began to take action against Stephen.[108] Stephen appealed to the Holy See, and Pope Lucius directed to the Archbishop of Canterbury the following letter:

> Constitutus in praesentia nostra . . . Ideoque, quia pro nostro officio volumus providere, ne qui gratiam meruit poenam sustineat, fraternitati tuae per apostolica scripta praecipiendo mandamus, quatenus, si legitime tibi de huiusmodi assertione constiterit, praefatum debitorem, ut eum a praedicta intercessione sine dilatione prorsus absolvat, omni gratia et timore postposito, nullius appellatione obstante ecclesiastica censura compellas. Quia vero diversa experimenta morborum varia nos compellunt remedia invenire, praesentium quoque auctoritate iniungimus, ut, si forte debitum vel accessiones ille negaverit, consuetudine, quae est legi contraria, non obstante, iuramentum calumniae subire cogatur. Praeterea, quia difficile foret intercessori suos testes in

107 Canon 1566, § 2.

108 *Casus* ad c. 3, X, *de fideiussoribus,* III, 22. For Peter of Blois, cf. *The Catholic Encyclopedia* (15 vols., Index, and 2 Supplements, New York, 1907-1922), XI, 765; also Fabricius, *Bibliotheca Latina Mediae et Infimae Aetatis* (3 vols., Florentiae, 1858), III, 234.

Angliam ducere, iudicibus Bononiensibus satisdatione idonea a cancellario ipso accepta, quod ad testes audiendos vadat, vel mittat infra terminum competentem, litteris tuis significes, ut eos vice tua recipiant, et examinent et interrogent diligenter, et depositiones eorum transmittentes inclusas significent, quanta fides possit instrumentis vel testibus adhiberi. Ceterum si iam dictus P. citatus praesentiam tuam adire vel iudicio stare contempserit eum infra XXX dies post harum litterarum susceptionem reddas beneficio alienum et reditus eius in debitorum solutionem convertas, quousque fuerit creditoribus satisfactum.[109]

Thus the Archbishop was ordered to look into the case. If on investigation he found the situation to be as alleged, he was to force his chancellor, even by censure, to meet his debts. If the chancellor denied his indebtedness, the Archbishop was to institute a trial for the settlement of the case between the chancellor and Stephen, the professor at Bologna. Since it would be difficult for Stephen to have his witnesses go from Bologna to England, the Archbishop was to commission judges at Bologna to receive the testimony of these witnesses. The decretal letter then outlined certain formalities that were to be observed in the taking of this testimony.[110]

First of all, if the chancellor contested the charge, he was to be required to take an oath to shun all calumny.[111] The decretal itself indicated the reason for having the testimony of the witnesses

[109] C. 3, X, *de fideiussoribus,* III, 22; cf. Jaffé, JL, n. 14963.

[110] *Casus, loc. cit.*

[111] The oath to shun calumny originated in Roman Law procedure; cf. Moriarty, *Oaths in Ecclesiastical Courts,* The Catholic University of America Canon Law Studies, n. 110 (Washington, D. C.: The Catholic University of America, 1937), p. 9. It played an important rôle in the decretals, but Honorius II (1124-1130) forbade its use with reference to spiritual matters. It covered five points: (1) the litigant swore to his belief in the justice of his cause; (2) he swore that, when interrogated, he would not deny that which he believed to be true; (3) he swore that he would not knowingly use false proofs; (4) that he would not seek a fraudulent delay; (5) that he had not given, nor would give, that he had not promised, nor would promise, anything save to those to whom the law permitted him to give or promise. Cf. Moriarty, *op. cit.,* pp. 3-4. It seems from the wording of the decretal *Constitutus* that already at that time (c. 1180-1184) in some places a custom was in force contrary to the taking of this oath. Moriarty (*op. cit.,* p. 28) cited Schmalzgrueber as saying that it was already out of use in his day (1663-1735).

taken outside of the place of the trial: it stated that it would be difficult to have the witnesses brought to England. Both Hostiensis [112] and Ioannes Andreae [113] understood this difficulty to consist especially in the necessity, on the part of the one calling the witnesses, to pay all the expenses of the witnesses he called.[114]

After the oath to shun all calumny, Peter of Blois was required to give a surety in a suitable amount that he would personally go, or that he would send a proxy to Bologna, for the hearing of the witnesses. When he first wrote his *Apparatus,* Bernard of Parma held the view that the surety had to be given provided the chancellor wished to go to Bologna or send a proxy. But if he preferred to relinquish his right in this regard, he could do so, and thus would not be required to give the surety, and the testimony would go unquestioned.[115]

Later, and under the influence of Innocent IV, Bernard added that it could well be that the surety had to be given in any event. For this statement he gave two reasons: First, it could have been required for the purpose of keeping Peter of Blois from trying to maliciously wear out his adversary by way of additional labors and expenses, and if he did not wish to give the bond, it would have been an indication that he did have such a malicious intention. But this reasoning Bernard rejected, for, if the chancellor lost the trial, he would have had to pay all the expenses of the plaintiff whether or not he went to Bologna. In other words, the additional bond for the trip to Bologna would not have meant any additional safeguard against possible malicious intentions; the chancellor could

112 *Commentaria,* Lib. III, tit. 22, c. 3, n. 3.

113 *Commentaria Novella,* Lib. III, tit. 22, c. 3.

114 Cf. c. 3, § 40, C. IV, q. 2 et 3; c. 11, *de rescriptis,* I, 3, in VI°.

115 "Hoc si voluerit, alias non compellitur, sed sufficit quod ei denuncietur, ut mittat vel vadat ad ipsos videndos, alias reciperentur in termino constituto." —*Glossa Ordinaria* s. v. *satisdatione,* ad c. 3, X, *de fideiussoribus,* III, 22. According to Van Hove (*Prolegomena,* p. 474) the *glossa ordinaria* of Bernard of Parma was finished shortly after 1245. According to Kuttner and Smalley there were at least four versions of Bernard's *Glossa*: first redaction, 1234-1241; second, 1243-1245; third, 1245-c. 1253; final, 1263-1266; cf. Kuttner and Smalley: "The 'Glossa Ordinaria' to the Gregorian Decretals"—*The English Historical Review,* LX (1945), 97-105.

have given the bond and then have refused to go to Bologna or to send a proxy, and after the trial, even if he lost, he would have received back his bond with no additional loss to himself. Consequently Bernard evolved the second reason, which he appears to have accepted, namely, that the chancellor was to be compelled to go to Bologna, either himself or through a proxy, and for this he was to be compelled to put up a suitable bond. Thus his possible losses would have included the expenses of the trip to Bologna in addition to the expenses of the plaintiff and the debt in question.[116] Hostiensis offered the explanation for the necessity of the bond as accepted by Bernard, but he added that if the chancellor lost the trial after paying the bond, then the latter could have been applied for expenses. He stated further that this interpretation regarding the mandatory character of the surety had to be adopted, since otherwise only an absurd interpretation could have resulted.[117]

Ioannes Andreae declared that Hostiensis saw in the optional granting of the bond about the trip to Bologna an extorted interpretation of the decretal for the reason that, if the debtor had been constrained simply to give the bond about the debt itself and the expenses of the trial, he would still have been suspect, and would still have been under the necessity of being cited to go to Bologna. Ioannes Andreae then reported another possible explanation for the necessity of the bond, which explanation was ascribed by Bernard

[116] "Vel forte ideo cautionem praestare debet: quia praesumptio erat contra cancellarium ne in fraudem malitiose debitum ei negaret, ut adversarium fatigaret laboribus et expensis: ut si eam praestare nollet, hoc ipso tamquam suspectus compelleretur ad satisfaciendum. Sed hoc non videtur: quia sive vadat sive non, nihilominus tenetur adversario in expensis, immo debet compelli ut vadat vel mittat, ut ipse magis puniatur: quia tunc gravatur in suis propriis expensis et etiam adversarii."—*Glossa Ordinaria* s. v. *satisdatione,* ad c. 3, X, *de fideiussoribus,* III, 22. According to Ioannes Andreae this portion of the *glossa* to the word *satisdatione* was added under the influence of Innocent IV; cf. *Commentaria Novella* (Venetiis: Ioannes et Gregorius de Gregoriis de Forlivio, 1489), Lib. III, tit. 22, c. 3. In fact, the Oxford MS of the *Glossa Ordinaria* (dated 1241) does not have this continuation "vel forte," etc. (Information here was kindly supplied by Mr. W. M. Hunt, Keeper of MSS. at the Bodleian Library.) Cf. also Innocentius IV, *Apparatus super Libros Decretalium* (Argentorati, 1478), Lib. III, tit. 22, c. 3.

[117] *Commentaria,* Lib. III, tit. 22, c. 3, n. 4.

de Montmirat (Abbas Antiquus, d. 1296) to his teacher, namely that, if the parties were properly cited for the taking of the testimony, an objection could sometimes be lodged against the testimony on the grounds that one of the parties was unavoidably absent; this surety would then make certain the attendance of the party or of his proxy, and would eliminate the possibility of such an objection.[118]

Ioannes Andreae was of the opinion that in his day the question of counteracting the malicious intentions of parties in demanding or in making necessary the testimony of distant witnesses had been solved by Innocent IV at the Council of Lyons in 1245, when he ruled that the one who requested the testimony of a witness should be prepared to meet his expenses.[119]

Panormitanus, however, was not convinced that the problem had been solved by Innocent IV, as Ioannes Andreae had suggested. The law given by Innocent IV, Panormitanus said, took care of the case in which a party, himself, deliberately insisted on the securing of the testimony of witnesses either to secure unnecessary disturbance to the witnesses or to play for time. It did not, so he claimed, provide for the case in which a party, by his denial of something, caused the other party to secure the testimony of distant witnesses. Thus according to Panormitanus the remedy as proposed through the surety that was demanded of the chancellor at Canterbury was still to be used. But, he concluded, when the parties acted with malicious intentions, then the judge could refuse their request and feel free of all care in the event that an appeal was invoked.[120]

Regarding the formalities to be observed in the taking of the testimony by the judge at Bologna, the decretal of Lucius III merely stated that it had to be done diligently. Decretalists pointed to a subsequent decretal of Innocent III to show what was meant by a diligent examination. An examination was such if it prudently inquired into all the pertinent circumstances of the question.[121] In

118 *Commentaria Novella,* Lib. III, tit. 22, c. 3.

119 *Glossa Ordinaria* s. v. *a producente* et *expensas,* ad c. 11, *de rescriptis,* I, 3, in VI°.

120 *Commentaria,* Lib. III, tit. 22, c. 3, nn. 8-9.

121 Hostiensis, *Commentaria,* Lib. III, tit. 22, c. 3, n. 4; Ioannes Andreae,

this respect Ioannes Andreae added that the witnesses should also be interrogated according to the questions proposed by the adversary.[122]

Tancredus (d. 1234 or 1236) agreed that testimony could be taken on commission in contentious cases, and in substantiation of this he referred to the Roman Law *"Iudices,"* [123] but he insisted that it could not be done in criminal cases, and in support of this claim he referred to the Roman Law known as *"Apud Eloquentissimum."* [124] In criminal cases, he said, the witnesses had to appear in the presence of the judge of the trial to give their testimony.[125]

Regarding the impossibility of taking testimony on commission in criminal cases, there was the following canon in the *Decree* of Gratian:

> Testes per quamcumque scripturam testimonium non proferant, sed praesentes de his, quae noverunt et viderunt, veraciter testimonium dicant. Nec de aliis causis vel negotiis dicant testimonium, nisi de his, quae sub praesentia eorum acta esse noscuntur.[126]

The ordinary interpretation of this was that it referred to criminal cases.[127] This canon was ascribed by Gratian to Pope Callixtus I (217-222), but apparently was pseudo-Isidorian in origin.[128]

Subsequent authors agreed with Tancredus that testimony should not be taken on commission in criminal cases. Hostiensis added that the taking of testimony should not be delegated to others, and both of these restrictions should be observed in marriage cases. However, he further added that the taking of testimony in marriage cases was through customary usage delegated to others.[129]

Commentaria Novella, loc. cit. Reference is made to c. 37, X, *de testibus et attestationibus,* II, 20; cf. Potthast, n. 2824.

[122] *Commentaria Novella,* Lib. III, tit. 22, c. 3; he gives as a reason for this statement c. 2, *de testibus et attestationibus,* II, 10, in VI°.

[123] C. (4, 21) 18.

[124] Nov. (90, 5).

[125] Cf. *Glossa Ordinaria* s. v. *transmittentes,* ad c. 3, X, *de fideiussoribus,* III, 22.

[126] C. 15, C. III, q. 9.

[127] *Glossa Ordinaria* s. v. *sed praesentes,* ad c. 15, C. III, q. 9.

[128] Cf. Jaffé, JK, n. 86; Hinschius, p. 137.

[129] *Commentaria,* Lib. III, tit. 22, c. 3, n. 4. Cf. also Ioannes Andreae,

Panormitanus seemed to understand Ioannes Andreae in the sense that the latter together with Ioannes Monachus permitted the taking of testimony on commission in criminal cases.[130] While Ioannes Andreae did perhaps see some difficulty by way of comparison with the Roman Law, which required that witnesses should not be called from the provinces to give testimony, he seemed rather to state that witnesses as well as the accused person were to be sent to the competent tribunal before which the accused was to be tried.[131]

Finally, before the depositions of the witnesses were to be returned to the judge of the trial, the judge who had taken the testimony was instructed to add an annotation regarding the measure in which the testimony merited belief.[132] In this respect an interesting addition of an unknown author was made to the *glossa ordinaria*, namely, that the judge who took the testimony was not to indicate whether or not the testimony merited belief, but rather he was to note the characteristics of the witnesses and any circumstances which would permit the judge of the trial to determine whether or not the testimony was belief-worthy.[133] Panormitanus held that the judge who took the testimony was to note whether the witness was hesitant or alarmed, or whether the witness was to be considered suspect in the mind of the judge. He added that the rendering of a judgment on this point did not belong to the one who took the testimony, since that had to be left to the other judge.[134]

Section 2. From the Council of Trent to the Code

Before the Council of Trent the doctrine of the canonists on the taking of testimony on commission was fairly well set. Because of

Commentaria Novella, Lib. III, tit. 22, c. 3; Panormitanus, *Commentaria*, Lib. III, tit. 22, c. 3, n. 10.

130 *Commentaria*, Lib. II, tit. 20, c. 37, n. 22; cf. also Lib. III, tit. 22, c. 3, n. 10.

131 *Commentaria Novella, Liber Sextus*, Lib. II, tit. 2, c. 1, n. 9.

132 *Glossa Ordinaria* s. v. *quanta fides*, ad c. 3, X, *de fideiussoribus*, III, 22.

133 Additio ad *glossam ordinariam*, c. 3, X, *de fideiussoribus*, III, 22.

134 *Commentaria*, Lib. III, tit. 22, c. 3, n. 5.

the difficulties involved in appearing before the judge of the trial, witnesses in other parts could be cited by the judges of their own territories at the request of the original judge of the case, and they could give their testimony, which then was returned to the judge who had requested it. The glossators regarded the practice as non-permissible in criminal cases, and they did not in any way qualify this restriction of the use of the rogatory commission for the taking of testimony in criminal trials. Even before the Council of Trent, however, there were indications that the use of the rogatory commission could be pressed into service in criminal trials under certain conditions.[135]

From the Council of Trent until the nineteenth century it was the more common doctrine among the canonists that in the taking of testimony on commission the general principle was to be followed, namely, testimony in criminal trials was not to be heard by authorization through a rogatory commission. In order that crimes might not go unpunished and that truth might not be hidden, such authorization could obtain in cases of necessity, for example, when the witnesses were in a different territory and could not be persuaded to appear before the judge who was hearing the case.[136]

Barbosa (d. 1649) [137] and Remigius Maschat a S. Erasmo (d. 1747) [138] still held to the unqualified statement that testimony was not to be taken on commission in criminal trials. But already in the seventeenth and eighteenth centuries authors treated of the taking of testimony on commission to the exclusion of any limitation

[135] Ioannes Bertachini, who died in 1506, stated that the testimony of an absent witness could not be taken on commission in a criminal case except in a case of necessity; cf. *Repertorium* (5 vols., Venetiis, 1570), s. v. *Remissio.* Prosper Farinacius (d. 1618) among many romanists cited also Felinus Sandeus (d. 1503), a canonist, as following this opinion; cf. *Tractatus de Testibus* (Venetiis, 1609), Q. LXXVII, n. 92.

[136] Farinacius, *Tractatus de Testibus,* Q. LXXVII, n. 92; Pellegrini, *Praxis Vicariorum* (Venetiis, 1706), Pars IV, Sect. IV, nn. 54, 60; Pirhing, Lib. II, tit. 20, n. 188; Reiffenstuel, Lib. II, tit. 20, n. 436; Schmalzgrueber, Lib. II, tit. 20, n. 100.

[137] *Collectanea Doctorum tam Veterum quam Recentiorum,* Lib. III, tit. 22, c. 3, n. 5.

[138] *Institutiones Canonicae* (4 vols. Florentiae, 1854), Lib. II, tit. 20, n. 10.

with reference to criminal cases. They thought that, when witnesses were outside of the territory in which the trial was being held, the judge of the trial was to request the judge of the territory of the witnesses' actual residence to send them to the place where the trial was being heard. If this could not be done, then the judge of that place was to take the testimony himself. In this matter they made no distinction between contentious and criminal cases.[139] It was this doctrine which became the common one in the nineteenth century, and it continued as such until the advent of the present Code.[140]

On various occasions during the nineteenth century the Roman Congregations issued Instructions on the taking of the testimony of absent witnesses through the instrumentality of their proper ordinaries. These Instructions made particular reference to marriage cases.[141] In 1883, in an Instruction to the United States of America on the course of procedure in the criminal and disciplinary trials of clerics, the Sacred Congregation for the Propagation of the Faith specifically provided that even in criminal trials the testimony of witnesses could be taken on commission. According to this Instruction, the testimony was to be thus taken when the witnesses lived either at a great distance from the scene of the trial or in a different diocese.[142] In the norms of procedure set up for the Sacred Roman Rota in 1910 the taking of testimony on commission stood acknowledged as part and parcel of judicial procedure. No distinction was invoked between contentious and criminal cases.[143]

[139] Engel, Lib. II, tit. 20 et 21, n. 2; Schmier, Lib. II, tract. 3, c. 5, n. 69; Pichler, Lib. II, tit. 20, n. 17.

[140] De Angelis, *Praelectiones Iuris Canonici,* Lib. II, tit. 20, n. 3; Bouix, *Tractatus de Judiciis Ecclesiasticis,* II, 220; Wernz, *Ius Decretalium,* V, n. 99; Lega, *De Iudiciis Ecclesiasticis,* II, n. 323.

[141] S. C. S. Off., instr. (ad Ep. Rituum Orient.) a. 1883, tit. III, n. 15—*Codicis Iuris Canonici Fontes* (9 vols., Vols. I-VI, ed. cura Emi Card. Gasparri; Vols. VII-IX, ed. cura et studio Emi Iustiniani Card. Serédi, Romae-Civitate Vaticana: Typis Polyglottis Vaticanis, 1923-1939), n. 1076 (hereafter cited *Fontes*) ; S. C. C., instr. 22 aug. 1840—*Fontes,* n. 4069; S. C. Ep. et Reg., instr. 11 iun. 1880—*Fontes,* n. 2005.

[142] S. C. de Prop. Fide, instr. a. 1883, n. 19—*Fontes,* n. 4900.

[143] Regulae servandae in iudiciis apud S. R. Rotae Tribunal, 4 aug. 1910,

In his detailed treatment on the taking of testimony on commission in civil cases, Farinacius (d. 1618) listed some forty-two authors, all of whom held that the judge of the case was obliged to grant permission for the taking of testimony in such a fashion when the witness in question was outside of the territory where the trial was being held.[144] Then, indicating his thought that in cases of necessity the testimony of witnesses could be taken on commission in criminal cases also, he reported the discussion among authors on the point whether in criminal cases it was to be left to the discretion of the judge or whether it was obligatory for him, even as in civil or contentious cases, to invoke the use of the rogatory commission. He, himself, adopted the latter view, namely, that the judge had to authorize the taking of testimony in criminal cases on commission. He did, however, consider the judge to be free of all obligations on this score when the latter suspected evil intentions on the part of the one who requested that the testimony of absent witnesses be taken.[145]

Farinacius then described the procedure to be followed by the judge in this matter. After the request by the party had been made, the adversary was to be cited in order to be present, if he wished, for the decree of the judge which permitted the testimony of the absent witnesses to be taken elsewhere. The adversary was also to be cited in order that he might present interrogatories on which the absent witnesses were likewise to be questioned, in order that he might be present when the letters were being closed, in order that he might be present when the messenger who was to carry the letter was put under oath, and in order that he might see that the letter was consigned to the messenger. The letter was to be directed only to a judge who had jurisdiction in the territory where the testimony was to be taken. When the letter had arrived, the adversary or his proxy was to be cited again in order that he might be present for the opening of the letter and for the administration of the oath to

§ 14, nn. 4-5; § 106, n. 3; § 110; § 143.—*Acta Apostolicae Sedis* (Romae, 1909—), II (1910), 788 (hereafter cited *AAS*); *Fontes,* n. 6461.

144 *Tractatus de Testibus,* Q. LXXVII, n. 2.

145 *Ibidem,* nn. 92-97.

the witnesses. The sworn deposition of the witnesses was then to be returned under seal to the judge of the case.[146]

A very detailed account of the limitations put on the use of the rogatory commission in the securing of testimony was given by Pellegrini (d. 1678). Treating of the institute in general, he taught that according to the usage and practice of the Roman Curia its use was granted except in the following cases:

(1) when it was possible to prove by means of documents what the party wished to prove by means of witnesses;

(2) when with the testimony of absent witnesses the party wanted to prove the contrary of what had been proved through documents;

(3) when the testimony of absent witnesses was desired as a hindrance for the taking of possession of the property received through a will;

(4) when the conclusion of the case had been reached so that a definitive decision could be rendered;

(5) when with the testimony of absent witnesses the party sought to establish proof for some juridical fact which had been accepted as such for a hundred years;

(6) when the matter for which proof was sought was of no practical consequences;

(7) when there was a well-founded suspicion that calumny would result; and

(8) when other witnesses were easily obtainable.

According to Pellegrini the concession for or the refusal of the taking of testimony on commission depended on the discretion of the judge, but in a case of doubt he was to grant rather than to withhold the concession. If the testimony was to be taken in a different territory, the party who requested the taking of the testimony was to make a deposit of money for the expenses involved, and likewise was to take an oath that his request was not motivated by improper reasons, such as the seeking of a delay in the trial or the using of some fraudulent means. The taking of testimony could be com-

[146] *Ibidem*, nn. 117-143.

mitted to any and all competent tribunals whether ecclesiastical or civil.[147]

Pellegrini held to the general principle that testimony was not to be taken on commission in criminal cases. However, he also held that this principle did not oblige when the witnesses resided outside of the territory where the criminal trial was being prosecuted, and could not rightfully be constrained to make a personal appearance at the trial. He claimed that the cause of equity was better served through the taking of testimony on commission even at the concomitant risk that the guilty party escape conviction than through the waiving of the testimony at the concomitant risk that the innocent party incur condemnation.[148]

Thereupon Pellegrini enumerated the postulated conditions for the taking of testimony on commission in criminal cases:

(1) before invoking the use of the rogatory commission in favor of any party through the issuing of a decree to that effect, the judge had to cite the adverse party to be present in the court, since it did not suffice simply to offer to the adverse party the possibility of reviewing the allegations (*articuli*) on which the testimony was to be taken;

(2) the adverse party had to be granted a hearing relative to the judge and the place where the testimony was to be taken;

(3) the adverse party was to be cited in order to be present for the closing of the letter, in order to supply further questions on which the witnesses were to be interrogated, and in order to be a witness of the oath taken by the messenger who was to carry the letter;

(4) the adverse party was to designate a proxy to be present at the taking of the testimony;

(5) the judge was not to issue his decree which permitted the taking of the testimony by another tribunal until he had first studied the reason for its request;

(6) the allegations *(articuli)* concerning which the witnesses were to be questioned had to be presented to the judge in order that he might determine whether or not they were pertinent to the case;

[147] *Praxis Vicariorum,* Pars II, Sect. II, subsectio 7, nn. 10-34.

[148] *Praxis Vicariorum,* Pars IV, Sect. IV, nn. 58-60.

(7) the party who requested the decree had to take the oath to shun all calumny in the event of a well-founded suspicion of evil intentions, but any slight or nebulous suspicion in the case could be ignored as non-existent.

(8) the one who made the request had to put up a bond or make a deposit of money for the expenses involved;

(9) the commission which authorized the taking of the testimony had to become vested in an ecclesiastical dignity or in a person who could exercise ecclesiastical jurisdiction;

(10) the judge had to set a determinate period of time for the presenting of the letter to the one who was to take the testimony; and

(11) the adverse party or his proxy had to be cited for presence in the place where the testimony was to be taken, in order that he might be an onlooker at the opening of the letter and at the taking of the oath by the witness who was to be interrogated.[149]

Beginning about with the time of Engel (d. 1674) authors no longer offered lengthy descriptions of the procedure for the taking of testimony on commission, but were content with the statement that such testimony had to be taken in accordance with the ordinary rules for the taking of the testimony of witnesses, and that the judge who had taken the testimony was to send it closed and under his seal to the original judge of the case.[150] Schmalzgrueber, presupposing that the testimony of the absent witnesses was to be taken with all the precautions ordinarily taken when the witnesses were interrogated, added that the judge who had taken the testimony was then also to make note of the important observations relating to the witness, e. g., whether he was frightened while giving his testimony, or whether he wavered or changed his mind.[151]

The various nineteenth century Instructions, as given by the Roman Congregations in their treatment regarding the taking of the testimony of absent witnesses, stated that this task was to be

149 *Ibidem,* nn. 69-70.

150 Engel, Lib. II, tit. 20 et 21, n. 2; Reiffenstuel, Lib. II, tit. 20, nn. 433-435; Schmier, Lib. II, tract. 3, c. 5, n. 69; De Angelis, *Praelectiones Iuris Canonici,* Lib. II, tit. 20, § 3.

151 *Ius Canonicum Universum,* Lib. II, tit. 20, n. 99.

performed in accordance with the norms which regulated the taking of the testimony of witnesses in the presence of a judge who was himself conducting the trial.[152] In the Instruction of the Sacred Congregation of the Council in 1840 it was also stated that, after the testimony of the absent witness had been taken, the deposition was to be signed and sealed before it was dispatched.[153]

Various terms were used in designation of the letter which requested another tribunal to take the testimony of a witness who was actually resident within its territory. Pellegrini employed the phrases *"litterae hortatoriae"* and *"litterae rogatoriae."*[154] The phrase *"litterae requisitoriales"* was also in use.[155] The special norms which were enacted in 1910 for the regulation of the procedure at the Sacred Roman Rota employed the phrases *"litterae rogatoriae"* and *"litterae remissoriales,"*[156] The phrase *"litterae mutui compassus"* was employed for a letter requesting the citation of a witness who was of another jurisdiction but whose presence was required at the scene of the trial.[157]

Article 5. The Rogatory Commission in the Execution of a Sentence

Section 1. Before the Council of Trent

In the period of the glossators, discussion also turned about the execution of a judicial sentence by means of a commission. This discussion can be divided into two parts: first, with reference to an interlocutory sentence; and secondly, with reference to the final sentence.

[152] S. C. S. Off., instr. (ad Ep. Rituum Orient.) a. 1883, tit. III, n. 15—*Fontes*, n. 1076; S. C. Ep. et Reg., instr., 11 iun. 1880, n. 19—*Fontes*, n. 2005; S. C. de Prop. Fide, instr. a. 1883, n. XIX—*Fontes*, n. 4900.

[153] S. C. C., instr. 22 aug. 1840—*Fontes*, n. 4069.

[154] *Praxis Vicariorum*, Pars IV, Sect. IV, n. 43.

[155] Cf. Wernz, *Ius Decretalium*, V, n. 99; Lega, *De Iudiciis Ecclesiasticis*, II, n. 323.

[156] Cf. Regulae servandae in iudiciis apud S. R. Rotae Tribunal, 4 aug. 1919, § 106, n. 3; § 110; § 143—*AAS*, II (1910), 788; *Fontes*, n. 6461.

[157] Cf. Engel, Lib. II, tit. 20 et 21, n. 2; Reiffenstuel, Lib. II, tit. 20, n. 433; Pichler, Lib. II, tit. 2, n. 17; De Angelis, *Praelectiones Iuris Canonici*, Lib. II, tit. 20, § 3.

In the case of the interlocutory sentence the discussion centered around the decree against contumacy in contentious trials. In criminal trials, as has been seen, attention was given to the actual presence of the accused in the court, which presence was to be secured, if possible, even with the help of another tribunal. Pope Innocent III (1198-1216) had legislated rather extensively in reference to the procedure to be followed in contentious trials in the event of contumacy. He provided that, if the defendant was contumaciously absent from the court before the joinder of the issue had taken place, the possession of the litigated property could be given to the plaintiff by means of an interlocutory sentence.[158]

This was called quasi-possession.[159] It simply served the purpose of custody. Within a year the defendant could appear in court and, having paid the expenses incurred by his absence and having given guarantees that he would pursue the case, he was again to receive the possession of the property until the case was decided.[160] If there was no property which could be transferred in this fashion, the court could inflict a censure, but if the contumacy occurred before the joinder of issue, the court could not proceed to the final sentence.[161]

Similar provisions concerning the taking over of property which was in the possession of a contumacious defendant had already been made in the *Digest* of Justinian through the law *"Heres absens."* [162]

The ordinary interpretation of this law as given by Accursius (d. 1260) permitted that, if the defendant had no property in the territory where the trial was taking place, any property he had elsewhere could be given in quasi-possession by the tribunal of that place.[163] Accursius stated, however, that there were some who con-

[158] C. 3, X, *ut lite non contestata non procedatur ad testium receptionem vel ad sententiam definitivam,* II, 6.

[159] *Glossa Ordinaria* s. v. *possessionem recuperet,* ad c. 5, § *in aliis vero casibus,* X, *ut lite non contestata etc.,* II, 6; s. v. *possessor,* ad c. 11, X, *de officio iudicis ordinarii,* I, 31.

[160] C. 3, X, *de eo, qui mittitur in possessionem causa rei servandae,* II, 15.

[161] C. 3, X, *ut lite non contestata etc.,* II, 6.

[162] D. (5, 1) (19, 1).

[163] *Glossa Ordinaria* s. v. *ibi se debebit,* ad D. (5, 1) (19, 1).

tended that the application of this law had to be restricted to property within the territory where the trial was taking place. Iacobus Balduinus (d. 1235), for example, seemed to share this opinion.[164]

Their argument was based upon the law of the *Digest*, "*Cum unus*,"[165] which definitely treated of an interlocutory sentence, and in which the taking over of the property of a contumacious defendant was expressly restricted for its execution solely in the territory where the trial was being conducted.[166] But Accursius was of the opinion that the law "*Cum unus*" needed also to be interpreted in such a way that, if the contumacious defendant had no goods in the territory of the trial, then any goods he had elsewhere could be taken over through recourse to the local tribunal.[167] Whether or not there were any canonists who followed the opinion that, in the case of contumacy before the joinder of issue in a contentious case, the goods which the defendant had in another diocese could not be given in quasi-possession seems impossible to determine from the sources available to the writer. However, this opinion was definitely rejected by ecclesiastical legislation,[168] as enacted by Pope Innocent IV (1243-1254) in § *Contrahentes* of the decretal *Romana*.[169]

This decretal of Innocent IV was clearly understood in the sense that it permitted the taking of possession of the goods of a contumacious defendant in a contentious trial on the part of a tribunal of the place where these goods were found.[170] Regarding the property outside of his diocese, the judge of the trial was not to issue

[164] According to Hostiensis. Hostiensis seemed to agree with his teacher on the interpretation of the Roman Law in question, but held that due to new legislation the situation was different at least for Canon Law. Cf. *Commentaria, Liber Sextus*, Lib. II, tit. 2, c. 1, n. 12.

[165] D. (42, 5) (12, 1).

[166] *Glossa Ordinaria* s. v. *is qui*, ad D. (42, 5) (12, 1).

[167] *Glossa Ordinaria* s. v. *is qui*, ad D. (42, 5) (12, 1). Cf. also Bartolus, *In Digestum Commentaria* (6 vols., Venetiis, 1585), D. (42, 5) (12, 1) (tit. *De bonis auto. iud. possi.*, Lex XII, § *Is qui possidere*), n. 1.

[168] *Glossa Ordinaria* s. v. *noscuntur*, ad c. 1, *de foro competenti*, II, 2, in VI°. Cf. also Hostiensis, *Commentaria*, Lib. II, tit. 2, c. 14, n. 1.

[169] C. 1, §, 3, *de foro competenti*, II, 2, in VI°; cf. *supra*, p. 12.

[170] Cf. *Casus* ad c. 1, *de foro competenti*, II, 2, in VI°; Ioannes Andreae, *Commentaria Novella, Liber Sextus*, Lib. II, tit. 2, c. 1, n. 6; also, *supra*, footnote 168.

any precept, nor was he to effect any execution; he was merely to issue against the contumacious party a decree which he then sent to the judge of the other territory for execution. He, himself, was not able to enforce the execution through another, unless he was the other's superior.[171]

Turning now to the point regarding the execution of the final sentence by means of a commission, one finds that the principle legislation in this matter was contained in the decretal *Postulasti* of Innocent III. This decretal provided that, in trials concerning crimes which also called for the penalty of the loss of an office or a benefice, the trial was to be conducted and the sentence was to be given where the crime had been committed, but the execution of the sentence was to take place in the diocese where the convicted one held the office or the benefice.[172]

The principle as here implied, namely, that a sentence given in one tribunal was to be duly honored through its acceptance by any other tribunal, was already basically established in the Roman Law[173] and in Gratian. In Gratian, however, this principle had not been stated clearly and apodictically; rather, it was there simply stated that a cleric who was deposed for subversive activity against his own bishop should be deposed without any hope of being reinstated,[174] and that a cleric who had been deposed for disciplinary reasons while he was in a heretical sect was to observe the same penalty on being received into the Catholic Church.[175] In the canons of Gratian no direct mention was made of a second trial, but undoubtedly it was implied that, if such cases were brought

[171] Ioannes Andreae, *loc. cit.*

[172] C. 14, X, *de foro competenti,* II, 2; cf. Potthast, n. 4722. This decretal of Innocent III was issued on April 29, 1213.

[173] Cf. D. (12, 2) 13; C. (7, 16) 41.

[174] C. 31, C. XI, q. 1. The authenticity of this canon is doubtful. It was ascribed by the Pseudo-Isidorians to Pope Fabian (236-250). Cf. Jaffé, JK, n. 93; Hinschius, p. 165.

[175] C. 39, C. XXIV, q. 1. This is an extract from a letter of St. Augustine written about 398 to Eusebius; cf. *Opera Sancti Aurelii Augustini Hipponensis Episcopi,* opera et studio Monachorum Ordinis S. Benedicti et Congregationis S. Mauri (18 vols., Venetiis, 1756-1769), II, 89-91.

before a second tribunal, this tribunal had to recognize and accept the decision of the original tribunal.

In the decretal *Postulasti* there was stressed another underlying principle, namely, that a sentence given by one tribunal could be executed by another tribunal.[176] This principle had already been found in the Roman Law of the *Digest*.[177]

Bernard of Parma, when commenting on the Decretal *Postulasti*, took the position that, when an accused was being tried for a crime which by law entailed the punishment of deprivation of office or benefice, and the accused had an office or a benefice in a diocese other than where he was tried, the judge of the trial was to pass sentence merely about the crime. He was not to make any judicial disposition regarding the office or the benefice in the other diocese.[178] After the accused was found guilty, the diocese in which he held his benefice was to take up the question of the deprivation of that benefice, and to pass sentence, and then to deprive him of the benefice. It was in this sense that the doctrine of Bernard was understood.[179]

The opinion of Innocent IV lacked full clearness in its expression, but it seemed to approximate the doctrine of Bernard. The accused was to be tried and sentenced. If there was incurred a *latae sententiae* penalty, it took effect immediately, and in this sense the accused could stand deprived even of a church or a benefice which he held in another diocese. Any specific decision, however, about any particular church or benefice which he had in another diocese was left to the judge of the place where the church or benefice was situated. In the meantime, he was actually suspended, even per-

176 *Glossa Ordinaria* s. v. *executio facienda*, ad. c. 14, X, *de foro competenti*, II, 2.

177 D. (42, 1) (15, 1). This law of the *Digest* was ascribed to Ulpian (d. 228). Dionysius Gothofredus (1549-1622), a civilist, stated that from this law there originated what he called the *litterae requisitoriae*, today known as the rogatory letter; cf. Dionysius Gothofredus, *Corpus Iuris Civilis cum notis integris* (Coloniae Allobrogum, 1781), D. (42, 1) (15, 1) (tit. *De re iudicata*, Lex XV, *A Divo*, ad § *Sententiam*), n. 8.

178 *Glossa Ordinaria* s. v. *deliquit*, ad c. 14, X, *de foro competenti*, II, 2.

179 Gulielmus Durantis, *Speculum Iuris*, Lib. II, Partic. III, *De Executione sententiae*, 2, § *Nunc dicendum*, n. 13.

petually if the penalty was such, but the execution of the sentence consisted in a specific judgment to that effect by his proper bishop.[180]

Beginning with Hostiensis, however, the more common opinion held that the judge of the trial, if he found the accused guilty of a crime which called for suspension from any office or benefice he might have, was to render the sentence of *guilty,* and was also to impose the punishment of the law, inclusive of the decision about any particular benefice or office or church he might have even in another diocese.[181]

Ioannes Andreae declared that in the favor of those following the opinion of Hostiensis was the fact that the letter which occasioned the decretal *Postulasti* had also touched the question of benefices, and that, although the execution of the sentence was to take place in the diocese where the church or benefice was, the decretal did not specifically demand that the decree of privation had to be issued there.[182] Durantis, some years earlier, had also followed the doctrine of Hostiensis.[183] Panormitanus specifically rejected the opinion of Innocent IV as leading to too much confusion. According to Panormitanus, it seemed that the execution of a sentence in such a case consisted in the actual depriving of the convicted person of his benefice after he had been declared deprived of it by the judge who had issued a sentence of *guilty* against him.[184]

Having seen the various restrictions and the corresponding necessity for the co-operation between tribunals in the execution of sentences, one may ask whether in this co-operation there really was need of a rogatory commission. In other words, was the execution to be effected at the specific request of the tribunal which had originally tried the case, and was such a specific request essential for the execution?

180 Innocentius IV, *Commentaria,* Lib. II, tit. 2, c. 14; also Lib. V, tit. 31, c. 11.

181 Hostiensis, *Commentaria,* Lib. II, tit. 2, c. 14, n. 1; Ioannes Andreae, *Commentaria Novella,* Lib. II, tit. 2, c. 14.

182 *Loc. cit.*

183 *Speculum Iuris,* Lib. II, Partic. III, *De Executione sententiae,* 2, § *Nunc dicendum,* n. 13.

184 *Commentaria,* Lib. II, tit. 2, c. 14, n. 7.

There is no doubt that with reference to the case considered in the decretal *Postulasti* Hostiensis felt that the execution was to be effected at the request and in accordance with the decree of the original judge of the case.[185] Ioannes Andreae seemed to subscribe to the same opinion.[186]

Durantis, however, reported that many held a contrary opinion, which, according to him, implied that even without a letter of request from the judge of the case the judge of the diocese where the church or the benefice was located could execute the sentence which had been given in a different diocese. Indeed, he did not deny the competence of the local judge of the seat of the benefice in executing the sentence merely on his own authority in the case envisioned by the decretal *Postulasti*, but he considered that competence as arising in this particular case from the close connection that existed between the sentence to be executed and other matters that were under his jurisdiction.[187] Panormitanus also ruled out the necessity of a rogatory commission in this case. He gave for his reason that it was the duty of a judge to employ his power and office in cases of crimes and in questions concerning benefices. Yet, even so, he left room for the use of the rogatory commission in this case.[188]

Allowance could be made for a different manner of procedure with reference to contracts when at least a part of them had to be fulfilled in a territory other than where they were entered into. Likewise, a different means of procedure became applicable for excommunications which of their nature obliged everywhere, and for cases that were substantially alike with the case that was contemplated in the decretal *Postulasti*. But, having thus made allowance for the exceptional cases, Durantis held that for the execution of a judicial sentence in a place other than where it was issued the request was not to be made by the judge who had issued the sentence, but rather the request was to derive from the interested party, who would enter a new judicial suit, called the *"actio in*

[185] *Commentaria,* Lib. II, tit. 2, c. 14, n. 1.

[186] *Commentaria Novella,* Lib. II, tit. 2, c. 14.

[187] *Speculum Iuris,* Lib. II, Partic. III, *De Executione sententiae,* 2, § *Nunc dicendum,* n. 13.

[188] *Commentaria,* Lib. II, tit. 2, c. 14, n. 18.

factum," before the judge of the place where this party desired to see the execution carried into effect. In this suit all the formalities of a trial were to be observed, and the plaintiff needed to furnish convincing proof of the other party's obligation.[189]

Having given his own opinion, Durantis pointed without comment to another opinion prevalent in his time. The one in whose favor a decision had been granted in one place could seek the execution of that decision in another place by means of an *actio in factum,* or by means of an *actio iudicati,* or by himself calling upon the judge in his official capacity to effect the execution. The first two means, namely the *actio in factum* and the *actio iudicati,* could be utilized anywhere, since anyone who had the right to invoke these suits could at his own option call upon their use. The third means, namely, of calling upon the judge for an effective assistance in the executing of the sentence, could be utilized only by a private individual, and with relation simply to that judge who had authority over the party who had lost the case. As an alternative it was still possible for the judge who had heard the case to address an appeal or a formal request to the judge of the place where the execution was to be effected.[190]

[189] *Speculum Iuris,* Lib. II, Partic. III, *De Executione sententiae,* 2, § Nunc dicendum, n. 14.

[190] *Speculum Iuris,* Lib. II, Partic. III, *De Executione sententiae,* 2, § *Nunc dicendum,* n. 14. An *actio in factum* was an action permitted originally by the praetor when there was no definite action recognized in the album, and yet equity pointed to the need of some available judicial action; cf. Wenger, *Institutes of the Roman Law of Procedure* (revised and translated by Fisk, New York: Veritas Press, 1940), p. 162, footnote 12; also *Glossa Ordinaria* s. v. *subiecta,* ad C. (4, 64) 3. In the *actio iudicati,* which represented the more common means of executing a sentence, the proceedings in the beginning were like those of an ordinary controversial proceeding, but then a deviation resulted when the debtor acknowledged the judgment debt that had been declared in the major issue, and the magistrate thereupon issued a decree for execution; cf. Wenger, *op. cit.,* p. 228. The appeal to the judge or to the *officium iudicis* here bespeaks a request made to the judge for effective and, if necessary, physical assistance in the execution; cf. D. (6, 1) 68. At least in the thirteenth century, when Accursius wrote the *Glossa Ordinaria,* the military force mentioned in D. (6, 1) 68 was not understood to connote an appeal to the army to effect the transfer of goods by the active assistance of soldiers, but rather

Who held this opinion in the time of Durantis, it is impossible to determine from the sources at hand. It was, however, practically the same opinion that was later adopted by Bartolus a Saxoferrato (d. 1357), and after him by Panormitanus. These two writers sought to confirm this doctrine by means of a clarification. The original opinion, as described by Durantis, had permitted, so it seemed, an appeal by the victorious party himself to any judge who had proper authority over the party who had lost the suit. The appeal, of course, sought intervention through the *officium iudicis* for the effective execution of the sentence. Bartolus and Panormitanus stated that any judge whose duty it was by the universal law to effect the execution could do so if requested by the victorious party. But, on the simple score of the *officium iudicis,* no other judge who was not commissioned by the universal law could effectively execute the sentence of another judge apart from the latter's request.

For a possible effective intervention through the *officium iudicis* on the part of a judge who had not issued the sentence, or who otherwise was not empowered by law, a letter of request from the original judge of the trial was necessary. A judge who intervened on his own authority overstepped his bounds. For the victorious party to expect such intervention simply on his own request would have been presumptuous, since an effective execution of the sentence could derive merely from the judge who had heard the case (and probably also from him who by the universal law was qualified for executing the sentence), and even then only on the score of equity. But the option with reference to the possible invoking of the *actio in factum* or the *actio iudicati* remained available before ecclesiastical judges in general.[191]

the effective assistance given in the execution by means of executors, since only if further assistance had been needed would military aid have been requested; cf. *Glossa Ordinaria* s. v. *transfertur,* ad D. (6, 1) 68.

191 Bartolus, *In Digestum Commentaria,* D. (42, 1) 15 (tit. *De re iudicata,* Lex XV, *O Divo,* § *Sententiam Romae*), n. 2; Panormitanus, *Commentaria,* Lib. II, tit. 2, c. 14, n. 18. Cf. also *Additio* to the *Glossa Ordinaria* s. v. *transfertur,* ad D. (6, 1) 68; D. (1, 10) (1, 1).

Section 2. From the Council of Trent to the Code

In the immediately preceding section there was mention of the *actio in factum* and the *actio iudicati.* When for reasons other than that of appeal a decision had not become executed, for example, inasmuch as the decision awaited its execution in a territory other than the one in which the trial had been conducted, then the victorious party could avail himself of the *actio iudicati* or the *actio in factum* before any tribunal which was competent over the person, the property, or the thing about which the execution was concerned. Such a suit had to be entered before the tribunal as any other suit, i. e., with all the juridical formalities. After the judge of this tribunal had issued the sentence, he could then proceed to the execution.

From this manner of securing the execution of a sentence in a different territory the writer wishes to prescind in the discussion regarding the rogatory commission after the Council of Trent. After the Council of Trent, as before, one could pursue his rights before any competent tribunal. The post-Tridentine authors were in agreement that in a contentious case the joinder of issue gave rise to a quasi-contract between the parties. This quasi-contract called not only for the prosecution of the case to the conclusion, but also for the fulfillment of the conditions inherent in the rendered judgment.[192] Some authors made specific mention of the *actio iudicati.*[193]

It seemed to be a generally accepted principle, after the Council of Trent as before, that a judge could not execute the sentence that he had rendered if that execution had to be effected in the territory of another. A judge could not execute his own sentence outside his own territory. A few authors explicitly stated this, and concluded therefrom that a recourse to the tribunal of the place where the

[192] Engel, Lib. II, tit. 5, n. 4; Pirhing, Lib. II, tit. 5, n. 27; Schmier, Lib. II, tract. 3, c. 1, n. 62; Reiffenstuel, Lib. II, tit. 5, n. 32; Schmalzgrueber, Lib. II, tit. 5, n. 8; Bouix, *Tractatus de Judiciis Ecclesiasticis,* II, 103; Sebastianelli, *De Iudiciis Civilibus,* n. 103; Lega, *De Iudiciis Ecclesiasticis,* I, n. 421; Santi, *Praelectiones Juris Canonici,* Lib. II, tit. 5, n. 7; Wernz, *Ius Decretalium,* V, n. 460.

[193] Reiffenstuel, *loc. cit.;* Santi, *loc. cit.*

execution awaited its dispatch was a matter of necessity.[194] Other authors took it for granted that a judge could not execute his sentence outside of his territory when they insisted that in such a case the judge had to request the proper authority of the other territory for the effecting of the execution.[195] Thus it was the universal and common teaching of the canonists from the Council of Trent to the promulgation of the present Code of Canon Law that, to execute a sentence outside of his own territory, a judge had to make a request to that effect to the authority of the territory where the execution was to be dispatched. In addition, it was agreed that that request had to be honored, and could not be refused.[196]

Not only could the assistance of other ecclesiastical tribunals be requested for the execution of the sentence, but also the help of the civil authority could be sought. Since the Church by itself had no way of employing physical force to effect the execution of a sentence, the help of the civil authority had at times to be reckoned as a matter of necessity. According to the authors who had treated this question, the request of the Church for such needed assistance from the state or municipal authorities necessitated for the latter an act of compliance with the request. In order to enforce such compliance, the Church could invoke the use of ecclesiastical censures.[197]

194 Tuschus, *Practicae Conclusiones Iuris in Omni Foro Frequentiores*, Littera E, concl. 494, n. 1; Barbosa, *Collectanea Doctorum tam Veterum quam Recentiorum*, Lib. II, tit. 2, c. 14, nn. 9-10; Pirhing, Lib. II, tit. 2, nn. 66-68.

195 Fagnanus, *Commentaria in V Libros Decretalium*, Lib. I, tit. *de treuga et pace*, c. 1, n. 8; Engel, Lib. II, tit. 27, n. 29; Reiffenstuel, Lib. II, tit. 27, n. 167; Schmier, Lib. II, tract. 3, c. 12, n. 172; Schmalzgrueber, Lib. II, tit. 2, n. 60; Pichler, Lib. II, tit. 27, n. 28; Ferraris, *Prompta Bibliotheca*, s. v. *Forum*, n. 12; De Angelis, *Praelectiones Iuris Canonici*, Lib. II, tit. 27, c. 3, § *De Executione Sententiae;* Lega, *De Iudiciis Ecclesiasticis*, II, n. 324; Wernz, *Ius Decretalium*, V, n. 290.

196 Engel, Lib. II, tit. 27, n. 29; Reiffenstuel, Lib. II, tit. 27, n. 167; Pirhing, Lib. II, tit. 2, n. 67; Pichler, Lib. II, tit. 27, n. 28; Schmalzgrueber, Lib. II, tit. 3, n. 23; De Angelis, *Praelectiones Iuris Canonici*, Lib. II, tit. 27, c. 3, § *De Executione Sententiae;* Lega, *De Iudiciis Ecclesiasticis*, II, n. 324.

197 Cf. Engel, Lib. II, tit. 27, n. 29; Schmier, Lib. II, tract. 3, c. 12, n. 173; Pichler, Lib. II, tit. 27, n. 28.

Granted, then, the need of the assistance which was to be given by a second tribunal to the first, was it necessary for the first tribunal to present a formal request for the effecting of the execution? This problem was discussed by very few authors. Cardinal Tuschus (d. 1620) proposed the general principle that before one judge could execute the sentence of another judge, the latter had to request the former to do so. But he also adverted to the fact that some judicial decisions carried with them their own automatic execution outside of the territory wherein they were rendered. By way of example he pointed to judicial decisions which involved the penalty of a *latae sententiae* excommunication.[198]

Reiffenstuel treated the matter at greater length. After stating that a judge could not execute the sentence of another tribunal apart from the latter's request, he pointed out the following exceptions: (1) a judge who by the universal law was authorized for the execution of the sentence had no need of the permission of the judge who had rendered the decision; (2) the ordinary judge had no need of any permission from his judicial delegate for effecting the execution of the latter's sentence; (3) in the interest of the common good a judge could *ex officio* be under constraint and necessity to execute a sentence which had been rendered elsewhere, as in the case of someone's deposition from a benefice, and then he had no need of any permission from the judge who had decreed the deposition; and, finally, (4) the effect of an incurred excommunication could be executed freely by any judge.[199]

In all other cases a judge who desired to execute a sentence given by another judge of a different territory could act only when he had been requested to do so.[200] Such a request was made by means of a letter called *"litterae requisitoriales."* In the execution of the request of another, the second judge had faithfully to follow

[198] *Practicae Conclusiones Iuris in Omni Foro Frequentiores,* Littera E, concl. 494, n. 8.

[199] Reiffenstuel, Lib. II, tit. 2, n. 52.

[200] Reiffenstuel, *loc. cit.*

the instructions given to him. In a word, he was to proceed in the manner of a simple delegate.[201]

Article 6. The Uniting of the Various Uses of the Rogatory Commission into a Single Juridical Institute

It has been seen that the authors, both before and after the Council of Trent, understood and interpreted the law of the Church in the sense that there was to be mutual help and assistance between tribunals both in contentious and criminal cases. The main reason for the necessity of this help and assistance lay in the territorial limitation of judicial or contentious jurisdiction. An additional reason derived from the fact of the convenience that benefited the witnesses if it remained unnecessary for them to appear before the original judge of the case.

In large measure this help and assistance between tribunals was discussed with reference to particular factors. The discussion related, for example, to the citation of the parties and of the witnesses, to the extradition proceedings, to the taking of testimony, and to the execution of decrees and definitive sentences. The ensuing relationship between the tribunals was truly juridical in the sense that the one tribunal could be juridically obliged and forced to grant the desired aid to the other tribunal which requested it.[202]

In the doctrine of Schmalzgrueber these different types of needed assistance between tribunals served as material which could be fused into a single dominant juridical concept. According to him, each jurisdictional territory was obliged to be of assistance to any other jurisdictional territory in the measure of the assistance that was needed.[203] This general principle became the adopted doctrine

[201] Lega, *De Iudiciis Ecclesiasticis,* II, n. 324.

[202] Cf. Engel, Lib. II, tit. 27, n. 29; Reiffenstuel, Lib. II, tit. 27, n. 167, and Lib. II, tit. 2, n. 54; Pichler, Lib. II, tit. 27, n. 28; De Angelis, *Praelectiones Iuris Canonici,* Lib. II, tit. 27, c. 3, § *De Executione Sententiae.*

[203] "Nam una jurisdictio per aliam adjuvanda est, et sicut manus manum fricat, ita unus magistratus alterius armis indiget."—Lib. II, tit. 3, n. 23; cf. also Lib. II, tit. 2, n. 63.

of Lega[204] and of Wernz,[205] and eventually became incorporated in the Code of Canon Law.[206]

[204] "Fundamentum huius conclusionis est in *subsidio iuris* quod iudices inter se *coordinati* praestare sibi debent in bonum universae reipublicae."—*De Iudiciis Ecclesiasticis,* IV, n. 166.

[205] "Quare unumquodque tribunal ecclesiasticum ius et obligationem habet requirendi ab alio tribunali in processu canonico actus legitimos suae competentiae subductos."—*Ius Decretalium,* V, n. 99.

[206] Canon 1570, § 2.

Part Two

Canonical Commentary

CHAPTER II

THE JURIDICAL PRINCIPLES NECESSITATING THE ROGATORY COMMISSION

Article 1. The Power of Jurisdiction can be Exercised Directly only over Subjects

Authority is the power of directing and obliging the members of a society toward the attainment of the proper end of that society.[1] From its very nature, it deals with the members of the society over which it is exercised. By its nature it has no direct power over anyone who is not a member of that society. Authority arises from the necessity of directing toward the common end those who are united together to attain that end. A specific end is desired which is unattainable by individual effort. There is effected a union of the individuals who desire the attainment of that end. Authority becomes necessary to direct the efforts of the many to the attainment of the common goal. The power of authority, therefore, extends over the members of the society. Directly it does not affect anyone outside of that society.

The Church is a juridically perfect society. As a society it must have authority. Authority in the Church, in its nature of a juridically perfect society, is called jurisdiction. Jurisdiction is a public

[1] Cf. Ottaviani, *Institutiones Iuris Publici Ecclesiastici* (2 vols., Vol. I, 3. ed., Civitate Vaticana: Typis Polyglottis Vaticanis, 1947), I, n. 28; Cappello, *Summa Iuris Publici Ecclesiastici* (4. ed., Romae: Apud Aedes Universitatis Gregorianae, 1936), n. 50.

power of ruling the members of the Church in the attainment of the peculiar end of the Church, namely, the sanctification of souls.[2]

The power of ecclesiastical jurisdiction is vested primarily in the Roman Pontiff. When the Church is looked upon as one society, juridically perfect, the power to rule that universal society is vested in the Bishop of Rome. Admission to that society is by valid baptism. Every validly baptized person of whatsoever position is a member of the society of which the Roman Pontiff is the head. He has immediate power over all the faithful.[3]

Besides the universal organization there are within the Church other societies, imperfect inasmuch as their end is directly subordinated to the end of the Church as a whole, but truly juridical. Bishops who by divine institution were intended to preside over particular churches have the charge of dioceses, which for the most part are territorial units.[4]

Other territories canonically erected but not included in any diocese are under the care of abbots and prelates *nullius*.[5] Still other territories which have not been erected into the status of dioceses are under the direction of apostolic vicars and prefects.[6] In addition to these, certain religious groups have been exempted from the local authority and placed under authorities of their own.[7]

All of the superiors mentioned partake of the public power of the Church.[8] They are true authorities over the faithful who have been committed to their charge. They are to direct their subjects in the attainment of their end, eternal salvation; to this end they are able to make demands upon the faithful, judge infractions of law and right according to law, and use coercive measures to enforce the law or to punish delinquents.

The jurisdiction of bishops, abbots and prelates *nullius*, apostolic vicars and prefects, and exempt clerical religious superiors has the

[2] Ottaviani, *op. cit.*, I, n. 113; Cappello, *op. cit.*, n. 187.
[3] Canon 218, §§ 1, 2.
[4] Canon 329, § 1.
[5] Canon 319.
[6] Canon 293, § 1.
[7] Canons 615; 501, § 1.
[8] Canons 335, § 1; 294 § 1; 323 § 1; 501, § 1.

same purpose as authority in any society, that is, to direct the members of that society in the attainment of their common goal. Jurisdiction and subjects therefore are correlative terms. Jurisdiction has been given by God to the Church in general for the governing of the faithful in general. Jurisdiction has been given to lesser prelates in the Church for the governing of their particular subjects. This is the purpose and the nature of jurisdiction. Therefore it follows that whatever jurisdiction a prelate possesses he cannot exercise it over those who are not his subjects,[9] or over those who are not members of the society of which he is the authority. The fact that jurisdiction can be exercised only over one's subjects derives from the very nature of jurisdiction itself.[10] Since it is of the nature of jurisdiction that it cannot be used over those who are not subjects, its use with reference to them would be invalid.[11]

Canon 94 establishes in general the manner in which one becomes a subject of a particular ordinary.[12] As a general rule, therefore, ordinaries are able to directly exercise their jurisdiction over only those who in their territory have a domicile or a quasi-domicile, or who actually reside there, lacking a domicile or a quasi-domicile anywhere. But as it is the universal law which determines who is subject to a particular ordinary, so the universal law can make exceptions. This it does in canon 14, § 1, 1°, which makes travelers directly subject to the ordinary of the place where they are

[9] Canon 201, § 1.

[10] Blat, *Commentarium Textus Codicis Iuris Canonici* (5 vols. in 6, Vol. II, 2. ed., 1921; Vol. IV, 1927, Romae: Libraria del Collegio "Angelico"), II, n. 150; De Meester, *Juris Canonici et Juris Canonico-Civilis Compendium* (nova editio, 3 vols. in 4, Brugis: Sumptibus et Typis Societatis Sancti Augustini, 1921-1928), I, n. 464; Oesterle, *Praelectiones Iuris Canonici* (Vol. I, Romae: In Collegio S. Anselmi, 1931), I, 109; Regatillo, *Institutiones Iuris Canonici* (2 vols., Vol. I, 2. ed., 1946; Vol. II, 1942, Santander; Sal Terrae), I, n. 362.

[11] Canon 1680, § 1. Sometimes, however, jurisdiction is prorogued; cf. canon 1628, § 1.

[12] Canons 111-117 give the norms for the affiliation of a secular cleric with his diocese; canons 538-586 treat of the admission of a candidate to a religious society; canon 641 treats of the reception and possible incardination of a former religious into a diocese; canon 672 relates to the similar reception of a dismissed religious.

traveling as far as laws are concerned which prescribe formalities for acts or which concern the public order. Similarly, by committing a delict one becomes subject, at least as far as the delict and its punishment are concerned, to the ordinary of the place where the delict was committed.[13] Also, in making a contract one becomes subject to the ordinary of the place where the contract is made or is to be carried out, at least as long as the contracting party who was not otherwise subject to him remains in his territory.[14]

Another exception to canon 94 is had in canon 1565, § 2, which permits contracting parties in the act of making the contract to choose an ordinary to whom they will be subject in any question that might arise in regard to the obligations springing from the contract. Here it is not any law as such that subjects the contracting parties, but the law permits the contracting parties to make their own choice of the one who will have power over them.

In all the cases mentioned so far, the exercise of the jurisdiction is one of direct application. Its exercise extends exclusively over subjects, whether these be subject by reason of domicile, of quasi-domicile, or of actual presence which at the same time connotes a lack of domicile or quasi-domicile anywhere or by reason of a special prescription of law in individual cases of delicts or contracts.

Besides its direct use which relates only to subjects, jurisdiction can have also an indirect effect which relates to non-subjects. When jurisdiction is exercised directly over persons or things subject to the authority, non-subjects frequently will be affected. This holds true in real property cases,[15] in cases involving a necessary forum,[16] and in marriage cases when one of the parties is not baptized or has his domicile or quasi-domicile in another diocese. In all these cases, the general principle remains true, namely, that jurisdiction

[13] Canon 1566, §§ 1, 2.

[14] Canon 1565, § 1; *Pontificia Commissio Interpretationis* (hereafter cited P. C. I.), 14 iul. 1922, ad XIII—*Acta Apostolicae Sedis* (Romae, 1909—), XIV (1922), 529 (hereafter cited *AAS*). Other cases of subjection of the traveler to the local ordinary are exemplified in canons 33, § 1; 804, § 3; 1251, § 1; 1303, §§ 2-4; cf. Hammill, *The Obligations of the Traveler according to Canon 14*, pp. 126-128.

[15] Canon 1564.

[16] Canon 1560.

can be exercised only over subjects; it is simply by reason of the legitimate use of this jurisdiction over subjects that non-subjects become indirectly affected.[17]

In relation to canon 201, § 1, a difficulty arises in regard to the granting of dispensations from the general law when the favor relates to travelers. Travelers are not delineated in canon 94 as subjects of the local ordinary in whose territory they are traveling. Nevertheless the Code itself provides that in some cases an ordinary can dispense travelers from the general law.[18] Certainly the granting of a dispensation is an act of jurisdiction, for it implies the release of someone from subjection to a given law. How can a local ordinary place an act of jurisdiction in favor of travelers who, as it may seem, are not his subjects? Some give the answer that as far as a dispensation is concerned travelers as such become subjects of the local ordinary where they are traveling by the very fact that they are passing through his territory or remaining there for a short time.[19] Others deny that the local ordinary cannot dispense travelers as such. They base their opinion on canon 201, § 1.[20] De Smet (d. 1927) stated that the dispensing of travelers is an exception.[21]

The opinion that travelers are always subject to the local ordinary where they are traveling as far as a dispensation is concerned, and this by reason of their actual presence in his territory, has no foundation in law. The Code implies that travelers are not under

[17] Prümmer, *Manuale Iuris Canonici* (3. ed., Friburgi Brisgoviae: Herder & Co., 1922), p. 123; Regatillo, *Institutiones Iuris Canonici,* I, n. 362; Toso, *Ad Codicem Iuris Canonici . . . Commentaria Minora* (5 vols. in 2, Romae: Marietti, 1920-1927), II, 170.

[18] Canons 1245, § 1; 1043; 1045.

[19] Cf. Michiels, *Normae Generales Juris Canonici* (2 vols., Lublin: Universitas Catholica, 1929), II, 494-495; anonymous, "Questioni Matrimoniali"—*Il Monitore Ecclesiastico* (Romae, 1876—), XXXVII (1925), 204-209.

[20] Cf. Chelodi, *Ius de Personis* (3. ed., curavit P. Ciprotti, Trento: Libraria Moderna Editrice, 1942), n. 87; De Smet, *Tractatus Theologico-Canonico De Sponsalibus et Matrimonio* (4. ed., Brugis: Car. Beyaert, 1927), nn. 773-775; Van Hove, *Commentarium Lovaniense in Codicem Iuris Canonici,* Vol. I, tom. 5, *De Privilegiis-De Dispensationis* (Mechliniae-Romae: H. Dessain, 1939), n. 433.

[21] *Op. cit.,* n. 775.

the jurisdiction of the ordinary of the place where they are traveling except in the cases specifically stated by the universal law.[22] In certain specific cases travelers are subjected to the local ordinary for the gaining of dispensations.[23] But nowhere in the Code is there any mention or statement of the general subjection of travelers to the ordinary of the place where they are traveling simply by reason of their actual presence in his territory.

On the other hand, there cannot be any exception to the principle that jurisdiction can be exercised only over subjects. This principle inheres in the very concept of jurisdiction and therefore cannot leave room for any exception.

The answer to the difficulty is to be found in a distinction made by Wernz- (d. 1914) Vidal (d. 1938),[24] namely, that although delegated power also has to be exercised over subjects, these must be subjects primarily of the one delegating the power. Only secondarily are they subjects of the one delegated. They are then subjects of the delegate inasmuch as he has been delegated, and not inasmuch as he possesses over them any jurisdiction of his own.

When a traveler on a journey is being dispensed by a local ordinary, he is definitely a subject of the Roman Pontiff whose jurisdiction is being exercised in the grant of the dispensation. He is a subject of the local ordinary inasmuch as the local ordinary acts as a delegate of the Roman Pontiff. He is not a subject of the local ordinary inasmuch as the latter is the head of a particular diocese. Thus there is no conflict with canon 201, § 1, whose universal validity remains unimpaired. Thus also there is no creation of a new title of subjection. What subjects the local ordinary is to have when exercising delegated jurisdiction depends not primarily on the extent of his territory but on the will of the Roman Pontiff who delegates him. To find out who the subjects of his delegated jurisdiction are, the local ordinary or any delegate must have recourse to the law or the special faculties which

[22] Canon 14.

[23] Canons 1245, § 1; 1043; 1045.

[24] *Ius Canonicum* (7 vols. in 8, Vol. II, 3. ed. a P. Aguirre recognita, 1943; Vol. V, 3. ed. a P. Aguirre recognita, 1946; Vol. VI, 1927, Romae: Apud Aedes Universitatis Gregorianae), II, n. 375.

afford him the power of granting the dispensation. In this discussion delegation is understood in the light of the principles of public law rather than in the peculiar meaning that this word has in the positive law of canon 197, § 1; consequently, it includes any power that permits a lower authority to dispense from the laws of a higher authority even though that power is granted by law and is exercised by reason of an office.

ARTICLE 2. JUDICIAL POWER CANNOT BE EXERCISED OUTSIDE THE TERRITORY

The Code adopted the previous legislation in regard to the territorial limitation of contentious jurisdiction. In the Code, however, a slightly different terminology is used. Contentious jurisdiction is called judicial power.[25] Judicial power is jurisdiction which is exercised according to the judicial formalities which are found in *Liber IV, Pars Prima,* of the Code.[26] Before the Code contentious jurisdiction extended to all things which required a judicial hearing by a tribunal.[27] Therefore the terms, contentious jurisdiction and judicial power, represent the same concept. Modern commentators recognize this limitation of judicial power to the proper territory of the judge as the principle found in the *Digest* of Justinian and ascribed to the jurist, Paul: *"Extra territorium ius dicenti impune non paretur."* [28]

After the publication of the Code arose the question whether acts of judicial jurisdiction if placed contrary to canon 201, § 2, would be invalid or merely illicit. Noval (d. 1938) thought that

[25] Canon 201, § 2.

[26] Coronata, *Institutiones Iuris Canonici* (2. ed., 5 vols., Taurini: Marietti, 1939-1947), I, n. 282; Regatillo, *Institutiones Iuris Canonici,* I, n. 358; Wernz-Vidal, *Ius Canonicum,* II, n. 375; Toso, *Ad Codicem Juris Canonici . . . Commentaria Minora,* II, 171.

[27] Cf. *supra,* pp. 5-6, footnotes 19 and 20.

[28] D. (2, 1) 20. Cf. also Coronata, *loc. cit.;* Toso, *loc. cit.;* Cocchi, *Commentarium in Codicem Iuris Canonici* (8 vols. in 5, Vol. II, 4. ed., 1937; Vol. VII, 3. ed., 1940, Taurinorum Augustae: Marietti), II, n. 124; De Meester, *Juris Canonici et Juris Canonico-Civilis Compendium,* I, n. 464; Wernz-Vidal, *loc. cit.*

such acts would be illicit but not invalid. He based his opinion on the absence of an invalidating clause in canon 201, § 2.[29] Against Noval authors quite commonly teach that such acts would be invalid.[30]

Noval's argument is not without some weight. The presumption of law is for the validity of acts until the invalidity is definitely proved. Canon 201, § 2, has no invalidating clause. Canon 1894, 4°, speaks about the affixing of the name of the place to the final sentence; without the name of the place, the sentence would be invalid. The canon, however, says nothing about a sentence being invalid if it was given by a judge who at the time was outside of his territory. The *"nequit"* in canon 201, § 2, does not give conclusive proof that a contrary action would be invalid.[31] Nor is it immediately evident that the territorial limitation belongs to the essence of judicial power.[32] One could envision a bishop holding a trial between two of his subjects in a place outside of his own territory where witnesses might be more available.

29 *Commentarium Codicis Iuris Canonici,* Liber IV, *De Processibus,* Pars I, *De Iudiciis* (Augustae Taurinorum-Romae: Marietti, 1920), n. 232 (hereafter cited as *De Iudiciis*). Sipos follows Noval's opinion, but admits that the contrary opinion is the more common one; cf. *Enchiridion Iuris Canonici* (3. ed., Pécs: Ex Typographia "Hâladas R. T.," 1936), p. 862, footnote 9.

30 Roberti, *De Processibus* (2 vols., Vol. I, 2. ed., Romae: Apud Custodiam Librariam Pontificii Instituti Utriusque Iuris, 1941; Vol. II, Romae: Apud Aedes Facultatis Iuridicae ad S. Apollinaris, 1926), I, n. 167; Cappello, *Summa Iuris Canonici* (3 vols., Vols. I, II, 4. ed., 1945; Vol. III, 2. ed., 1940, Romae: Apud Aedes Universitatis Gregorianae), III, n. 80; Toso, *Ad Codicem Juris Canonici . . . Commentaria Minora,* II, 171; Lega-Bartoccetti, *Commentarius in Iudicia Ecclesiastica iuxta Codicem Iuris Canonici* (3 vols., Romae: Anonima Libraria Cattolica Italiana, 1938-1941), I, 55, 268, 270 (hereafter cited as *Commentarius in Iudicia Ecclesiastica*); Berutti, *Institutiones Iuris Canonici* (5 vols., Vol. II, Taurini-Romae: Marietti, 1943), II, 321; Eichmann, *Lehrbuch des Kirchenrechts auf Grund des Codex Iuris Canonici* (2. ed., Paderborn: Ferdinand Schoningh, 1926), p. 568; Cocchi, *Commentarium in Codicem Iuris Canonici,* VII, 106; Regatillo, *Institutiones Iuris Canonici,* II, n. 416; Vermeersch-Creusen, *Epitome Iuris Canonici* (6. ed., 3 vols., Mechliniae-Romae: H. Dessain, 1937-1946), III, n. 71.

31 Coronata, *Institutiones Iuris Canonici,* I, 35, footnote 6.

32 This against Roberti (*De Processibus,* I, n. 167).

Nevertheless, one must conclude with Roberti[33] that judicial acts of jurisdiction placed outside of the proper territory of the judge hearing the case would be invalid. The law placing the territorial limitation on judicial power was already present in the pre-Code legislation. It must therefore be interpreted according to the pre-Code authors.[34] Under Decretal Law contentious jurisdiction was essentially bound up with the territory of a diocese, so that outside of that territory the judge had no such jurisdiction. From then to the time of the Code authors understood the use of contentious jurisdiction outside of the proper territory of the judge to be invalid. No pre-Code author ever contradicted this.[35] Therefore canon 201, § 2, must be understood in the sense that any act of judicial power if placed outside of the proper territory of the judge would be invalid.

Before the Code there was one notable exception to the limitation of judicial power to the territory of the judge. With the consent of both parties a judge could sit in judgment in another's territory, provided that the latter also gave his consent. This was known as the *forum prorogationis*.[36] There is no doubt that, according to the law of the Code, competence can still be prorogued. If a judge does not advert to the fact that he is relatively incompetent and the parties do not raise any exception in this regard, the competency is prorogued.[37]

The *forum prorogationis,* itself, however, was abolished by the Code.[38] In no manner is it listed among the titles of competence enumerated in the Code.[39] In no case can an accused be cited

[33] *De Processibus,* I, n. 167.

[34] Canon 6, §§ 2, 3.

[35] Cf. *supra,* pp. 7-9.

[36] Cf. c. 18, X, *de foro competenti,* II, 2; c. 40, X, *de officio et potestate iudicis delegati,* I, 29; c. 11, *de rescriptis,* I, 3, in VI°; Schmalzgruber, Lib. II, tit. 2, n. 143 ff.; Reiffenstuel, Lib. II, tit. 2, n. 122 ff.

[37] Cf. Roberti, *De Processibus,* I, n. 61; Lega-Bartoccetti, *Commentarius in Iudicia Ecclesiastica,* I, 72.

[38] Cf. Noval, *De Iudiciis,* I, n. 69; Coronata, *Institutiones Iuris Canonici,* III, n. 1100; Roberti, *De Processibus,* I, n. 61; Besté, *Introductio in Codicem* (3. ed., Collegeville, Minn.: St. John's Abbey Press, 1946), p. 779.

[39] Cf. canons 1560-1568.

except for one of the titles of competence listed.[40] Before a judge proceeds to cite an accused to appear before his court he must first make a judgment as to his competence by reason of at least one of the legitimate titles.[41] Therefore a judge cannot proceed to conduct a trial outside of his territory on the ground that he is competent by reason of the *forum prorogationis,* for no such title of competence any longer exists.

If a judge actually proceeded to conduct a trial outside of his territory either because the parties so desired or with their consequent failure to raise an exception in due time, would his competence be prorogued? It must be answered that competence in this case would not be prorogued,[42] since the case does not involve the question of relative incompetency. When a judge is relatively incompetent, competence can be prorogued according to canons 1610, § 2, and 1628, § 1, but relative incompetence is had when there is not present any of the titles of competence mentioned in canons 1560-1568. Rather, the case of the judge outside of his territory seems to be attended with absolute incompetence. Absolute incompetence points to the incapacity of the judge,[43] and is imposed by reasons of the public good.[44]

It has been seen that the restriction on the use of his jurisdiction outside of his territory was of such a nature that the judge was considered deprived of his power when he was outside of his territory, and reduced to the state of a private person.[45] In other words,

[40] Canon 1559, § 1.

[41] Canon 1609, § 1.

[42] Roberti, *De Processibus,* I, n. 167. Roberti (*loc. cit.*) seems to regard Lega-Bartoccetti as being of the opposite opinion. Lega-Bartoccetti (*Commentarius in Iudicia Ecclesiastica,* I, 269-270), however, appears to agree that, if the place where the judge acts is outside of his territory, competence is not prorogued. But they say that the situation is different if the judge acts in an exempt place, for in such a case he is not absolutely incompetent unless the exempt place forms part of a prelacy *nullius.*

[43] Wernz-Vidal, *Ius Canonicum,* VI, n. 63, footnote 46; Lega-Bartoccetti, *Commentarius in Iudicia Ecclesiastica,* I, 40.

[44] Lega-Bartoccetti, *Commentarius in Iudicia Ecclesiastica,* I, 72; Noval, *De Iudiciis,* n. 59; Vermeersch-Creusen, *Epitome Iuris Canonici,* III, n. 10; Coronata, *Institutiones Iuris Canonici,* III, n. 1094.

[45] Cf. *supra,* p. 7; also Roberti, *De Processibus,* I, n. 167.

he was *incapax*. This limitation was imposed for reasons of the public good, as a means of preventing confusion between neighboring territorial jurisdictions.[46] Therefore the incompetency of the judge outside of his territory must be called absolute.

A confirming argument that a judge is absolutely incompetent outside of his territory[47] can be drawn from the universal opinion of the authors before the Code, and the almost universal opinion of authors since the Code, that acts placed by a judge outside of his territory are invalid.[48] Acts placed by a judge who is absolutely incompetent are always invalid, whereas, if he is only relatively incompetent, his acts must be considered valid if an exception is not brought against his incompetence in due time.[49]

Canon 1636 states that a bishop can within his diocese set up a tribunal in any place which is not exempt. It has been seen that a bishop is relegated to the position of a private person as far as judicial power is concerned as soon as he leaves his diocese. Does this take place when he passes into a place or territory that is exempt?

If the territory is actively exempt, such as a prelacy or abbacy *nullius*, there is no doubt that the bishop has no judicial power. This is clear from canon 319, which states that prelates and abbots *nullius* have their own territory separate from any diocese. A bishop passing from his own diocese into such a territory is definitely outside of his own territory, and therefore entirely without judicial jurisdiction.

Is a bishop in an exempt territory of religious also outside of his diocese, and consequently incapable of placing an act of judicial jurisdiction? Neither before the Code nor after has there been any unanimity of opinion in this matter.[50] Coronata prefers the

[46] Lega-Bartoccetti, *Commentarius in Iudicia Ecclesiastica,* I, 55.

[47] With due regard for the exceptions mentioned in canon 201, § 2.

[48] Cf. *supra,* pp. 8-9.

[49] Noval, *De Iudiciis,* n. 58; Vermeersch-Creusen, *Epitome Iuris Canonici,* III, n. 10; Lega-Bartoccetti, *Commentarius in Iudicia Ecclesiastica,* I, 72; Coronata, *Institutiones Iuris Canonici,* III, n. 1094.

[50] Ramos, "De Conditione Saecularium in Domibus Religiosorum," *Commentarium pro Religiosis* (Romae, 1920-1934; ab anno 1935: *Commentarium pro Religiosis et Missionariis*), VI (1925), 28-33.

opinion that the territory on which the houses and churches of exempt religious have been erected is altogether separated from the territory of the local bishop.[51] He contends that this view fully conforms to the doctrine expressed in pontifical documents, which regard the territory of exempt religious as separated from that of the diocese.[52]

More commonly such property of exempt religious is considered as being in the diocese but not of the diocese, the exemption of the property being merely by reason of the persons. Accordingly, acts of judicial jurisdiction could validly be undertaken there by the local ordinary.[53] The argument for this opinion is based on a reply of the Sacred Congregation of the Sacraments, which stated that the exempt churches of religious Orders can be considered as being of the territory of the local pastor or ordinary relative to assistance at marriages.[54]

Weighing the arguments for and against the validity of the acts of judicial power performed in the territory or houses of exempt religious, one is not able to come to a definite conclusion. In the light of canon 1636 such acts certainly seem to be illicit, especially if performed without the consent of the local superior.[55] Since the arguments whether for or against their validity do not induce certitude, a *dubium iuris* results, and thus in consequence

[51] *Institutiones Iuris Canonici,* I, p. 826, footnote 1.

[52] "Sed quod eorum [regularium] domus habitae fuerint iuris fictione quasi territoria quaedem ab ipsis dioecesibus avulsa."—Leo XIII, Const. *Romanos Pontifices,* 8 maii 1881, § 7; cf. *Fontes,* n. 582.

[53] Vermeersch-Creusen, *Epitome Iuris Canonici,* III, n. 71; Cappello, *Summa Iuris Canonici,* III, n. 80; Regatillo, *Institutiones Iuris Canonici,* II, n. 416; Besté, *Introductio in Codicem,* p. 798; Roberti, *De Processibus,* I, n. 167. Lega-Bartoccetti (*Commentarius,* I, 269-270) are not unmistakably clear in their statement, but they contend that in a case of sickness the taking of the testimony of a monk or of a nun would be licit as well as valid; they add that as a general principle acts placed in the territory of exempt religious would be relatively null and therefore remediable.

[54] S. C. de Sacramentis, decr. 13 mart. 1910, ad VIII—*Fontes,* n. 2101; cf. Chelodi, *Ius de Personis,* n. 281, footnote 4; Regatillo, *Institutiones Iuris Canonici,* II, n. 416.

[55] Cappello, *Summa Iuris Canonici,* III, n. 80.

of the ruling of canon 209 such acts would have to be considered as valid.[56]

So far individual judicial acts have been considered. Both before the Code [57] and after [58] there was the opinion that, although individual acts of a local judge in the territory of exempt religious might be valid, nevertheless an entire process conducted there would be invalid. The reason given was a decision of the Congregation of Bishops and Regulars of September 15, 1741: "Praevia circumscriptione processus, tamquam compilati in loco immuni et exempto, Ordinarius procedat ex integro ad sententiam inclusive." [59] Rather than signifying that the process was null, this decision in reality implied its validity, for *circumscribere* connotes a nullifying or rescissory action rather than a declaration of nullity.[60] Consequently, this opinion can safely be disregarded, as it has been after Augustine.

Article 3. Justice Must Be Procured With the Least Possible Inconvenience

The ideal and scope of judicial processes is the complete and evident triumph of right against wrong.[61] In judicial controversies regarding the rights of individuals the process is called civil or contentious. If a penal law has been violated, then a criminal trial is held with a view to declaring or inflicting the needed punishment.[62] In either case, in order that the victory of truth and right may be

[56] Cf. Cocchi, *Commentarium in Codicem Iuris Canonici,* VII, n. 54.

[57] Wernz, *Ius Decretalium,* V, n. 315.

[58] Augustine, *A Commentary on the New Code of Canon Law* (8 vols., Vol. VII, St. Louis and London: Herder, 1921), VII, 84.

[59] *Analecta Iuris Pontificii* (Romae, 1855-1869; Parisiis, 1872-1891), XI (1872), 1094.

[60] Aegidius Forcellinus, *Lexicon Totius Latinitatis* (3. ed., 6 vols., curaverunt F. Corradini et I. Perin, Patavii: Typis Seminarii, 1940), s. v. *circumscribo,* II, 2, c. Cf. also Lega-Bartoccetti, *Commentarius in Iudicia Ecclesiastica,* I, 270.

[61] Taparelli, *Saggio Teoretico di Dritto Naturale* (2 vols., Romae, 1855), n. 1195.

[62] Canon 1552, § 2.

complete, these must be made manifest to the public authority. This vindication of truth and right by means of a judicial process provides for the *social* triumph of justice.[63]

In order that the triumph of justice may be truly complete, it strictly should be accomplished without any inconvenience to the innocent party. The innocent party not only has the right to obtain that which rightfully belongs to him, but he also has the right to obtain it without inconvenience from others.[64] Every inconvenience that the innocent party suffers connotes an imperfection in the process, and hence must be avoided as much as possible. The accused in those matters in which he is innocent, and the parties in general inasmuch as they act in good faith, must be protected from unnecessary molestation. However, to achieve the social triumph of justice as well as the private, the avoidance of all inconvenience is not absolutely achievable. The maximum of perfection in the judicial order is humanly impossible.[65]

In setting up a judiciary system the lawgiver must never forget that not only must the system serve to attain truth, but the truth itself must likewise be uncovered with the least possible inconvenience to him whose right is in jeopardy. It is unfortunate that the vindication and maintenance of right are attended with difficulty. There remains the task to reduce this difficulty to a minimum.[66]

[63] Cavagnis, *Institutiones Iuris Publici Ecclesiastici* (2 vols., Romae, 1882-1883), I, n. 138.

[64] Taparelli, *op. cit.*, n. 1196.

[65] Taparelli, *op. cit.*, n. 1196.

[66] Cavagnis, *op. cit.*, n. 138; Ottaviani, *Institutiones Iuris Publici Ecclesiastici,* I, n. 54.

CHAPTER III

THE USE OF THE ROGATORY COMMISSION IN FORMAL CASES

ARTICLE 1. THE IMPOSSIBILITY OF ATTAINING JUSTICE IF THE LIMITATIONS OF JURISDICTION ARE STRICTLY APPLIED

IN a juridically perfect society judicial power, like all jurisdiction, is fundamentally and essentially one, and this is in the possession of the supreme authority in that society. Since, however, the members of a juridically perfect society are generally very numerous, not all can expect to achieve justice at the court of that supreme authority. It is necessary that inferior courts be established, and that to these inferior courts there be assigned a proper competence.[1] While other judges of lower courts thus come to participate in the judicial jurisdiction of the juridically perfect society, their participation obtains in such a way as to preserve the unity of the society; their power to judge is derived from the supreme authority, and, therefore, remains dependent on it.[2]

In the Church the Pope possesses the supreme and complete power of jurisdiction. Partly by divine positive law, and partly by ecclesiastical positive law, bishops, abbots and prelates *nullius*, apostolic vicars and prefects, and superiors and chapters of exempt clerical religious societies participate in this power to judge.[3] Despite this participation, the Church remains one. The Pope is the supreme judge of all the faithful, and in all ecclesiastical trials the approach to his tribunal is left open.[4]

[1] Taparelli, *Saggio Teoretico di Dritto Naturale*, nn. 1188-1189; Cavagnis, *Institutiones Iuris Publici Ecclesiastici*, I, n. 138.

[2] Taparelli, *loc. cit.*

[3] Cf. *supra*, p. 54.

[4] Canons 218, § 1; 1569, § 1; Concilium Vaticanum, sess. IX, c. III, *de vi et ratione primatus Romani Pontificis*—H. Denzinger-C. Bannwart-J. B. Umberg, *Enchiridion Symbolorum Definitionum, et Declarationum de Rebus Fidei et Morum* (21.-23. ed., Friburgi Brisgoviae: Herder & Co., 1937), n. 1830.

For practical reasons, and especially for the maintenance of peace and order, definite limits are assigned to the jurisdictions which those who are subordinate to the Roman Pontiff possess by virtue of their participation in the supreme power of the Church.[5] For the most part these limits are of a territorial character. This is the case with residential bishops, abbots and prelates *nullius*, and apostolic vicars and prefects.

The territorial limitation of judicial jurisdiction is twofold. First, it can be exercised only over subjects, i. e., over those who in some legally recognized permanent fashion are connected with that territory. This limitation comes from the very nature of jurisdiction; it suffers no exceptions.[6] Secondly, it cannot be validly exercised outside of the territory.[7]

Within the sphere of competence allotted by the Code, the judicial jurisdiction exercised by the superiors of exempt clerical religious societies is limited solely by the general principle that jurisdiction can be exercised only over subjects. Subjection to the religious superior arises not by reason of any connection with a territory, but by reason of a personal relationship to that superior. By a so called tacit agreement or quasi-contract, novices, and by reason of religious profession, the other religious are under the jurisdiction of their proper superiors.[8]

That ordinaries, religious and secular, should have a limited sphere of competence in the exercise of their jurisdiction is a matter of necessity. At the same time, if this limitation were to be rigidly applied, it would lead in many cases to a paralysis in the

[5] Roberti, *De Processibus*, I, n. 60.

[6] Canon 201, § 1; cf. *supra*, p. 55.

[7] Canon 201, § 2; cf. *supra*, p. 61. Canon 201, § 2, lists two exceptions to the principle that a judge must be in his territory to judge. If he is forcibly expelled from his territory or impeded from exercising his jurisdiction there, he can proceed against those who expelled him or impeded him, even though he is in another's territory. The second exception is that those who have ordinary power to hear confessions can exercise that power anywhere. These two exceptions are not of importance to the discussion of the rogatory commission.

[8] Schaefer, *De Religiosis* (3. ed., Romae: S. A. L. E. R., 1940), nn. 250, 263; Coronata, *Institutiones Iuris Canonici*, I, nn. 585, 589.

administration of justice.[9] Every time that the elements of proof would lie outside of the sphere of jurisdiction of the judge of the case, the victory of justice, which is the end and purpose of judicial power, would be endangered. Witnesses not subject to the judge of the trial could not be constrained to give testimony.

Unattainable, likewise, would be the testimony of witnesses who, although subject to the judge's power, nevertheless are outside of his territory and are hindered from coming to the seat of the trial. The same could be true of the interrogation of one of the parties of the trial. Important documents or other matters of proof which are outside of the territory could not be inspected. The execution of a sentence could become impossible in consequence of the fact that the things or persons in question are outside of the jurisdictional reach of the one who has decided the case. Thus the very participation of many in the securing of justice would lead to a frustration of justice because of the necessary limitation of their jurisdiction.

Article 2. The Rogatory Commission

The rogatory commission is a juridical institute by which a competent tribunal in the prosecution of a particular trial consigns to another tribunal certain judicial acts which are necessary for the rendering of a just sentence, but which are outside of the former's and fall under the latter's jurisdiction. Between different grades of ecclesiastical tribunals there is a definitely established subordination which permits appeal from the lower courts to the higher courts. The purpose of this appeal is to safeguard justice from human failings and from the possible evil intentions of individual judges.[10] As tribunals are subordinated to one another for the triumph of justice, they are for the same purpose co-ordinated. In the interest

[9] Baldassari, *Enciclopedia Italiana di Scienze, Lettere ed Arti* (36 vols. and Appendice, Roma: Istituto Giovanni Treccani, 1929-1939), s. v. *Rogatoria interna;* Pugliese, "Le Rogatorie e i Poteri del Tribunale Delegato," *Salesianum* (Torino, 1939—), VI (1944), 53.

[10] Cavagnis, *Institutiones Iuris Publici Ecclesiastici,* I, n. 138; Cappello, *Summa Iuris Publici Ecclesiastici,* n. 231; Ottaviani, *Institutiones Iuris Publici Ecclesiastici,* I, n. 53.

of the administration of justice, tribunals mutually assist each other by placing judicial acts which are within their own sphere of jurisdiction but beyond the power of the tribunal hearing the case.[11]

The co-ordination of ecclesiastical tribunals is provided for in Canon Law by canon 1570, § 2, which reads as follows:

> Quodlibet tamen tribunal, quod attinet ad partium et testium examen aut citationem, documentorum vel rei controversae inspectionem, decretorum intimationem aliaque huiusmodi, ius habet in auxilium vocandi aliud tribunal, quod normas pro singulis actibus iure praescriptas servare debet.

The assistance provided for in this canon will be a matter of necessity in two cases: (1) if an act of jurisdiction must be placed in reference to a person who is not a subject of the judge of the trial, e. g., a non-subject must be cited as a witness; or (2) if an act of jurisdiction must be performed outside of the territory of the judge of the case. The necessity for placing an act of jurisdiction in another territory may be either physical or moral in its character. An example of physical necessity is realized when judicial access or inspection must be carried out beyond the borders of the diocese where the trial is being conducted. An example of moral necessity is had when a witness is outside of the diocese and because of serious inconvenience is excused from appearing at the court of the trial.

Whenever in a judicial procedure an act of jurisdiction would be required for the proper triumph of justice, and at the same time the judge of the trial is unable to place that act of jurisdiction because of the lack of power over the person in question, he is empowered by the Code to call upon another tribunal to place that act of jurisdiction. Thus, if a witness belongs to another diocese, the judge can call upon the tribunal of that diocese to cite the witness to appear at the court where the trial is being conducted. The witness cannot disregard a citation given in this manner, for it comes from his own superior.

Wherever in a judicial process an act of jurisdiction would have to be performed in another's territory, the judge of the trial has the

[11] Lega-Bartoccetti, *Commentarius in Iudicia Ecclesiastica,* I, 103.

right to call upon the tribunal of that territory to execute the required act. Thus, a tribunal would carry out a judicial access or inspection, or would take the testimony of a witness who would be unable or excused from appearing at the court of the trial, when it was requested to do so by the original tribunal of the case.

ARTICLE 3. THE NATURE OF THE POWER USED IN THE EXECUTING OF A ROGATORY COMMISSION

There is much confusion of ideas in the writings of canonists on the nature of the power that is used in the execution of a rogatory commission. Haring (d. 1945) apparently held that the tribunal which executes a rogatory commission does so from power that is delegated by the original judge of the case. This is deduced from his terminology, and from his failure to object to the point of delegation in the argument that he who has ordinary power is able to delegate it totally or in part. This argument was alleged with a view to proving that a tribunal could commit an entire process to another tribunal.[12]

The French civil lawyer, Maurice Billecard, also held the same opinion as Haring.[13] While Pugliese in one place states that the power to execute a rogatory commission is actually delegated to the other tribunal,[14] in another place he says that in rogatory commissions delegations and subdelegations are no longer necessary.[15] Lega-Bartoccetti seems to adhere to the doctrine of the delegated power,[16]

12 "Delegation eines Eheprozesses"—*Theologisch-practische Quartalschrift* (Linz, 1848—), LXXXIII (1930), 140-142.

13 *Les Commissions Rogatoires en Droit International Privé* (Paris, 1902), pp. 6, 7, 15.

14 ". . . in quanto la rogatoria essenzialmente equivale a un mandato di delegatione, col quale il delegante circoscrive la richiesta nella sostanza e nelle modalità accidentali, salvo le disposizioni legali che vigono nel luogo della delegazione, conferendo al delegato i poteri necessari."—"Le Rogatorie e i Poteri del Tribunale Delegato," *Salesianum*, VI (1944), 54.

15 *Ibidem*, p. 52.

16 "Auxilium expostulant iudices per litteras *rogatorias* seu *remissoriales*, quae nimirum continent remissionem seu *remissoriam* cuiusdam negotii litigiosi alteri iudici datam, qui nisi delegaretur ad certum iudicii actum, nullam sane

but at the same time states that the necessity of the rogatory commission lies in this, that a judge ordinarily is not able to exercise jurisdiction in another diocese.[17]

Roberti denies that a rogatory commission ordinarily is executed with delegated power; according to him, it is the Code itself that supplies the power for this purpose.[18] On another occasion, however, he leaves the impression that a tribunal executes a rogatory commission with its own ordinary power, for he says that before the promulgation of the Code it was the common opinion that one tribunal had the right to call upon another to place acts that were under the latter's competence.[19]

The theory of the delegated power appears untenable. If, according to canon 201, § 2, a judge cannot use his jurisdiction outside of his territory, it follows that he cannot delegate anyone else to act outside of his territory in his stead. A delegate acts with the power of the one who delegated him. If the power of the one delegating is restricted to his own territory, the power of the delegate would be likewise restricted. Authors, even those who speak of the execution of the rogatory commission by way of delegated power, hold that the reason for the necessity of the rogatory commission lies in the restriction of the judicial power to the territory of the judge.[20] Then, again, if it is delegated power that is used in the execution of a rogatory commission, there is no reason why the Code should speak only of tribunals being called upon for the rendering of assistance. The tribunal of the case could imme-

haberet competentiam . . . Etenim in huiusmodi casu iudex agit tamquam delegatus, et hinc sedulo delegationis limites cognoscere debet et revereri, iuxta principia can. 1917."—*Commentarius in Iudicia Ecclesiastica,* I, 103-104.

17 ". . . quia iudex in aliena dioecesi, ordinario, iurisdictionem non potest exercere."—*op. cit.,* I, 103.

18 "Nec tamquam delegationes intelligendae sunt litterae rogatoriae, ad quas exsequendas potestas recipitur ab ipso Codice, nisi agatur de causis quas quis cognoscit delegata potestate."—*De Processibus,* I, 451, footnote 1.

19 "Doctores ius et obligationem statuerant pro unoquoque tribunali requirendi et exigendi ab alio tribunali actus legitimos propriae competentiae subductos."—*op. cit.,* I, n. 89.

20 Lega-Bartoccetti, *Commentarius in Iudicia Ecclesiastica,* I, 103; Pugliese, "Le Rogatorie e i Poteri del Tribunale Delegato"—*Salesianum,* VI (1944), 62; Billecard, *Les Commissions Rogatoires en Droit International Privé,* p. 2.

diately delegate clerics in outlying districts of other territories, just as it does in its own territory according to canon 1770 § 2, 4°. Consequently, the prohibition of canon 201, § 1, on the use of delegated as well as ordinary judicial power outside of the territory must also be observed in the issuing of rogatory commissions.

Equally unsatisfactory is the theory that the Code supplies the power to execute a rogatory commission. Canon 1570, § 2, makes no mention of such power. It speaks merely of the right to which corresponds an obligation to effect the execution. But between the obligation to execute and the power to execute there is a real distinction. It cannot be said that the obligation presupposes the power and that the power is therefore implied in the obligation which is imposed. It is true that the obligation presupposes the power, but it does not have to be supplied by the legislation of the Code. For ordinary cases the proper jurisdiction of the tribunal is sufficient to execute the rogatory commission. For cases reserved to Rome, the power can be delegated when the commission is issued.

More acceptable is the opinion that in ordinary cases, when a tribunal executes a rogatory commission, it does so by reason of the ordinary power that it possesses and exercises over its own subjects. This seems to be the opinion of Wernz-Vidal,[21] and Roberti appears to understand other canonists in this light.[22] In this way one has a better explanation of canon 1570, § 2, which speaks of one tribunal calling upon another for assistance. The second tribunal must have some efficacy or power of its own to give the required assistance. The same thought was implied in the Instruction of the Sacred Congregation of Bishops and Regulars of June 11, 1880, which stated that absent witnesses were to be examined by the authority of the place where they were.[23] This appeal to the authority would lose much of its significance if the authority was not understood to bring its own proper power to bear.

Authors generally agree that the reason for the rogatory com-

[21] "Quare unumquodque tribunal ecclesiasticum ius et obligationem habet requirendi ab alio tribunali in processu canonico actus legitimos suae competentiae subductos."—*Ius Canonicum*, VI, n. 72.

[22] Cf. *supra*, footnote 19.

[23] S. C. Ep. et Reg., instr. 11 iun. 1880, n. 19—*Fontes*, n. 2005.

mission lies in the fact that a judge has no power outside of his territory. To act in an effective manner outside of his territory, he must request assistance.[24] The tribunal from which the assistance is requested actually has jurisdiction over its own subjects within its own territory. The logical conclusion is that, in giving the assistance required, the tribunal uses the jurisdiction that it ordinarily has.

The opinion that is here adopted, namely, that a tribunal executes a rogatory commission by means of its own jurisdiction, holds true for ordinary cases. In matters for which a tribunal is absolutely competent for the reason that the Holy See has reserved them to itself, it will have to be delegated by the competent authority in Rome, or subdelegated by another who had been previously delegated by the Roman authority; in such cases competence cannot be prorogued. However, there is no objection to delegation, for the jurisdiction of the Holy See is universal; nor to subdelegation, for the jurisdiction of a delegate of the Holy See is without territorial limitation unless the contrary is expressly stated.

The Roman Rota has competence, or is specially commissioned by the Roman Pontiff, to judge cases[25] in which the lower tribunals are absolutely incompetent.[26] While in these cases the Rota has the right from canon 1570, § 2, to call upon a local ordinary to constitute a tribunal and to draw up certain acts, nevertheless, it will have to delegate the local ordinary to grant the required assistance. Attention is called to this delegation in the procedural norms of the Rota.[27] It cannot be maintained that the need of this

[24] Lega-Bartoccetti, *Commentarius in Iudicia Ecclesiastica,* I, 103; Coronata, *Institutiones Iuris Canonici,* III, n. 1113; Pugliese, "Le Rogatorie e i Poteri del Tribunale Delegato," *Salesianum,* VI (1944), 53-54; Cappello, *Summa Iuris Canonici,* III, n. 23; Cocchi, *Commentarium in Codicem Iuris Canonici,* VII, n. 15; De Meester, *Juris Canonici et Juris Canonico-Civilis Compendium,* III, 2, n. 1514; Ferreres, *Institutiones Canonicae* (2. ed., 2 vols., Barcinone: Eugenius Subirana, 1920), II, n. 538; Prümmer (*Manuale Iuris Canonici,* p. 554) mentions only the difficulty of distance.

[25] Canon 1599, § 2.

[26] Canons 1577, §§ 2, 3; 1588.

[27] Normae S. R. Rotae Tribunalis, 29 iun. 1934, art. 93, § 1; 102—*AAS,* XXVI (1934), 473, 475.

delegation by the Rota is outmoded, as Roberti [28] and Pugliese [29] imply, for without this delegation any acts placed by lower tribunals in trials in which they are absolutely incompetent would be null and void. Jurisdiction is never prorogued in the case of absolute incompetence.

Equally outside of the proper competence of the ordinary diocesan tribunals is the preparing of such processes as for the dispensation from a non-consummated marriage or the declaration of the nullity of Sacred Orders and all cases that are reserved to the Sacred Congregations.[30] Usually the Sacred Congregations commit to local ordinaries the task of preparing the acts of these cases. In doing so the Sacred Congregations actually delegate the particular ordinaries to execute the work that they commit to them.[31] Without this delegation the acts would be invalid.[32] Consequently, when the tribunal which was delegated by the Holy See calls upon another tribunal for assistance in preparing the acts, subdelegation will have to be given.[33]

In ordinary cases one tribunal calls upon another tribunal for assistance, as is provided for in canon 1570, § 2. When delegated tribunals prepare processes for the Sacred Congregations, they do not call upon other tribunals directly for assistance, for these tribunals are incompetent in these matters. Rather, the request is made

[28] "Quare in casibus ordinariis non videntur necessariae repetitae delegationes et subdelegationes quae in nonnullis legibus (NoSRR a. 93 § 1, 102) et apud quaedam tribunalia adhuc servantur, non obstante Codicis dispositione"—*De Processibus*, I, n. 89.

[29] "Consequentamente, non sono più necessarie le innumerevoli deleghe e subdeleghe che, per una spiegabile sopravvivenza del passato non ancora perfettamente armonizzato col diritto vigente, sembrano conservate nelle antiche *Norme proprie* della S. R. Rota (art. 93 § 1, 102)."—"Le Rogatorie e i Poteri del Tribunale Delegato," *Salesianum*, VI (1944), 52.

[30] Canons 1963, § 1; 249, § 3.

[31] "Contra bene intelligitur cur SS. Congregationes de delegatione loquantur, cum causas sibi reservatas vel tribunalibus ordinariis instruendas committunt."—Roberti, *De Processibus*, I, p. 244, footnote 5.

[32] Canons 249, § 3; 1557, § 3; 1558.

[33] "Nec tamquam delegationes intelligendae sunt litterae rogatoriae . . . nisi agatur de causis quas quis cognoscit delegata potestate."—Roberti, *De Processibus*, I, 451, footnote 1.

to the local ordinary to set up a tribunal to fulfill the request.[34]

There can be no objection when a tribunal which is delegated by the Holy See subdelegates another local ordinary on the ground that the one who is preparing the process is acting outside of his territory when he subdelegates. As a delegate of the Holy See, his jurisdiction is without territorial limit, although generally he will prepare the acts in the customary hall of sessions of his own territory. When one local ordinary who has been delegated by the Holy See calls upon another local ordinary to constitute a tribunal for the purpose of lending assistance in the process, his request for assistance is made not because of any limited jurisdiction on his part, but simply in view of the difficulties occasioned by the distance that separates the persons in question from the usual scene of the preparation of the acts.

The opinion has been advanced by the writer that the local tribunal, in executing a rogatory commission in ordinary cases at the request of another local tribunal, acts by reason of its own proper power of jurisdiction. A further question touches the particular juridical effect of the rogatory commission. If a tribunal executes a rogatory commission by means of its own jurisdiction, why must it wait till that commission is given before it can act? Why must the tribunal execute the rogatory commission according to the instructions of the judge of the case?

In practice, it will frequently happen that one tribunal alone will be competent in a particular case. In that event all other tribunals will be incompetent. However, it can happen that many tribunals would be competent. Should this be so, the first that cites the defendant excludes all other tribunals from competence in the case.[35] In both cases, therefore, all tribunals other than the one where the trial is being conducted are relatively incompetent to place

[34] S. C. de Sacramentis, *Regulae servandae in processibus super Matrimonio rato et non consummato,* 7 maii 1923, n. 23—*AAS,* XV (1923), 396; S. C. de Sacramentis, *Regulae servandae in processibus super nullitate sacrae ordinationis vel onerum sacris ordinibus inhaerentium,* 9 maii 1931, n. 14—*AAS,* XXIII (1931), 461; S. C. pro Ecclesia Orientali, *Instructio ad conficiendos processus super matrimònio rato et non consummato,* 10 iun. 1935, n. 25—*AAS,* XXVII (1935), 339.

[35] Canons 1568; 1725, 2°.

acts in that trial. Should they in reality attempt to conduct any acts in that trial, those acts could not even be called judicial, since that particular judge is not sitting in judgment to administer justice.[36]

In order to answer these difficulties, it is suggested that the particular effect of the rogatory commission is such that from the force of law the committing of judicial acts to another tribunal causes that tribunal to become competent to place the acts that are requested. In other words, canon 1570, § 2, creates a title of competence, not to conduct an entire trial as do canons 1560-1568, but merely to conduct such acts as are requested in the rogatory letter. The extent of the competence depends, according to the will of the legislator, on the extent of the request. What is requested of it a tribunal is competent to grant, but it remains incompetent in all other matters.

To make the requested tribunal competent to grant the assistance is not identical with supplying to that tribunal the power of jurisdiction. The titles of competence in canons 1560-1568 do not confer jurisdiction; rather, they specify how and to what extent the ordinary jurisdiction of a tribunal can be used. Canon 1570, § 2, extends the ordinary power of a tribunal so that it may grant assistance to other tribunals, and it makes a tribunal competent to give that assistance when and to what extent it is requested. This is in accord with the principle that the power of the local bishop is ordinary, but it remains for the Holy See in many instances to determine the extent of its competence.[37]

When a tribunal executes a rogatory commission, it acts in unison with the original tribunal of the case. The exercise of its jurisdiction is intimately joined with the exercise of the other's jurisdiction, so that it becomes part and parcel of the same trial. Thus, the acts which a tribunal undertakes in executing the rogatory commission are truly judicial, for they are conducted in a trial, and by one who acts in the place of the judge.[38] Just as an auditor acts in the place of the judge when the judge is able to dele-

36 Cf. Reiffenstuel, Lib. II, tit. 1, n. 24.

37 Ryan, *Principles of Episcopal Jurisdiction*, p. 87.

38 ". . . ut eos vice tua recipiant."—c. 3, X, *de fideiussoribus*, III, 22.

gate him, so the judge of another territory acts in the place of the judge of the trial where the latter cannot himself act or delegate another. All acts, however, are conducted in the same trial, and are, therefore, truly judicial.

The opinion that canon 1570, § 2, gives a title of competence best explains how a tribunal that is otherwise relatively incompetent in a case can conduct acts that have full judicial value before the tribunal that is actually prosecuting the case. Acts conducted on a rogatory commission do not have their force simply in consequence of the failure of the parties to advance an objection or through the rejection of an exception by the judge. In addition, it is contended that the opinion that canon 1570, § 2, gives a title of competence for a tribunal to use its own proper jurisdiction best explains the universal practice of ecclesiastical curias and the common teaching of the doctors that to a specific tribunal there are to be committed only such acts as fall within the jurisdiction of that tribunal.

Article 4. The Right to Request and the Obligation to Execute a Rogatory Commission

Section 1. The Nature of the Right and of the Obligation

The right to request and the obligation to execute a rogatory commission come from the provision of positive law as stated in canon 1570, § 2.[39] The various ecclesiastical tribunals of the same grade would not, of themselves, have any right or obligation to mutual assistance.[40] Dioceses, abbacies and prelacies *nullius*, apos-

39 Roberti, De Processibus, I, n. 89; Wernz-Vidal, *Ius Canonicum*, VI, n. 71; Pugliese, "Le Rogatorie e i Poteri del Tribunale Delegato"—*Salesianum*, VI (1944), 52.

40 Certain civil lawyers subscribed to the doctrine that, even in the absence of positive legislation, secular courts would be obliged in the interest of justice to fulfill a request for the execution of a rogatory commission; cf. Contuzzi, *Il Digesto Italiano* (24 vols. in 49, Torino: Unione Tip. Editrice Torinese, 1884-1921), s. v. *Commissione Rogatoria*, n. 47; Billecard, *Les Commissions Rogatoires en Droit International Privé*, p. 4. Justice would demand some remedy for the limitation of judicial power, but it is doubtful that the rogatory commission would be the only possible remedy.

tolic vicariates and prefectures, and exempt clerical religious institutes are, under the Roman Pontiff, autonomous and independent of each other. The one has not any authority over the other, and therefore cannot impose any obligation on the other.[41] Their superiors have completely, but also simply, whatever power the government of their respective units requires.[42] Among tribunals, therefore, of the same grade, the one cannot put an obligation on the other, nor could a tribunal oblige its own subjects to assist another tribunal, for its own power is restricted within the consideration of the proper good of its own people.

While one diocese is not obliged in justice to further the good of another diocese,[43] nevertheless, each diocese can be obliged to further the end of the universal Church. An inferior subordinate society is obliged to assist in a positive manner its superior society.[44] The triumph of justice is the concern of the universal Church, and especially when that justice is unattainable in the lower courts. For this reason the juridical institute of judicial appeal was established. Consequently, too, in the common interest of justice, there is the institute of mutual assistance between tribunals.

Immediate mutual assistance between tribunals, as provided for in canon 1570, § 2, was not the only way in which the Church could have arranged for the possibility of achieving justice when justice was frustrated as a result of the limited jurisdiction of ordinaries. It could have provided that the entire trial be brought before an Apostolic tribunal which was not hampered by any like limitations, since it possessed universal jurisdiction. Another possibility would have been that in such cases a request be sent to Rome for the purpose of securing authorization for those acts of jurisdiction which were beyond the power of the original judge of the case. Justice, therefore, demanded a remedy for the limitation of jurisdiction in minor judges, but did not point exclusively to the rogatory commission. The institute of the rogatory commission

[41] "Cum par in parem non habeat iurisdictionem."—Wernz-Vidal, *Ius Canonicum,* VI, n. 71.

[42] Ryan, *Principles of Episcopal Jurisdiction,* p. 79.

[43] Cappello, *Summa Iuris Publici Ecclesiastici,* n. 102.

[44] Cappello, *op. cit.,* n. 103.

is therefore of the positive law; probably it was decided upon in the common interest of the economy of time and labor.

Section 2. The Subject of the Right

Canon 1570, § 2, gives to every tribunal the right to call upon another tribunal for assistance. Apparently this right is given only to ecclesiastical tribunals, for the relations between ecclesiastical and secular tribunals are regulated by concordats.[45]

The right is vested in a *tribunal.* The word tribunal is used in various senses: it can signify the place in which court sessions are usually conducted; it can point to the principal person or persons of the court, namely, the judge or judges; it can denote the judge or judges together with those persons who must be present at the trial in order that the acts may be truly judicial.[46]

In canon 1570, § 2, the word tribunal must be understood as signifying the judge or judges together with those persons who are required for the proper exercise of judicial power.[47] Essentially an ecclesiastical tribunal is composed of the office of the judge and the office of a notary.[48] Frequently the presence of other persons, such as the defender of the bond or the promoter of justice, is necessary for the proper conduct of a trial. In some trials, too, there is question of the function of an auditor, or a beadle (*cursor*), or a marshal (*apparitor*). If these are used in a particular trial, they truly belong to the personnel of the tribunal.

The need for the assistance of another tribunal may derive from the inability of any one of the members of a tribunal to fulfill his assigned task because of the territorial limitation of judicial power or because of physical or moral impossibility occasioned by the element of distance. Not only is a judge incapable of exercising his

[45] Cf. Concordat between the Holy See and the Republic of Austria, Art. VII, § 5—*AAS,* XXVI (1934), 259.

[46] Noval, *De Iudiciis,* n. 93; Vermeersch-Creusen, *Epitome Iuris Canonici,* III, n. 25.

[47] Wernz-Vidal, *Ius Canonicum,* VI, n. 66; Lega-Bartoccetti, *Commentarius in Iudicia Ecclesiastica,* I, 95.

[48] Roberti, *De Processibus,* I, n. 92; Coronata, *Institutiones Iuris Canonici,* III, n. 1110.

jurisdiction outside of his territory, but the same territorial limitation is put upon a notary, or actuary, as he is called in judicial procedure.[49] The defender of the bond and the promoter of justice serve to safeguard justice and the common good by the assistance which they give to a particular bishop or to him who takes his place; [50] consequently their activity must be confined within the restrictions that affect the one who exercises the judicial power. The beadle is permitted to enter the territory of another diocese to deliver a citation,[51] but this permission is of little practical value if the diocese wherein the citation is to be delivered is a thousand miles distant. The marshal could hardly enter another diocese to effect a sequestration, even though he was ordered to do so by the judge of the court to which he was attached.

The victory of justice could be frustrated in consequence of the limited activity of any one of those who constitute the tribunal, who are necessary for its valid functioning, or who actually assist in the judicial process. It is the tribunal with all its necessary and accessory personnel that has need of the assistance of another tribunal to place such acts as fall outside of its ordinary jurisdiction. It is, therefore, the tribunal as properly constituted that must be said to have the right to call upon another tribunal for assistance; when canon 1570, § 2, states that each tribunal has the right to call upon another tribunal for help, the word tribunal must be understood in this comprehensive sense.

With the conclusion accepted that a tribunal as mentioned in canon 1570, § 2, must be understood as a collegiate body of all those who are necessary for the performance of the judicial acts, it may next be asked what tribunal has the right under this canon to assistance from another tribunal. The answer is not difficult: the right is possessed by every ecclesiastical tribunal without distinction. Distinctions must not be introduced when the lawgiver himself gives no indication of them. The word *quodlibet* furnishes added and conclusive proof that no tribunal can be denied the right to assistance whenever assistance is needed.

[49] Canon 374, § 2.
[50] Canon 363, §§ 1, 2.
[51] Canon 1717, § 2.

No question could possibly arise regarding the right of a diocesan tribunal to assistance when it is presided over by the local bishop either singly or in union with other judges. What is true of the local bishop is also true of the abbot and prelate *nullius*,[52] and the same must be said of the vicar capitular,[53] and the vicar general [54] or the one who rules the diocese, according to canon 429, when the bishop is impeded from ruling it because of captivity, banishment, exile, or incapacity, and is not able to communicate with it even by letter.

In all these cases the ones who are mentioned are true local ordinaries,[55] and the local ordinary is the judge of the first instance in every diocese.[56] The tribunals over which anyone of these presides are true tribunals, and, therefore, are able to call upon other tribunals for assistance. Inasmuch as tribunals of second instance are to follow the same rules or procedure that are followed by tribunals of first instance,[57] they too have the right to commit the performance of judicial acts to other tribunals whenever such action appears necessary.

In their own territories, apostolic vicars and prefects are judges of the first instance.[58] The tribunals which they constitute either

[52] Canon 215, § 2.

[53] Canons 327, § 1; 432, § 1; cf. Roberti, *De Processibus,* I, n. 83; Coronata, *Institutiones Iuris Canonici,* III, n. 1115; Noval, *De Iudiciis,* n. 110; Vermeersch-Creusen, *Epitome Iuris Canonici,* III, n. 32. What is affirmed of the vicar capitular also holds for the diocesan administrator in those dioceses where consultors take the place of the cathedral chapter; cf. canon 427.

[54] Ordinarily the vicar general cannot act as a judge except in a small diocese, in which judicial cases are few in number and in which he has also been named *officialis* in accordance with canon 1573, § 1; if the vicar general should act in the capacity of a judge in the ordinary functioning of a diocese without having been appointed as *officialis* or delegated with the judicial power, he acts invalidly according to Roberti (*De Processibus,* I, n. 96); according to Coronata (*Institutiones Iuris Canonici,* III, n. 1116) he would act illicitly but validly. From the wording of canon 1573, § 1, the opinion of Roberti appears more probable.

[55] Canon 198, § 1.

[56] Canon 1572, § 1.

[57] Canon 1595.

[58] Canon 294, § 1; Vermeersch-Creusen, *Epitome Iuris Canonici,* I, n. 415;

on single occasions or in a permanent manner, as the demands of their territory may necessitate, must not be deprived of the rights which diocesan tribunals enjoy especially in the matter of issuing a rogatory commission. Religious tribunals[59] possess this right to call upon other tribunals, either secular or religious, for assistance,[60] as do also delegated tribunals, especially those which have been delegated by local or religious ordinaries. All of these are truly ecclesiastical tribunals and must of necessity possess the right which canon 1570, § 2, confers on every ecclesiastical tribunal.

While the tribunals of the Holy See follow their own laws and regulations,[61] nevertheless, it seems that none of them must be excluded from the right for assistance in the preparation of the judicial acts. But while they possess the same right as other tribunals, they must, with reference to the tribunal to which they look for assistance, share with it the actual faculty of drawing up the desired act. This rule obtains when the Holy See has reserved certain processes to itself, as when there is question of the possible granting of a dispensation from a non-consummated marriage, or of the rendering of a judicial decision concerning the validity of Sacred Orders or the binding force of the obligations arising from the same.[62] The same rule also obtains when the Holy Father, or his delegate, or the tribunals of the Holy See try the cases of those persons who are mentioned in canon 1557, for in these cases the lower tribunals are absolutely incompetent.

Special mention is made of this right to assistance from other tribunals in the procedural norms of the Roman Rota[63] and the Apostolic Signatura.[64] Similar mention is made in the rules issued

III, n. 32; Roberti, *De Processibus,* I, n. 83; Coronata, *Institutiones Iuris Canonici,* III, n. 1115; Noval, *De Iudiciis,* n. 110.

[59] Canons 1579, §§ 1, 2; 1594, § 4; 655.

[60] Noval, *De Iudiciis,* n. 104; Blat, *Commentarium Textus Codicis Iuris Canonici,* IV, n. 26.

[61] Canon 243, § 1.

[62] Canons 1963, § 1; 249, § 3.

[63] Normae S. R. Rotae Tribunalis, 29 iun. 1934, art. 93, § 1; 102—*AAS,* XXVI (1934), 473, 475.

[64] Regulae servandae in iudiciis apud Suprem. Signaturae Ap. Tribunal, 6 mart. 1912, art. 16—*AAS,* IV (1912), 192.

on May 7, 1923, by the Sacred Congregation of the Sacraments with reference to the preparation of a process for a dispensation from a non-consummated marriage,[65] in the rules issued by the same Congregation on June 9, 1931, for the preparation of processes concerning the nullity of Sacred Orders or the lack of the obligations arising from the reception of Sacred Orders,[66] and in the Instruction of June 10, 1935, of the Sacred Congregation for the Oriental Church with reference to the preparation of a process for a dispensation from a non-consummated marriage.[67]

All of the tribunals that have been enumerated above must be said to possess the right to call upon other tribunals for assistance in their judicial activity. Granted that the law confers this right, the fundamental reason why they must be said to possess the right is that they are truly tribunals, i. e., tribunals about whose jurisdiction there can be no question.[68] Where there is no jurisdiction, there is no tribunal, and consequently, too, there is no right to assistance from other tribunals.

To possess jurisdiction in general does not suffice as a claim to the right in question. There must also be jurisdiction for the particular trial that is being conducted. In other words, competence is required. If competence is lacking in a particular trial, then to the extent in which it is lacking, the incompetent tribunal has not the power to judge, and therefore it would not have the right to call on another tribunal to be of assistance in the matter. In this point, however, special attention must be given to the distinction between absolute and relative incompetence.

If a tribunal is absolutely incompetent, that incompetence per-

[65] S. C. de Sacramentis, *Regulae servandae in processibus super matrimonio rato et non consummato,* 7 maii 1923, n. 23—*AAS,* XV (1923), 396.

[66] S. C. de Sacramentis, *Regulae servandae in processibus super nullitate sacrae ordinationis vel onerum sacris ordinibus inhaerentium,* 9 iun. 1931, n. 14—*AAS,* XXIII (1931), 461.

[67] S. C. pro Ecclesia Orientali, *Instructio ad conficiendos processus super matrimonio rato et non consummato,* 10 iun. 1935, nn. 6, 25—*AAS,* XXVII (1935), 334-5, 339.

[68] "Si tamen de eius iurisdictione certo constat."—Noval, *De Iudiciis,* n. 101.

sists. Competence is never prorogued in such a case.[69] The sentence is irremediably null and void,[70] and all of the acts are of the same null and void character.[71] Lacking all right to prosecute a case when it is absolutely incompetent, a tribunal also lacks the right to request assistance from others. The reason is that in that particular trial wherein it is absolutely incompetent, the tribunal really is no tribunal, for it lacks jurisdiction. Consequently, it does not possess the rights of tribunals, at least as far as that particular case is concerned.

In relative incompetence, the situation is quite different. Even here jurisdiction cannot validly be exercised except over subjects, and a judge is not able to cite any defendant to his tribunal unless he is competent by reason of one of the titles established by law. However, if no title of competence is actually present, and the parties fail to bring an exception against the competence of the judge before the joinder of issue, competence is supplied by the Code.[72] If an objection is lodged by one of the parties against the relative incompetence of the judge, and the judge declares in favor of his own competence, again jurisdiction and competence are supplied by the law, even though from a purely objective approach it actually was lacking.[73] Although other remedies may be invoked against a sentence given by such a judge,[74] a complaint of nullity is never possible in the case of relative incompetence.

Unless a judge actually declares himself incompetent, competence always is prorogued in cases of relative incompetence. The relatively incompetent tribunal becomes competent by a prescription of law. This supplying of competence by the Code takes place either at the time of the decision of the judge in rejecting an ex-

69 Noval, *De Iudiciis,* n. 58; Roberti, *De Processibus,* I, n. 60; Coronata, *Institutiones Iuris Canonici,* III, n. 1099.

70 Canon 1892, 1°.

71 Coronata, *Institutiones Iuris Canonici,* III, n. 1418.

72 Canon 1628, § 1; cf. Lega-Bartoccetti, *Commentarius in Iudicia Ecclesiastica,* I, 72.

73 Canon 1610, § 2; cf. Lega-Bartoccetti, *Commentarius in Iudicia Ecclesiastica,* I, 72; Noval, *De Iudiciis,* n. 193; Wernz-Vidal, *Ius Canonicum,* VI, nn. 63, 144, footnote 3; Besté, *Introductio in Codicem,* p. 794.

74 Canons 1625, § 1; 1880, 6°; 1905, 4°.

ception of incompetence,[75] or at the time of the joinder of issue, after which the raising of the exception of relative incompetence is ordinarily no longer admitted.[76] From this moment of the supplying of competence, the previously relatively incompetent tribunal is now competent with all the rights of a competent tribunal. From that moment, therefore, even with a purely objective outlook, it has a true right to call upon other tribunals to assist in prosecuting the case.

What must be said of the tribunal which actually was relatively incompetent before the competence was supplied at the time of the rejection of the exception of incompetence or at the time of the joinder of issue? In reality, up to the point of the supplying of the competence, the tribunal did not have any competence in that particular case, and therefore did not have any right to assistance from other tribunals in prosecuting the case. Acts performed by an incompetent tribunal before competence was supplied to it must be regarded as having been invalid.[77] For this reason a judge is

[75] Canon 1610, § 2.

[76] Canon 1628, § 1. While the raising of an exception against the relative incompetence of the judge is possible, according to canon 1628, § 1, under certain conditions even after the joinder of issue, this will rarely happen, since the relative incompetence which arises after the joinder of issue does not change the forum of the trial; cf. canon 1725, 1°-3°; also Roberti, *De Processibus,* I, n. 149. If such an exception is brought after the joinder of issue and the judge declares himself incompetent, all the acts of the case up to that point will be invalid; if he rejects the exception of incompetence with just cause, the acts will have been valid; if, however, he rejects the exception when in reality he was relatively incompetent, competence will be supplied him from that point, because the law permits no appeal or complaint of nullity. What must be said about the acts of the case that had been placed in the trial up to that point? It is the opinion of the writer that just as the decree which rejects the exception of relative incompetence supplies competence for future acts in the case in the event that relative incompetence actually existed, so it also remedies all the acts of the case up to that point.

[77] The invalidity is affirmed from the general principle of canon 201, § 1, namely, that jurisdiction can be directly exercised only over subjects. Before the jurisdiction is supplied, the acts are invalid. This opinion is confirmed by the statements of authors that in relative incompetence acts have their value unless an exception of incompetence is brought forward and accepted. They seem to agree that, if such an exception was admitted by the judge, the

forbidden to cite anyone before he judges that he is competent. But, granted that the judge does act while he is incompetent, the same provision of law which supplies competence through the failure of the parties to object to his incompetence, or through the rejection of the exception of incompetence, must also be said to remedy the acts that were placed previous to this supplying of competence. The same reason which calls for the supplying of competence for future acts prevails also for the remedying of previous acts. It will also be remembered that each judge sits in judgment with reference even to his own competence,[78] and his competence, therefore, is not a matter which rests with another tribunal for a decision.

Section 3. The Subject of the Obligation

From the subject of the right to request assistance in the placing of judicial acts, one now turns to the subject of the corresponding obligation. The tribunal that is spoken of in canon 1570, § 2, as being called upon for assistance must be understood in the similar fashion of the tribunal that makes the request. Similarity, however, is not identity. Strictly, if a tribunal is to have a true right to assistance from another tribunal, it must be conducting a specific trial wherein justice cannot safely be achieved without the help of a second tribunal. Such a prosecution of a specific case presupposes a tribunal already properly constituted with the required personnel.

While the tribunal that makes the request must be already in existence with the necessary personnel, it may happen that the tribunal of which the request is made has not yet been constituted, and, therefore, is not capable of immediately granting the required aid. The law requires that such tribunals should always be in existence in dioceses, and in abbacies and prelacies *nullius*.[79] No such obligation is imposed on exempt clerical religious institutes; canon 503 states that they can appoint notaries, but apparently no obligation is present unless an occasion should arise when a notary

acts up to that point remain invalid. Cf. Lega-Bartoccetti, *Commentarius in Iudicia Ecclesiastica,* I, 41; Coronata, *Institutiones Iuris Canonici,* III, n. 1094.

[78] Canon 1610, § 1.

[79] Canons 1572, § 1; 1573, §§ 1, 2; 372, §§ 1, 3; 1585, § 2; 1586; 1591.

would be needed. Nor are apostolic vicars and prefects under an obligation to maintain a court continuously in existence.[80] But even in the case of exempt clerical religious institutes and of apostolic vicariates and prefectures, a rogatory commission is always sent to a tribunal. Tribunal here must also be understood in a strict sense, i. e., as constituted with the necessary personnel, not necessarily as already constituted, but simply as potentially constituted by the proper authority, should some need arise.

It is important to stress the notion that a tribunal makes its request for necessary assistance to a tribunal which is considered as being composed of a judge together with all the other persons who are necessary for the exercise of judicial acts. The Code uses the word tribunal, and this is the proper meaning of the word. The required assistance cannot be given by a tribunal which is considered merely in the sense of the judge or the ordinary who has judicial power. The word tribunal must include at least the notary, and, when their presence is required, also the promoter of justice, and the defender of the bond.

In the usual exchange of rogatory commissions between tribunals of different ordinaries, if an ordinary tribunal is already in existence under the ordinary to whom the request is directed, it is this tribunal which has the obligation to execute the rogatory commission. The Code says nothing about the constituting of a special tribunal to fulfill the requests that come in from other tribunals. If, however, a tribunal is not habitually in existence in the place to which the request is directed, canon 1570, § 2, considers that tribunal as potentially in existence, inasmuch as the proper ordinary would then be obliged to constitute it with the necessary personnel in order to give the assistance that was requested.

The constitution of a special tribunal is spoken of in rogatory commissions from the Roman Rota and from delegated tribunals which are to prepare processes concerning the non-consummation of marriages, or the validity of Sacred Orders, or the obligations that

80 Cf. canons 1572, § 1; 1573, §§ 1, 2; 372, §§ 1, 3; 1585, § 2; 1586; 1591. All of these canons speak of a bishop or a diocese, and, therefore, apostolic vicars and prefects are not included; cf. Coronata, *Institutiones Iuris Canonici*, III, n. 1116; also canon 215, § 2.

normally arise through the reception of Sacred Orders. In these cases the instructions prescribe that the rogatory commission be sent to the local ordinary; no mention is made of its being sent to a tribunal.[81] This is understandable, for in these processes, as well as in many cases treated by the Roman Rota, the ordinary local tribunals are absolutely incompetent.

It will be noticed that when canon 1570, § 2, points to the tribunal which has a right to request assistance it uses the word "*quodlibet.*" This word is not used in reference to the tribunal that is to honor the request. The tribunal that is to execute a rogatory commission must have the necessary power to do so, i. e., that which is requested must fall under its ordinary jurisdiction.

That that which is requested of another tribunal must come under the ordinary jurisdiction of the tribunal which is to honor the request derives from the very nature of the rogatory commission. The rogatory commission exists for the simple reason that a tribunal can exercise jurisdiction only over persons and things that are subject to it, and in consequence cannot act outside of its territory. Because of this limitation there is enlisted the aid of another tribunal. But that tribunal must have power in the matter or over the person in question, and must be able to act in the place where the judicial act has to be exercised.

When, therefore, a legitimate request that falls under its jurisdiction is made to a tribunal as understood in the sense described above, that tribunal has a duty to comply with the request. To every right there is a corresponding duty. To the right spoken of in canon 1570, § 2, there is the corresponding duty on the part of the tribunal to which the request is made, namely, to grant the assistance that has been asked for.

[81] Normae S. R. Rotae Tribunalis, 29 iun. 1934, art. 93, § 1; 102—*AAS*, XXVI (1934), 473, 475; S. C. de Sacramentis, *Regulae servandae in processibus super matrimonio rato et non consummato,* 7 maii 1923, n. 23—*AAS*, XV (1923), 396; S. C. de Sacramentis, *Regulae servandae in processibus super nullitate sacrae ordinationis vel onerum sacris ordinibus inhaerentium,* 9 maii 1931, n. 14—*AAS*, XXIII (1931), 461; S. C. pro Ecclesia Orientali, *Instructio ad conficiendos processus super matrimonio rato et non consummato,* 10 iun. 1935, n. 25—*AAS*, XXVII (1935), 339.

Article 5. The Committing of Judicial Acts to Another Tribunal

Section 1. The Judicial Acts That Can Be Committed to Another Tribunal

From the very wording of canon 1570, § 2, it is clear that the Code does not intend to give an exhaustive list of the various judicial acts that one tribunal can commit to another. Besides the examination and citation of the parties and the witnesses, the examination of documents or of the particular thing that is under dispute, and the notification of decrees, the words *"alia huiusmodi"* permit other possibilities. In particular, what other acts can be committed to other tribunals may best be determined after it is clear what cannot be committed to them.

Haring affirmed that one tribunal cannot delegate an entire process to another tribunal. He based this conclusion on two arguments. First, canon 1570, § 1, states that trials are to be conducted by the tribunals mentioned in canon 1572, and, on the other hand, canon 1570, § 2, speaks of committing individual acts of a trial to another tribunal. The juxtaposition of the two paragraphs of the same canon seemed, according to him, to rule out the possibility of delegating the conduct of an entire trial to another tribunal. Secondly, so he argued, only the competent tribunal is obliged to undertake a trial. If the entire process is delegated to another tribunal, the delegated tribunal would not be obliged to accept the delegation, since the two tribunals exist on an equal basis, so that the one cannot put an obligation on the other.[82]

Haring's conclusion is undoubtedly true. A tribunal that is competent in a particular trial cannot commit the conduct of that entire trial to another tribunal. Roberti also accepts this opinion.[83] A more potent reason, however, is the one that postulates competence for the conduct of a trial. From canon 1559, § 1, it is evident that

[82] "Delegation eines Eheprozesses," *Theologisch-praktische Quartalschrift,* LXXXIII (1930), 141.

[83] "At nullo modo potest unum tribunal alii tribunali committere integrum processum."—*De Processibus,* I, n. 89.

the list of titles for competence to conduct an entire trial, as given in canons 1560-1568, excludes the possibility of other titles. The fact that a tribunal which otherwise is incompetent, has received the commission from a competent tribunal to conduct the trial is not listed as a title by which a tribunal becomes competent to conduct that trial. Therefore, the tribunal which has none of the titles of competence mentioned in canons 1560-1568 could not conduct an entire trial simply upon the commission to do so as granted by a tribunal that has competence.

If a number of tribunals are equally competent, the tribunal which has received the plaintiff's petition cannot commission one of the other competent tribunals to hear the case unless the plaintiff was prevailed upon to withdraw his petition and present it to the other tribunal. If many tribunals are competent, it is the plaintiff who has the right of option.[84] The tribunal which has received the petition cannot refuse its services; it must honor the legitimate request of the plaintiff.[85] It cannot of its own accord commission another tribunal, even though this tribunal would be equally competent, to conduct a trial in answer to a petition that it, itself, has received. To do so would destroy the plaintiff's option.

As entire trials cannot be committed to other tribunals, so also the pronouncement of the final sentence cannot. The final sentence is the essence and purpose of the trial.[86] The preparation of the process with the gathering of proofs is but a means to that end. With the pronouncement of the final sentence, the tribunal completes its work.[87]

The very purpose of the titles of competence in the Code is that by a final sentence right may become defined by those whom the Code recognizes as competent to do so, that right in an individual case may be made publicly manifest through an official announcement made by a public authority recognized as competent to make that pronouncement. If only one tribunal is competent in

[84] Canon 1559, § 3.

[85] Canons 1608; 1625, § 1.

[86] Roberti, *De Processibus*, I, n. 25; Lega-Bartoccetti, *Commentarius in Iudicia Ecclesiastica*, I, 2.

[87] Lega-Bartoccetti, *op. cit.*, III, 79; cf. canon 1920, § 1.

a particular case, it is clear that the law intends that the final sentence be given by that tribunal. If from the beginning many tribunals are competent, that competence becomes restricted to one tribunal in consequence of the citation of the defendant to that tribunal. Besides frustrating the power of option that the plaintiff possesses, the act whereby one of the erstwhile competent tribunals is commissioned with the rendering of the final sentence would only restore to that tribunal the essence and major point that the Code itself has taken away, and relieve of its main duty that tribunal which the Code has recognized as properly competent for the case in question.

Another argument that the rendering of the final sentence cannot be committed to another tribunal may be drawn from the wording of canon 1570, § 2. There it is stated that one tribunal has the right to call upon another tribunal *for assistance*. If the original tribunal of the case commissioned another tribunal to pronounce the final sentence, this other tribunal would have the major and essential point of the trial. The original tribunal would not then be calling upon the other tribunal for assistance, but rather the opposite would be true, i. e., the tribunal acting on commission and doing the major work of the trial would then be receiving assistance from the first tribunal.

Besides the final sentence, also certain other acts, from the very fact that they fall under the exclusive jurisdiction of the authority conducting the trial, cannot be committed to other tribunals. Thus a local tribunal could not commission another local tribunal to take testimony or to execute a judicial access in the former's own territory. Of course, delegation could be given; but this would relate, not to a rogatory commission as it is considered in this work, but rather to the case envisioned in canon 1770, § 2, 4°. The subjects of the territory where the trial is being conducted could not be effectively cited by another tribunal, even though this tribunal was commissioned to take their testimony inasmuch as they could not return without serious inconvenience to the place of the trial. All acts which must be exercised in the territory where the trial is being conducted, or which purport to coerce those who are subjects of that territory alone, must be exercised by the competent tribunal of the case. They could not be committed to other tribunals, since these would lack the necessary jurisdiction from the viewpoint either of territorial competence or of personal subjection.

The position has been taken that an entire trial, the pronouncement of the final sentence, and such acts which must be exercised in the territory where the trial is being heard, or which purport to coerce those who are subjects exclusively of that territory, cannot be committed to another tribunal. The further opinion is now ventured that all other acts, besides those mentioned, can be committed to other tribunals. Four conditions are required for such a commission.

First, there must be a reason of necessity. A sufficient reason is required because one tribunal cannot be expected to inconvenience itself in the interest of the other tribunal without a proportionately grave reason. Usually this reason will be that the trial cannot be properly prosecuted, and justice cannot safely be achieved unless the other tribunal is called upon to exercise an act of jurisdiction in its own territory or to force its proper subjects to co-operate in the trial. Canon 1770, § 2, 3°, also states that the grave inconvenience which a witness would have to suffer in returning to the scene of the trial to give evidence would furnish a sufficient reason for calling upon the tribunal of the place of the witness' actual residence to take the testimony. Consequently, the avoiding of a serious inconvenience, or the attaining of a considerable advantage, would constitute a sufficient reason for issuing a rogatory commission.

Secondly, it must be a judicial act that is committed to another tribunal, i. e., an act which is to be exercised by a tribunal and which has a direct and formal bearing on the trial. For acts that are not judicial there is no necessity for calling on a tribunal as such. Thus tribunals can be called upon to cite witnesses, to take testimony, or to execute a judicial access. On the other hand, the assistance of a tribunal would not be necessary in the securing of transcripts from parochial or chancery archives, in the searching for possible witnesses who could testify in a case, in the drawing up of a mandate for an advocate, or in the edicted inserting of a summons in a newspaper. Frequently courtesy will prompt the members of different tribunals to assist each other in matters of this type, but a rogatory commission in a true sense is not had except in judicial acts.[88]

Thirdly, the act that is requested must be legitimate. There could be no obligation to perform an illegitimate act; as a matter of fact, there would be an obligation not to perform it. Thus one tribunal could not call upon another to cite a nun who was under its jurisdiction to leave the pontifical cloister to which she was obliged, and appear before the judge of the trial, even though the distance to the court in the other diocese was negligible.

Finally, the commission must be made to a tribunal that has the needed jurisdiction for exercising the desired acts, although it would otherwise be relatively incompetent in the particular trial in question. Apart from the possession of jurisdiction obligations could not be imposed, and the judicial acts would be without value. If the request is sent to a local tribunal, it must be for an act that is to be exercised within its proper territory. If the request is for an act that would place an obligation on a person, it must be made to the tribunal which has jurisdiction over that person.

That the presence of these four conditions will suffice for calling upon another tribunal to cite witnesses or parties, to take testimony, to execute a judicial access, or to notify decrees, is sufficiently clear from the wording of canon 1570, § 2, and from daily practice. About these acts there can be no question. A question could arise, however, regarding such procedural acts (*acta processus*) as the joining of the issue, the publication of the acts, and the closing of the evidence (*conclusio in causa*). The opinion is here ventured that even these acts can be committed to another tribunal in a case of necessity.

There is no reason to deny that whatever can be delegated to an auditor in the territory of the judge of the trial can also for a good reason be committed to another tribunal to be executed in its territory. But canon 1582 excludes from the auditor's acquirable competence simply the rendering of the final sentence. Noval's opinion that the closing of the evidence cannot be delegated to the auditor since a way must always be left open for the correcting

[88] Contuzzi, *Il Digesto Italiano*, s. v. *Commissione Rogatoria*, n. 51.

of any mistakes made by the auditor in the preparing of the process [89] is without foundation. In a case of necessity new proofs can be admitted after the closing of the evidence,[90] and even incidental questions can be corrected.[91]

It is admitted that a necessitating reason will not be had as often for the committing of such acts as the joinder of issue, the publication of the acts, and the closing of the evidence, to another tribunal as is had for the taking of evidence. But such a reason is not impossible. Canon 1770, § 2, 3°, considers serious inconvenience as sufficient for committing the hearing of witnesses to another tribunal. One could imagine a case wherein a right arising from a contract is being litigated in the place where the contract was made. After being cited, the defendant took up residence in a territory where the plaintiff and all of the witnesses also are in residence. It could be a grave inconvenience for the parties to have to appoint and properly instruct proxies to effect the joinder of the issue; it could be a grave inconvenience to be forced to wait till all of the evidence taken on commission is sent to the original tribunal of the case before it can be inspected; it could possibly also be a grave inconvenience to have to wait till the original tribunal of the case had sufficiently studied the acts in order to give the decree for the closing of the evidence, and to set the time for the parties to prepare their defense, when all this could have been done with equal proficiency by the tribunal that had prepared all the acts of the case on commission.

In the opinion of some authors,[92] the accepting of a decisive oath, the making of a settlement (*transactio*), or the administering of a judicial correction cannot be committed to others, since these would preclude the need of the rendering of a final sentence, and therefore be tantamount to the rendering of that sentence. While it is conceded that the judgment regarding the presence of the necessary

[89] *De Iudiciis,* n. 135; cf. also Coronata, *Institutiones Iuris Canonici,* III, n. 1121.

[90] Canon 1861, § 1.

[91] Canon 1841.

[92] Noval, *De Iudiciis,* n. 135; Vermeersch-Creusen, *Epitome Iuris Canonici,* III, n. 40; Besté, *Introductio in Codicem,* p. 787.

conditions and the admissibility of these extraordinary means of terminating a trial, at least as a general rule,[93] must be reserved to the judge of the case, there is no reason why the making of a settlement, the accepting of a decisive oath, and the administering of a judicial correction cannot be committed to others. As a matter of fact, the use of judicial correction is reserved, not to the judge as such, but to the ordinary.[94]

When a criminal trial is being prosecuted in the place where the crime was committed, and upon the confession of the accused in the trial the judge has considered judicial correction admissible under the circumstances, it is entirely feasible that the ordinary whose duty it would be to inflict the judicial correction should remit the guilty party to his own ordinary to receive the correction. Of course, the matter is then no longer connected with a rogatory commission in the strict sense; rather it connotes a mutual assistance between the two ordinaries, for in reality the judicial correction itself leaves the judicial sphere and enters the administrative.

As regards the reaching of a settlement by the contending parties, the Code itself suggests that ordinarily the judge should not personally preside, but should commit this matter to another.[95] If the parties are in another diocese, and it would be a serious inconvenience for them to come to the tribunal, the details for the reaching of the settlement could be committed to the tribunal of their actual residence. The same can be said for the details of the offering and the administering of the decisive oath after it had been approved by the judge of the trial.

Can the decision to admit a settlement, to accept a decisive oath, or to resort to a judicial correction be committed to another tribunal? The answer is closely connected with the question whether incidental questions can be committed to other tribunals. The opinion that is here adopted is that ordinarily only the exploration of proof will be committed to other tribunals; however, should a case of necessity arise, incidental questions, even those which would be

[93] "Contra nequeunt regulariter committi auditori omnes actus qui decisionem attingunt vel ei praeiudicant."—Roberti, *De Processibus,* I, n. 113.

[94] Canon 1950.

[95] Canon 1925, § 3.

settled by means of a sentence which has definitive force, and therefore also the judgment as to the admissibility of making a settlement, of accepting a decisive oath, or of administering a judicial correction, can be committed to other tribunals. Canon 1582 solely forbids the rendering of a definitive sentence to be committed to an auditor, and it is the opinion of the writer that what can be committed to an auditor, can, for a sufficient reason, be committed to another tribunal. If an injustice should arise, even in the case of an interlocutory sentence having a definitive force, it can be corrected by the original judge of the case before the final decision is given.[96]

Section 2. The Regular Uses of the Rogatory Commission

A. In the Taking of the Testimony

Canon 1766, § 1 indicates for every witness, if he has been properly cited, the obligation to make his appearance or to offer an excuse for his absence to the judge. Where that appearance is to be made is explained in canon 1770, § 1. The witness is to be examined in the court room. Apparently the court room of the tribunal which hears the case is implied, for in § 2, 3°, of the same canon a clear distinction is made between the tribunal of the diocese where the trial is being conducted and the tribunals of the various places where the witnesses are if they reside outside of the diocese.

Canon 1770, § 2, 3°, exempts from the obligation of undergoing the examination in the court room of the tribunal of the trial those who are outside of the diocese and cannot return and appear in the court room without serious inconvenience. From the word *"reverti"* it can be deduced that this exemption applies at least to those who in law pertain to the place where the trial is being conducted. Those who are subject to the jurisdiction of the place where the trial is being conducted are excused from returning there if they find it seriously inconvenient to do so. In this case the taking of their testimony is to be committed to the tribunal of the place of their

[96] Canon 1841; cf. Lega-Bartoccetti, *Commentarius in Iudicia Ecclesiastica,* II, 860-861.

actual residence. At the same time it is clear that, if after a proper citation it would not be seriously inconvenient for them to return, they would be obliged to do so.

A question arises as to the taking of the testimony of witnesses who are not under the jurisdiction of the place where the trial is being conducted. It seems that before the advent of the present Code there were three different opinions on this point.

Engel (d. 1674),[97] Reiffenstuel (d. 1703) [98] and Pichler (d. 1736) [99] distinctly held that a witness who was of another jurisdiction was not to be excused from giving his testimony at the court of the trial unless some special reason intervened, as sickness, the great distance to be traveled, etc. The same doctrine was followed by De Angelis (d. 1881) [100] and Lega (d. 1935).[101] This seems also to have been the doctrine of Pirhing, (d. 1699),[102] Schmalzgrueber (d. 1735) [103] and Remigius Maschat a S. Erasmo (d. 1747),[104] for they connected the excusing factor with the distance from the place of the trial, and did not indicate any special exemption for those of another jurisdiction.

Another opinion held that witnesses of other jurisdictions were always to be examined before their own proper tribunals. To this effect the judge of the trial was to commission the judge of the territory where these witnesses were. This was the opinion of Bouix (d. 1870),[105] Santi (d. 1885) [106] and Lombardi (d. 1908).[107]

A third and intermediate opinion was presented by F. Schmier (d. 1728). The witnesses of other jurisdictions were either to be sent to the original judge of the trial or subjected to examination

[97] *Collegium Universi Iuris Canonici,* Lib. II, tit. 20 et 21, n. 2.

[98] *Ius Canonicum Universum,* Lib. II, tit. 20, n. 433.

[99] *Ius Canonicum secundum Quinque Decretalum Titulos Explicatum,* Lib. II, tit. 20, n. 26.

[100] *Praelectiones Iuris Canonici,* Lib. II, tit. 20, n. 3.

[101] *De Iudiciis Ecclesiasticis,* I, n. 490.

[102] *Jus Canonicum in V Libros Decretalum,* Lib. II, tit. 20, n. 9.

[103] *Ius Ecclesiasticum Universum,* Lib. II, tit. 21, n. 9.

[104] *Institutiones Canonicae,* II, 398.

[105] *Tractatus de Judiciis Ecclesiasticis,* II, 220.

[106] *Praelectiones Juris Canonici,* Lib. II, tit. 21, n. 1.

[107] *Iuris Canonici Privati Institutiones,* III, 254.

by their own proper authorities. In this he gave no reason by which a choice was to be made between the two methods of procedure.[108] Sebastianelli (d. 1920) wrote in similar terms.[109]

After the publication of the Code the first two opinions continued to remain. Woywod (d. 1941)-Smith makes the unqualified statement that witnesses who live in other dioceses are to be summoned and examined by the court of their own diocese.[110] On the other hand, Coronata[111] and Blat[112] say that canon 1770, § 2, 3°, applies also for witnesses who are not under the jurisdiction of the place where the trial is being heard. According to this opinion, witnesses who are not under the jurisdiction of the judge of the trial, provided that they are properly cited, are not exempt from appearing before the tribunal of the trial unless serious inconvenience excuses them.

The latter interpretation of canon 1770, § 2, 3°, appears the more logical, and is to be followed. If witnesses of other jurisdictions were not included in this section of the canon, they would have no exemption at all from the general principle announced in canon 1770, § 1. Canon 1770, § 2, 3°, in its use of general terms states nothing about whether or not the witness is domiciled in the place of the trial. The word *"reverti"* does not necessarily imply a domicile in the place of the trial, for it could also apply to one who had merely visited there, or to one who at one time had a domicile there. The lawgiver may well have chosen it to explain how one can be a witness in a trial that is being conducted in another territory. Therefore, it is claimed that all witnesses, irrespective of the jurisdiction

108 *Jurisprudentia Canonico-civilis,* Lib. II, tract. 3, c. 5, n. 69.

109 *De Iudiciis Civilibus,* n. 146.

110 *A Practical Commentary on the Code of Canon Law* (revised and enlarged edition, 2 vols., New York: Joseph F. Wagner, Inc., 1948), II, n. 1715.

111 "Nihil refert utrum testes de iurisdictione sint tribunalis requirentis an non; testificationes taliter absentium semper recipi possunt per tribunal loci, dummodo accessus ad tribunal requirens grave incommodum importet."—*Institutiones Iuris Canonici,* III, n. 1298.

112 *"In dioecesim* hanc *reverti,* si ab ea, ad quam forsan pertineant, egressi fuerunt, idemque valet ac si numquam in ea fuerunt, sed illud erit de facto ut plurimum."—*Commentarium Textus Codicis Iuris Canonici,* IV, n. 278.

to which they belong, who are outside of the diocese and cannot without grave inconvenience go to the place of the trial must be heard by the tribunal of the place where they are. Likewise, if no serious inconvenience would be suffered, and no other excusing factor as mentioned in canon 1770, § 2, were present, all witnesses, irrespective of the jurisdiction to which they belong, would have to make a personal appearance at the scene of the trial. This supposes, of course, that they were properly cited.

The judgment regarding the existence of the grave inconvenience is to be made by the judge to whom it pertains to issue the citation.[113] As shall be seen, the one issuing the citation may be a person entirely different from the judge of the case who would receive the testimony, inasmuch as the citation has to be given by one who has jurisdiction over the witness. The gravity of the inconvenience will be judged according to the judgment of prudent men,[114] and especially the factor of time will have to be considered, as today, more than ever, "time is money."[115] This opinion as adopted in regard to canon 1770, § 2, 3°, is particularly practical, for frequently it happens that a witness can appear at the tribunal of a neighboring diocese with greater ease than he can go to his own. In the case of a doubt as to the gravity of the inconvenience, the proper ordinary of the witness could dispense, and free his subject from the necessity of appearing at the tribunal of another diocese.[116]

From the wording of canon 1770, § 2, 3°, there appears to be an obligation to hear the witness in the diocese where he actually sojourns if he would be seriously inconvenienced in going to the court room of the trial. This obligation is invoked in favor of the witness, and therefore he can relinquish his right. This interpretation has been given for marriage cases,[117] but it can be taken as an indication

[113] Noval, *De Iudiciis,* n. 489.

[114] Blat, *Commentarium Textus Codicis Iuris Canonici,* IV, n. 278; Lega-Bartoccetti, *Commentarius in Iudicia Ecclesiastica,* I, 103.

[115] Lega-Bartoccetti, *loc. cit.*

[116] Canon 15; cf. Noval, *De Iudiciis,* n. 489.

[117] S. C. de Sacramentis, instr. 15 aug. 1936, art 98, § 2—*AAS,* XXVIII (1936), 334.

of the meaning of the law in question. Consequently, if witnesses who are outside of the diocese consent to undergo a serious inconvenience in order to appear at the court of the trial, the parties have a right to call upon them to do so. But if the witnesses are willing, the decision to have them come to the scene of the trial will depend upon the party who will have to pay their expenses.[118]

When the conditions permit it, the appearance of the witnesses before the judge of the trial is preferable to the taking of testimony on commission. The judge who is conducting the trial is better acquainted with all the circumstances of it, and can better direct the examination. It may also be preferable in the second or higher instance if the court of first instance would have to be commissioned to take the desired testimony; here the human element could influence a judge from whose sentence an appeal has been made.[119]

A special problem arises in the taking of the testimony of exempt men religious who, as regards their persons as well as their homes, enjoy the privilege of exemption from the local ordinary.[120] All women religious who have this privilege would also be exempted from the obligation of making a personal appearance in a trial before the ordinary seat of the tribunal, since they would come under the category of *moniales*. The same exemption from appearing at the trial would obtain for exempt men religious in the event that they were impeded through sickness. In each case the testimony would have to be taken in their respective homes.[121] A bishop does not have the right to set up a tribunal in the exempt territory of religious,[122] and there is an opinion that such exempt places are entirely separated from the territory of the diocese.[123]

The more common opinion that the exempt homes and churches of regulars are in the diocese but not of the diocese would permit, at least as far as validity is concerned, that the judge of the case together with a notary conduct the examination in the exempt re-

[118] Canon 1787.

[119] Torre, *Processus Matrimonialis* (Neapoli: M. D'Auria, 1947), p. 90.

[120] Canon 615.

[121] Canon 1770, § 2, 2°.

[122] Canon 1636.

[123] Coronata, *Institutiones Iuris Canonici*, I, p. 826, footnote 1; cf. *supra*, pp. 63-64.

ligious house. This would not be contrary to canon 1636, for this canon deals with the setting up of a tribunal, while canon 1770, § 2, 2°, implies that the taking of testimony in a home is an act undertaken outside of a tribunal. The licitness of the act could readily be safeguarded through the granted permission of the religious superior of the place.[124] The opinion that the local tribunal can take testimony in the exempt religious houses of regulars was held by Wernz (d. 1914),[125] and is mentioned at the present time by Lega-Bartoccetti.[126] They base their opinion on a decision supposedly given at Rome on June 9, 1828.[127]

The suggestion is made that another solution of the problem would consist in commissioning the proper religious tribunal of the residence of the religious to take the desired testimony. Thus, the testimony of exempt women religious could also be received through the instrumentality of the tribunal which had jurisdiction over them. Ordinarily religious tribunals would not be competent in matters that are tried before diocesan tribunals, but the fact that they were commissioned by diocesan tribunals would extend their proper competence to cover such acts as are needed by diocesan tribunals. If in a particular case the intervention of a promoter of justice or a defender of the bond would be needed, he could be appointed by the religious ordinary, for one who has the right and the duty to exercise a judicial act must also be acknowledged as having the power to make an appointment which is necessary for the validity of that act.

It could be insisted that diocesan tribunals cannot call upon religious tribunals for assistance because of the latter's incompetence in matters that are tried before diocesan courts. This incompetence seems to arise from the lack of a title of competence, and there doesn't seem to be any place in the Code which describes the incompetence of religious tribunals in trials before diocesan courts

124 Cappello, *Summa Iuris Canonici,* III, n. 80.

125 *Ius Decretalium,* V, n. 315.

126 *Commentarius in Iudicia Ecclesiastica,* I, 270.

127 "Le juge d'instruction a le pouvoir de recevoir les dépositions juridiques pour les causes civiles ou criminelles dans les hôpitaux, monastères et autres lieux privilégiés, lorques les témoins ne peuvent pas sortir."—*Analecta Iuris Pontificii,* XIII (1874), 48.

as absolute. Canon 503 states that major superiors can appoint notaries only for ecclesiastical affairs of their own institute. But the taking of the testimony of its own subjects could not be said to be entirely foreign to a religious institute, even though this testimony is going to be used in a trial before a diocesan court. If it is denied that a religious institute can appoint notaries for the taking of testimony on commission from a diocesan court, the testimony of exempt religious could never be obtained by diocesan courts, unless they willingly consented to give it. Diocesan courts could not cite exempt religious, for these are not subject to their jurisdiction. For the religious superior to issue the citation, he would require a notary.[128]

When a trial is being conducted by a particular diocesan tribunal, not only religious but all other tribunals, diocesan as well, are incompetent in that process. When the judge of that trial issues a rogatory commission to another diocesan tribunal, this tribunal becomes competent to exercise the acts that receive mention in the letter of request. There seems to be no reason why the ordinary competence of a religious tribunal could not be prorogued in a similar fashion which will allow it to render necessary assistance to diocesan tribunals.

The use of the rogatory commission to secure the testimony of exempt religious becomes applicable only when the witness is not able to make an appearance at the diocesan tribunal. Exempt men religious who can conveniently appear at the scene of the trial are obliged to do so after they have been properly cited. If they are outside of the diocese where the trial is being conducted, and they cannot conveniently return, their testimony would have to be taken by the diocesan tribunal of the place where they are. Canon 1770, § 2, 3°, particularly specifies that absent witnesses are to be heard *"a tribunali loci in quo commorantur."* But here again, if they are impeded from appearing at the tribunal of their place of residence, one of the two ways suggested above could be used.

From the point of view of personal jurisdiction, similar to religious, are members of the armed forces who are under their own

[128] Canon 1715, § 2.

proper ordinary, a military vicar. When members of the armed forces are outside of the territory or diocese where a trial is being conducted, it appears that their testimony must be taken by the tribunal of the place where they are stationed, or where at the time they are staying, rather than by a delegate of the military vicar. This interpretation follows from the fact that the military vicar is not an *ordinarius loci*. It is argued, therefore, that the tribunal of the military ordinariate is not a *tribunal loci*, as canon 1770, § 2, 3°, postulates.

In the letter by which another tribunal is notified that it has been commissioned to take the testimony of a witness, there are to be sent the questions that are to be proposed to the witnesses. These will be drawn up in accordance with the canons which prescribe the procedure to be followed in this matter. Along with the questions will be included sufficient instructions about the nature of the case, the particular points of the commission, the financial status of the party desiring the testimony, and particularly whether gratuitous defense had been granted by the judge of the case. The tribunal will be asked to take particular note of the conduct of the witness during the trial, and to include in the acts mention of any points on which the judge of the case can form his opinion regarding the credibility of the witness. It seems advisable to commission the judge who is going to take the testimony to include his opinion, along with the points on which it is based, regarding the credibility of the witness. While this would be an act of judgment, and therefore pertain particularly to the judge of the trial, nevertheless it would only be an interlocutory decree which could be changed before the final sentence is rendered.

Since canon 1770, § 2, 3°, makes no distinction between contentious and criminal trials, there is no doubt that testimony can now be taken on commission in criminal trials.[129] However, the very reasons which forbade the use of the rogatory commission in criminal cases under the Decretal Law would suggest that a maximum of caution accompany the conceding and the executing of the rogatory commission in these cases.

[129] Cf. S. C. de Prop. Fide, instr. a. 1883, n. XIX.—*Fontes*, n. 4900.

B. In the Issuing of the Citation

A citation considered in a broad sense is the act of a judge by which he summons the parties, witnesses, or officials of the tribunal to appear in court and to co-operate in some judicial act.[130] In a stricter sense it pertains especially to the calling into court of the defendant in order to engage him in a lawsuit. Inasmuch as the citation of the defendant proceeds from the command of the judge, who orders him to appear, this summons must be considered as an act of jurisdiction.[131]

Under the law of the Code there will be little use for the rogatory commission for the summoning of the parties. As these are always subject to the jurisdiction of the judge of the case, provided he is competent, he will always be able to exercise his jurisdiction over them in the measure in which the prosecution of the trial demands it. For the most part, the assistance of another tribunal will not be necessary for the delivering of the summons, for the Code permits a judge to authorize his own beadle to deliver a summons even in the territory of another diocese.[132] If the distance be so great that the judge cannot send his own beadle, he can make use of registered mail provided he demand a return receipt, or of some other safe method according to the local laws and customs.[133]

The use of the rogatory commission for the summoning of the parties is not entirely excluded as a possibility. It could be that the distant place in which the defendant resides is without any registered mail service and offers no other safe way for the delivery of a summons except the employment of a beadle for that purpose. This could happen in mission countries. In this case, a petition to have the citation delivered could be presented to the local ordinary.

If both of the parties live in another diocese and at an inconvenient distance from the scene of the trial, the judge could commit the joinder of the issue to the tribunal of the actual residence of the parties. In this event it seems that he could commit to the

130 Noval, *De Iudiciis*, n. 392.
131 Cappello, *Summa Iuris Canonici*, III, n. 146.
132 Canon 1717, § 2.
133 Canon 1719.

other tribunal the summoning of the defendant, provided that the defendant was under its jurisdiction. Thus, the second tribunal would cite the parties to appear before its own court to effect the joinder of the issue in a trial to be conducted before another court. Then, too, the interrogation of the parties could be committed to this second tribunal. This case would explain why canon 1570, § 2, makes it allowable for one tribunal to call upon another for assistance in the citation and examination of the parties as well as of the witnesses.

The rogatory commission will be a matter of necessity whenever the witnesses to be cited are of a jurisdiction other than that of the judge of the trial and it is desired to bring force to bear to insure their appearance. The citation of a witness is an act of jurisdiction just as the citation of the defendant. It contains the judge's precept that the desired witness appear in court.[134] The judge must bring his authority to bear to give the citation its binding force.[135] There is no obligation for a witness to appear until he has been properly cited.[136] Therefore, since the citation of a witness is an act of jurisdiction, a judge can issue a citation only to his own subjects.[137]

That a judge could cite as witnesses only his own subjects, and that witnesses of other jurisdictions had to be cited by their own proper authorities, was the common doctrine before the Code.[138] No author either before the Code or since the Code has held a contrary position as far as the writer was able to ascertain. Since the Code, however, few authors take up the question. Wernz-Vidal[139]

134 "Quae praeceptum iudicis . . . factum ad comperendum exprimat"—canon 1715, § 1; cf. also canon 1765.

135 Noval, *De Iudiciis,* n. 392; Lega-Bartoccetti, *Commentarius in Iudicia Ecclesiastica,* II, 692.

136 Canon 1766, § 1.

137 Canon 201, § 1.

138 Engel, Lib. II, tit. 20 et 21, n. 2; Reiffenstuel, Lib. II, tit. 20, n. 433; Schmalzgrueber, Lib. II, tit. 21, n. 12; Schmier, Lib. II, tract. 3, c. 5, n. 69; Pichler, Lib. II, tit. 20, n. 17; De Angelis, *Praelectiones Iuris Canonici,* Lib. II, tit. 20, § 3; Santi, *Praelectiones Juris Canonici,* Lib. II, tit. 21, n. 1; Lega, *De Iudiciis Ecclesiasticis,* I, n. 490; Wernz, *Ius Decretalium,* V, n. 622.

139 "Si legitime citatur a iudice suo."—*Ius Canonicum,* VI, n. 460.

and Coronata [140] seem positively to teach that witnesses must be cited by tribunals which have jurisdiction over them.

The commissioning of another tribunal to cite one of its own subjects can be of importance when subjects of another jurisdiction are desired as witnesses, and they are not excused from appearing at the court because of serious inconvenience. Before the Code, the special name of *litterae mutui compassus* was used in designation of the letter by which a judge was requested to cite his own subject to go before a tribunal in another territory to give testimony.[141]

Concerning the citation of witnesses who pertain to other jurisdictions, but who are at the time in the territory of the tribunal where the trial is being conducted, there is no word in the pre-Code authors. Undoubtedly, this was due to the confusion of opinions in regard to the legal status of the traveler in relation to the jurisdiction of the place where he was traveling.[142] Under the law of the Code it is certain that the traveler is not subject to the jurisdiction of the authority of the place where he is traveling, with the exception of matters that touch the public order and the solemnities of acts.[143] Therefore, to effectively cite a witness who is not his subject, but who is temporarily in his territory, the judge will have to call upon the tribunal which has jurisdiction over that witness.

It is true that a valid citation is not necessary if a witness actually makes his appearance at the court and willingly responds to the questions proposed to him.[144] The analogy, however, between the parties and witnesses in this matter is not perfect. Canon 1711, § 2, which treats of the spontaneous appearance of the parties cannot be applied to witnesses without some restriction. If a

[140] "De iure vigente huiusmodi litterae [i. e., mutui compassus] non videntur amplius necessariae ex c. 1717, § 2, nisi testis non sit subditus tribunali eum citanti."—*Institutiones Iuris Canonici,* III, 212, footnote 1.

[141] Engel, Lib. II, tit. 20 et 21, n. 2; Reiffenstuel, Lib. II, tit. 20, n. 433; Pichler, Lib. II, tit. 2, n. 17; De Angelis, *Praelectionis Iuris Canonici,* Lib. II, tit. 20, § 3.

[142] Hammill, *The Obligation of the Traveler according to Canon 14,* pp. 49-58.

[143] Canon 14, § 1, 2°. Cf. Hammill, *op. cit.,* p. 118.

[144] Coronata, *Institutiones Iuris Canonici,* III, n. 1294

witness spontaneously offers to give testimony, there will be reason to be suspicious of the testimony, and the law leaves the question up to the discretion of the judge whether to admit or reject the witness.[145] Certainly punishments could not be used in order to enforce the appearance of a witness if he has not been properly cited.[146]

C. In the Executing of the Decrees and Sentences

Judicial jurisdiction actually involves two functions: first, the power of investigating and defining a controversy; and secondly, the power of enforcing the execution of the decrees and decisions of the judge. To the judge must be recognized a sufficient power of enforcement to fulfill his task of investigating and defining. To this end he is supplied with beadles and marshals.[147] When the final sentence has been given, and he has issued the decree for its execution, the judge has completed his work.[148] Under the present law of the Code the judge who has rendered the final sentence is not the executor of it.[149] Consequently, a distinction can be made between the execution of an interlocutory decree or sentence which is within the power of the judge, and the execution of a final sentence which is not in his power.

In regard to interlocutory decrees and sentences, mention has already been made of the execution of the decrees for the citation, and for the taking of testimony on commission. To these may be added many other instances wherein another tribunal could be called upon to assist in the execution of the interlocutory decrees and sentences of the judge of the trial. For example, the judge may have determined that the particular thing about which the trial is concerned should be sequestered; one of the parties may have been ordered to produce a document; judicial access may have been de-

145 Canon 1760.

146 Canon 1766.

147 Canon 1591, § 1.

148 Lega-Bartoccetti, *Commentarius in Iudicia Ecclesiastica,* I, 5; III, 77-79; Wernz-Vidal, *Ius Canonicum,* VI, n. 597.

149 Canon 1920.

cided upon, etc. All of these are strictly judicial acts, and, when necessity arises, another tribunal can be called upon to assist in their execution in accordance with canon 1570, § 2. To this end the other tribunal will be notified of the work that has been committed to it, and sufficient information about the case will be supplied in order that the request may be properly executed.

In regard to the final sentence, a new problem has arisen with the promulgation of the Code. Under the Code the execution is no longer a judicial act, but rather an administrative or executive act, which is committed to the ordinary of the place in which the sentence in first instance had been given.[150] The local ordinary, as far as the execution of the final sentence is concerned, must be understood in the sense of canon 198, §§ 1, 2, and includes the vicar general and the vicar capitular.[151] Since canon 1570, § 2, treats of the interrelationships between tribunals, it appears that the local ordinary, as executor of the final sentence, could not appeal to this canon if he should require the assistance of another local ordinary to effect the execution.

There is no canon which specifically prescribes that local ordinaries shall mutually assist each other when there is need of such assistance in the exercise of administrative or executive power. In the absence of such a provision, a norm must be taken from canon 1570, § 2. While this canon applies to judicial power, the similarity between mutual assistance in judicial matters and mutual assistance in administrative matters cannot be denied. In the execution of a sentence, co-operation between administrative powers is just as necessary for the triumph of justice as is co-operation between tribunals. Actually in the Church it is one and the same person who in his own name possesses and uses both the administrative and the judicial power, namely, the bishop.

Canon 1570, § 2, also exhibits a general principle of law, namely that the Church is one, and that there must be co-operation between the various jurisdictional units. Finally, it has been the common

150 Canon 1920, § 1; cf. Coronata, *Institutiones Iuris Canonici,* III, n. 1439.

151 Coronata, *loc. cit.;* Vermeersch-Creusen, *Epitome Iuris Canonici,* III, n. 251; Noval, *De Iudiciis,* n. 707; Lega-Bartoccetti, *Commentarius in Iudicia Ecclesiastica,* III, 88.

and constant opinion of doctors in canon law that the authorities of different territories must co-operate with each other in the execution of judicial sentences.[152] Basing an argument on canon 20, one can conclude that one local ordinary would be obliged to assist another in the execution of a final sentence if he were called upon to do so. With this conclusion, Wernz-Vidal,[153] Roberti[154] and Lega-Bartoccetti[155] are in agreement.

The original executor of the sentence is obliged to abstain from the execution of the sentence if the sentence is obviously unjust.[156] This would also apply to him who was called upon to assist in the execution of a sentence. An example of manifest injustice is had when the sentence goes beyond the jurisdiction of the judge, and infringes upon the jurisdiction of the ordinary who is called upon to execute it. Thus, if a law in a particular diocese prescribes the punishment of suspension from a particular office or benefice, a judge is not able to deprive a cleric, by force of that particular law, of an office or benefice which he perhaps holds in another diocese.[157] An ordinary, if called upon to assist another in the execution of such a sentence, would be justified in refusing and returning the request with his objection to the original executor.[158]

It will be noticed that the rogatory commission for the execution of a sentence is authorized by the local ordinary whose duty it is from the law of the Code to execute the sentence; it is made to another ordinary under whose jurisdiction the thing or person about which the execution is concerned exists. It is not a request which the judge who issued the sentence presents to the one who is to execute it, as had been the more common interpretation of the decretal *Postulasti*. The opinion of Reiffenstuel[159] has been received into the

152 Cf. *supra*, p. 49.

153 *Ius Canonicum*, VI, n. 660.

154 *De Processibus*, II, n. 548.

155 *Commentarius in Iudicia Ecclesiastica*, I, 104.

156 Canon 1921, § 2.

157 Canon 2282; cf. Coronata, *Institutiones Iuris Canonici*, IV, n. 1814.

158 "Et executiones quae ab alio tribunali sine Ordinarii loci iurisdictionis coarctatione fieri possunt."—Roberti, *De Processibus*, I, n. 89; cf. Pirhing, Lib. II, tit. 2, n. 67.

159 *Ius Canonicum Universum*, Lib. II, tit. 2, n. 52.

Code, namely, that the one who is appointed by the law to execute a sentence does not have to be requested to execute it. After the judge has issued the decree for the execution,[160] it immediately becomes the duty of the local ordinary in whose tribunal the sentence in first instance had been issued to effect the execution. His title to effect the execution is not the request from the judge to do so, but the sentence itself that had been issued.[161]

There is the final question whether a definitive sentence can be executed by others than those mentioned in canon 1920 without their being specifically requested to do so. This point has not been considered by the post-Code commentators. Since the present law commits the execution of the final sentence to administrative power, it seems that any ordinary on his own authority can execute that part of a judicial sentence which pertains to matters and persons that are under his jurisdiction; it is not necessary that he be requested to effect that execution by the one whom the law of the Code has appointed as executor.[162]

In enumerating those who are to execute sentences, canon 1920 states the obligation which these have in effecting the execution. From the obligation one can argue to a corresponding right. But it does not necessarily follow that that right is exclusive. By force of canons 1568 and 1725, 2°, exclusive competence is given in judicial matters to the tribunal which first cited the defendant. From this exclusive competence there arises the necessity of the actual request to another tribunal in order to prorogue its competence and to secure its assistance in judicial matters. The execution of a sentence, on the other hand, no longer belongs to the judicial power. Consequently, what the pre-Code authors stated concerning the necessity of a request before one judge could execute a sentence which was given by another judge is no longer in force, even if one considers the judge who had given the sentence as the one who was authorized by the pre-Code law to execute it.

160 Canon 1918.

161 Lega-Bartoccetti, *Commentarius in Iudicia Ecclesiastica,* III, 91.

162 Reiffenstuel (Lib. II, tit. 2, n. 52) taught that a judge could execute the decision of another judge without being requested to do so in cases wherein he could act *ex officio* and where the public good demanded the execution of the sentence.

An ordinary, therefore, without being requested to do so, can execute a sentence, although there be some other ordinary who is obliged to effect that execution by reason of canon 1920. He will, of course, effect the execution only in such measure as it falls under his jurisdiction. Even apart from a request he may become obliged to execute a sentence. This can happen when the public good of his own diocese demands that he execute the sentence, for example, in the case of a pastor being deprived of his office.[163] He can also be obliged to execute a sentence if he is requested to do so by the one who has the primary obligation. In every case he must be certain of the fact and of the nature of the sentence from an authentic copy of it, and the execution must pertain to persons and things that come under his jurisdiction.

Section 3. The Formalities in the Issuing of the Rogatory Commission

A rogatory commission is a request made by one tribunal to another to perform certain judicial acts which are necessary for the prosecution of a trial.[164] This request is made by means of a letter which is known by various names. In Canon Law it is known as *litterae remissoriales,* if sent to a tribunal of equal grade; *litterae imperatoriae* or *hortatoriae,* if sent to a tribunal of lower grade; and *litterae supplicatoriae,* if sent to a tribunal of higher grade.[165] Metropolitan courts are considered of higher grade than their suffragan tribunals only when they hear a case in second instance. When they hear a case in first instance, they are considered on an equal level with diocesan tribunals, and consequently the instrument requesting the assistance even of a suffragan is to be looked upon as effected between equal tribunals.[166] However, this distinction in terminol-

[163] Reiffenstuel, Lib. II, tit. 2, n. 52.

[164] Roberti, *De Processibus,* I, n. 185.

[165] Roberti, *De Processibus,* I, n. 89; Noval, *De Iudiciis,* n. 104; Coronata, *Institutiones Iuris Canonici,* III, n. 1113; Muñiz, *Procedimientos Eclesiásticos* (2. ed., 3 vols., Sevilla: Imp. y Lib. De Sobrino de Izquierdo, 1925-1926), III, n. 15.

[166] Muniz, *loc. cit.*

ogy is of little importance today, since all letters of request exchanged between tribunals, irrespective of their grades, are called rogatory letters (*litterae rogatoriae*) [167] or letters of request (*litterae requisitoriae*).[168]

The formulation and signing of the rogatory letter does not require an act of jurisdiction,[169] except when the tribunals of the Holy See delegate, or the tribunals delegated by the Holy See subdelegate other tribunals to exercise certain judicial acts. In ordinary cases the letter does not contain any strict command, but the obliging force of the letter derives from the law of the Code; it likewise does not contain any sharing of power, for it is sent to a tribunal which has power of its own, but which thus becomes authorized to use its power in this particular case for the execution of the request.

In a rogatory commission there always is question of one tribunal calling upon another for help in the exercise of certain judicial acts. As a general principle, it can be stated that whoever has the authority in the original tribunal of the case to exercise a certain act can, in a case of necessity, issue the letter of request to another tribunal for assistance in the exercise of that act. This principle does not obtain in the case of tribunals of the Holy See when they hear cases that are reserved to themselves, or in the case of tribunals delegated by the Holy See. These will have to follow the principles of delegation enunciated in canon 199.

The Code gives the right to every tribunal to call upon another tribunal for assistance. Therefore, in ordinary cases, he who has the power to act in the place of the tribunal should also be able to act in the name of that tribunal by calling upon another tribunal for assistance in a matter in which he himself has the power to act. In the absence of a specific prohibition in the Code, there is no reason to deny this principle. The power of subdelegating is restricted to certain limits in canon 199. But in the ordinary relations

[167] Roberti, *De Processibus,* I, n. 89; Coronata, *Institutiones Iuris Canonici,* III, n. 1113.

[168] Lega-Bartoccetti, *Commentarius in Iudicia Ecclesiastica,* I, 104.

[169] Pugliese, "Le Rogatorie e i Poteri del Tribunale Delegato," *Salesianum,* VI (1944), 54; Baldassari, *Enciclopedia Italiana di Scienze, Lettere ed Arti,* s. v. *Rogatoria interna.*

between tribunals, there is no delegation or subdelegation in the rogatory letter, for indeed there is no question of the actual conferring of power.

Ordinarily, it is the *officialis* who issues the rogatory commission. He will act in his capacity as presiding officer of the particular tribunal that has need of assistance from another tribunal. This is true whether the *officialis* is judging by himself, or in a collegiate body with others. In a collegiate tribunal, however, the *officialis* cannot do on his own authority alone what the collegiate body has reserved to itself.[170] If a collegiate tribunal has reserved some act to itself, the *officialis* cannot commit that act to another tribunal unless he is specially authorized to do so. What pertains to his proper sphere of activity, either from the law of the Code, or by reason of a mandate from the collegiate tribunal, he can commit to another tribunal whenever the necessary conditions are present. What is true of the *officialis*, is true also of the *vice-officialis*.

Can an auditor issue a rogatory commission? In answering this question one must remember that the power of the auditor is delegated, and depends entirely on the principal judge of the trial.[171] The auditor, therefore, can draw up only such acts as are clearly and legitimately delineated in his mandate,[172] at least implicitly. But whatever acts he is delegated to draw up in the process, he can also commit to another tribunal when the required conditions warrant it. What is affirmed of the auditor holds also for others who are delegated by diocesan or religious tribunals to draw up judicial acts.

About the power of the ordinary to issue a rogatory commission when he is acting as judge in a trial there cannot be any doubt. The same restriction affects his activity in a collegiate tribunal as

170 Roberti, *De Processibus*, I, nn. 107-108; Besté, *Introductio in Codicem*, p. 786; cf. also S. C. de Sacramentis, instr. 15 aug. 1936, art. 68, § 2—*AAS*, XXVIII (1936), 328.

171 Coronata, *Institutiones Iuris Canonici*, III, n. 1121; Besté, *Introductio in Codicem*, p. 787; Sipos, *Enchiridon Iuris Canonici*, p. 852; Wernz-Vidal, *Ius Canonicum*, VI, n. 100. Roberti (*De Processibus*, I, n. 113) holds that the power of the auditor is ordinary if he is stably constituted, but he also admits that the limits of his power always depend on the will of the judge.

172 Noval, *De Iudiciis*, n. 135.

affects the activity of the *officialis,* i. e., what is reserved to the collegiate body the ordinary cannot do without their authorization. Consequently, what he cannot do merely on the strength of his own authority, he likewise cannot commit to another tribunal without the authorization of the collegiate body.

Every rogatory commission is concerned with the execution of a decree or of an interlocutory sentence which the judge or the auditor has issued for the exercise of some judicial act. It is then seen that the act cannot be executed without the assistance of another tribunal, and thus the rogatory commission is issued. Lega-Bartoccetti states that rogatory commissions are concerned either with the execution of a decree or a sentence, or with the securing of evidence.[173] This distinction is not complete, for even the taking of testimony, the employment of experts, the use of judicial access, etc., are executions of judicial decrees which precede the securing of the evidence.[174]

Distinguishing from its other uses the use of the rogatory commission in the collecting of judicial proofs, one may draw attention to a point of value. In most other uses of the rogatory commission, e. g., in the citing of a witness who is of another jurisdiction, in the effecting of a sequestration, etc., there will be no alternative but to have recourse to the other tribunal. On the other hand, when one of the parties, the promoter of justice, the defender of the bond, or the judge *ex officio* proposes a means of proof which can be secured only through the instrumentality of another tribunal, the adverse party who is present either personally or by proxy at all of the sessions of the trial, unless prohibited in singular instances by the law,[175] may have serious objections to offer, and thus can give rise to an incidental question.[176] It may be objected that the securing of this proof by another tribunal on commission may delay the trial for an unwarranted duration of time, or may at least be intended as

[173] *Commentarius in Iudicia Ecclesiastica,* I, 104-105.

[174] Canons 1754; 1792; 1806.

[175] Lega-Bartoccetti, *Commentarius in Iudicia Ecclesiastica,* I, 280; II, 541; Wernz-Vidal, *Ius Canonicum,* VI, nn. 179, 199; Lega, *De Iudiciis Ecclesiasticis,* I, n. 391; cf. also canons 1640, § 1; 1771.

[176] Lega-Bartoccetti, *op. cit.,* I, 105.

a means for slowing the progress of the trial, or also may occasion uncalled for expense in view of the necessity of appointing a proxy or an advocate at the other tribunal.

If an objection is raised against a proposed securing of proof by another tribunal, that objection will be dealt with by the judge in accordance with the rules for the handling of incidental questions.[177] If the judge is convinced that the proof was requested simply with a view to delaying the trial, or that it was unnecessary inasmuch as other proofs by documents or witnesses were easily available or already secured, he must reject the petition for it.[178] In a case of doubt it would be better to accede to the request than to deny it.[179]

In the event that a petition for the taking of evidence on commission had been denied, a recourse could be invoked. From the decree of the judge a recourse could be made to the judge himself; from the decree of an auditor, to the judge or the collegiate tribunal of the trial; from the decree of the presiding judicial officer, to the collegiate tribunal. At any time before the final sentence is rendered, the decree could be withdrawn and corrected.[180] Judicial appeal, however, would not be permitted unless it could be proved that the decree had the force of a definitive sentence,[181] e.g., if the securing of a necessary means of proof had been denied.

If it is admitted, as has been proposed, that other procedural acts, such as the publication of the acts, the closing of the evidence, etc., can also be committed to other tribunals, an objection could be raised against such a commission. The auditor or the presiding official, to whom it pertained in the individual case to grant the commission, would hear the objection. Against his rejection of the objection a recourse could be invoked as in the case of the rejecting of the petition for the taking of evidence on commission.

After the decree or the interlocutory sentence has been issued for the exercise of a judicial act that cannot be executed without

177 Canons 1837-1841.

178 Canon 1749.

179 Pellegrini, *Praxis Vicariorum*, Pars II, Sect. II, subsectio 7, n. 19.

180 Canon 1841.

181 Canon 1880, 6°.

the assistance of another tribunal, the actual commissioning of the other tribunal will be in effect. This calling upon another tribunal for assistance is an act distinct from the decree for the exercise of the act. While in practice they may be joined together, this formal calling upon the other tribunal must never be omitted from the acts. It is an act of the judge [182] or of his delegate, and, therefore, a part of the trial. This act is not of little importance. It is the call for assistance which gives the other tribunal a title of competence to execute the request. An exception of incompetence can be raised against any acts that have been exercised in a trial by another tribunal if it was not properly commissioned. Therefore, the commissioning of the other tribunal will appear in the acts of the case with the signature of the one who issued the commission, along with the signature of the notary and the affixing of the date and the indication of the place.

With the actual rogatory commission completed, it then remains for the other tribunal to be notified of the fact. In this matter of notification, canons 1711-1723 with the necessary modifications will have to be followed.[183]

Usually the rogatory letter is addressed to the ordinary of the tribunal whose assistance is desired. The bishop represents his tribunal before all other ecclesiastical authorities, and in this capacity the rogatory letter is addressed to him.[184] This, however, is a matter of courtesy, since the letter could just as well be addressed to the *officialis*. But no matter to whom the letter is addressed, it should be clear that the desired assistance is that of the tribunal represented by the person, and not the personal attention of the addressee. The Code vindicates the right to assistance from a *tribunal;* it does not confirm the right to assistance from any particular individual. If a particular individual is singled out as commissioned to execute the request, it follows that he will have to do it personally unless he can delegate it. This is necessary when requests come from tribunals delegated by the Holy See, but it should not be made necessary in the ordinary relationships between diocesan tri-

182 Roberti, *De Processibus,* I, n. 185.

183 Canon 1724.

184 Roberti, *De Processibus,* I, n. 97.

bunals. It can easily be avoided if the letter is addressed to the bishop or to the *officialis,* but at the same time it is made clear that it is the assistance of the tribunal that is desired.

If a rogatory letter is addressed to the bishop or to the *officialis* without mention of the tribunal, it can be presumed that the letter is in accord with canon 1570, § 2, and the bishop or the *officialis* is addressed simply as representing the tribunal. If the letter is addressed to the bishop or to the *officialis,* and he is called upon to exercise an act or to delegate another to do so, this presumption falls in the face of the expressed intention of the one who issued the request.[185]

The rogatory letter will contain the names of the parties, the names and addresses of their proxies, mention of the point at issue, and also of the grounds on which the plaintiff is basing his claim. Mention will be made whether the party calling for this particular act had been granted gratuitous defense by the original judge of the case. The particular act or acts that are to be committed to the other tribunal will be clearly and specifically mentioned, and sufficient additional information and instructions will be given with reference to the execution of the commission. In the case of a request emanating from a tribunal delegated by the Holy See, subdelegation with the power of subdelegating again will be granted. Finally, the letter is to be signed by the judge or the auditor, whosoever had rightfully given the commission, and by the notary.[186]

In regard to the signing of the rogatory letter, mention is made of the custom of having the ordinary affix his signature in the place of the judge or the auditor, even though he is not acting as judge in the trial. While the signature of the ordinary does not eliminate the need of the signature of the notary, much can be said for this practice. That he can do so, there can be no doubt. In any diocese there is only one tribunal, and of that tribunal the bishop is the head, and he can replace the presiding judge at any time. As the ordinary represents his tribunal before all other ecclesiastical authorities in receiving rogatory letters, so also he can represent his tri-

185 Cf. Doheny, *Practical Manual for Marriage Cases* (New York, Milwaukee, and Chicago: The Bruce Publishing Company, 1938), p. 175.

186 Canon 1715, §§ 1, 2.

bunal in sending them. The letter, however, cannot be signed by the vicar general unless he rules the diocese in accordance with canon 429, or is at the same time the *officialis* in accordance with canon 1572. In the exclusive capacity of a vicar general he is removed from judicial matters, and therefore cannot represent the tribunal.

The signing of the rogatory letter by the ordinary can be of practical importance. Besides the added prestige that the letter will derive from his signature, there is the possibility that less doubt could arise as to the legitimacy of the tribunal from which the request is issuing. For this latter reason it is also possible to send the letter through the instrumentality of the Apostolic Delegate or Nuncio.[187] This will be useful especially when a request must be made to an ecclesiastical tribunal of another country and there is the possibility that the signature, even of an ordinary, would not be immediately recognized. Certainly, the use of diplomatic channels would satisfy the requirement of canon 1719, but there always remains the possibility of the use of the public mails as long as the letter is registered and a return receipt is requested.

Two copies of the rogatory letter will have to be drawn up. The one will be sent to the other tribunal as described; the other copy will be inserted in the acts of the pending case.[188]

Article 6. Conflict Between Tribunals

The obligation of a tribunal to accede to the request of another tribunal is not unconditional. As the right arises only under certain conditions, so too the obligation is measured by the same conditions. Any conflict between tribunals on the question of a rogatory commission will be concerning the presence or absence of these conditions, which are especially the following:

(1) The issuing of the rogatory commission must be necessary. One tribunal cannot be forced to assist another unless that assistance is necessary. Roberti[189] and Wernz-Vidal[190] insist that the tri-

[187] Muñiz, *Procedimientos Eclesiásticos*, III, n. 15.
[188] Canon 1716.
[189] *De Processibus*, I, n. 89.
[190] *Ius Canonicum*, VI, n. 73.

bunal issuing the rogatory commission is the sole judge of its necessity. As regards the necessity of a certain judicial act, certainly only the tribunal hearing the case can decide. It may not, however, always pertain to that tribunal to decide whether a judical act which is deemed necessary for the trial necessarily has to be exercised on commission. Each tribunal should be the best judge of the obligations of its own subjects. Consequently, a tribunal could judge that there was no necessity for itself to take the testimony of one of its subjects inasmuch as that person could very easily make a personal appearance before the tribunal in the neighboring diocese which desires the testimony.

(2) The assistance requested must be of a judicial nature. From the fact that the Code gives the right to one tribunal to call upon another for assistance, it follows that that assistance must be such as is proper to the activity of a tribunal. Generally this question will not arise, but, if it does, it seems that each tribunal has an equal right to voice its own opinion.

(3) The ecclesiastical tribunal making the request must be legitimate. Strictly considered, the tribunal making the request must also be competent. Since it is not within the competence of one tribunal to judge the competence of another tribunal every time that it receives a request for assistance from the latter,[191] it will suffice that the tribunal which makes the request possesses jurisdiction in general and that it is not certainly incompetent.[192] If the incompetence is evident and notorious, as it would be if a local tribunal took up any case mentioned in canons 1556-1557, there would be no obligation to fulfill the request. If a local tribunal has been delegated by the Holy See to conduct any case falling under canon 1557, it is necessary for that tribunal to make mention of that special delegation in forwarding a request for assistance to another tribunal.[193]

Rarely could a request be refused in view of certainty that the tribunal making the request was relatively incompetent. It is only after the joinder of the issue that witnesses are to be examined,

[191] Canons 1609; 1610.

[192] Noval, *De Iudiciis*, n. 104.

[193] From analogy with the ruling expressed in canon 1057.

documents to be inspected, or judical access to be executed. Usually, questions of relative incompetence have ceased to exist by the time of the joinder of issue.[194] If, however, a tribunal was called upon to assist in the citation and interrogation of one of its own subjects who was accused of a crime before another tribunal, and if it was certain and notorious that the other tribunal was relatively incompetent, the request for assistance could be refused.

(4) The tribunal of which the request is made must have the jurisdiction to exercise the judical act that is asked for. Even though it had been requested to do so, a tribunal could not exercise judical acts outside of its own territory, nor could it exercise jurisdiction over those who are not its subjects. A tribunal could take the testimony of a person traveling within its territory, for this is specifically provided for in law.[195] If the witness refused to appear of his own volition, the recourse for his citation would necessarily have to be invoked through his own tribunal. Since this citation is an act of jurisdiction, it cannot be exercised over non-subjects. The tribunal of which any request is made has the right to judge the sphere of its own jurisdiction.[196]

(5) That which the tribunal requests of the other tribunal must not be notoriously and evidently illegitimate. A tribunal should be presumed to make legitimate requests. A judge is cautioned by law not to admit the exploration of proofs which seem to be intended simply with the purpose of delaying the trial, or which are unnecessary,[197] and he should be presumed to act in that manner. However, when the matter that has been requested is notoriously and evidently illegitimate, that presumption falls, and the obligation to fulfill the request is non-existent. If that which is requested is actually forbidden by law, moral and legitimate civil law as well as canon law, for example, to propose questions to a witness that are manifestly cunning, captious or suggestive of the answer,[198] there would be no obligation to fulfill the request, or at least that part of it which

[194] Canons 1610; 1619; 1628, § 1.

[195] Canon 1770, § 2, 3°.

[196] Wernz-Vidal, *Ius Canonicum,* VI, n. 73.

[197] Canon 1749.

[198] Canon 1775.

is illegitimate. A tribunal cannot act illegitimately in the interest of another tribunal, just as it cannot do so in its own interest. If, by a prescription of law, that which is asked for is actually valueless, e. g., the depositions of those who, according to canon 1757, § 3, are incapable of being witnesses, there would be an obligation not to fulfill the request.[199] This conclusion is based on the principle of public law that authority can only demand of its subjects what is necessary or useful. Before executing a rogatory commission, a tribunal would have a right to judge whether the request was legitimate or not.[200]

If a tribunal has any objection against executing a rogatory commission, that objection should first be made known to the tribunal which has made the request.[201] If the dispute persists, and the one tribunal continues to demand that the commission be executed, and the other still refuses, the tribunal which has made the request can pursue its claim by means of a recourse.[202] Judicial appeal could not be used, since the refusal is a matter of extra-judicial character.[203] Appeal is allowable only from a judicial sentence or from a judicial decree which has the force of a final sentence.[204] The act by means of which the tribunal refuses to execute a rogatory commission is administrative in nature, and not judicial, for this act is not exercised *in a trial.* A similar instance of this is had in the rejection of a bill of complaint. In that case, too, a recourse is made available,[205] but not an appeal.

If an *officialis* refuses to execute a rogatory commission, recourse can be invoked with his proper ordinary. An ordinary could not proceed against his *officialis* for neglect of duty in executing a rogatory commission merely on the strength of canon 1625. A

199 Cf. Coronata, *Institutiones Iuris Canonici,* III, n. 1113.

200 Wernz-Vidal, *Ius Canonicum,* VI, n. 73.

201 Wernz-Vidal, *loc. cit.*

202 Reiffenstuel, Lib. II, tit. 20, n. 435; Schmalzgrueber, Lib. II, tit. 3, n. 23; Bouix, *Tractatus de Judiciis Ecclesiasticis,* II, 161; Lega, *De Iudiciis Ecclesiasticis,* II, n. 324; Wernz, *Ius Decretalium,* V, n. 100; Wernz-Vidal, *Ius Canonicum,* VI, n. 73.

203 Lega-Bartoccetti, *Commentarius in Iudicia Ecclesiastica,* I, 105.

204 Canons 1879; 1880, 6°.

205 Canon 1709, § 3.

strict interpretation of the words *ius dicere* in this canon points to the pronouncing of a sentence. Therefore, to proceed effectively against his *officialis* for neglect in this matter, an ordinary would have to issue a penal precept. If the obligation was not thereupon fulfilled, penal action could then be taken according to the punishment that had been threatened.

If the ordinary of a diocese refuses to execute a rogatory commission, recourse can not be interposed with the immediately superior tribunal, as Wernz-Vidal seems to allow and suggest.[206] Metropolitans have no right to receive disputes in the form of recourse unless some law confers this right on them.[207] They have only such rights as the Code explicitly vindicates for them.[208]

Although the Code does give metropolitans the right to settle certain disputes that are brought to them by way of recourse from suffragan bishops,[209] it makes no mention of any right of a metropolitan to settle disputes that may arise concerning the execution of a rogatory commission. Even before the Code, Lega doubted that a metropolitan could force his suffragan to execute a rogatory commission.[210]

Recourse, therefore, must be made to the Holy See. The Sacred Congregation of the Council ordinarily is competent in this matter; the recourse would, however, be directed to the Sacred Congregation for the Propagation of the Faith if the tribunal which refused to execute the rogatory commission belonged to a territory that was still subject to that Congregation, or to the Sacred Congregation of Religious, if the recusant tribunal was a tribunal constituted in a religious institute.

[206] *Ius Canonicum,* VI, n. 73.

[207] Cf. McClunn, *Administrative Recourse,* The Catholic University of America Canon Law Studies, n. 240 (Washington, D. C.: The Catholic University of America Press, 1946), pp. 74-75; Popek, *The Rights and Obligations of Metropolitans,* The Catholic University of America Canon Law Studies, n. 260 (Washington, D. C.: The Catholic University of America Press, 1947), p. 255.

[208] Canon 274.

[209] Canons 1709, § 3; 1710.

[210] *De Iudiciis Ecclesiasticis,* II, n. 324.

Article 7. The Execution of the Rogatory Commission

The rogatory commission must be executed by him who was commissioned to do so by the rogatory letter. Canon 1570, § 2, recognizes the right of every tribunal to call upon another tribunal for assistance. If it is the tribunal that is commissioned, then it will be the tribunal that will be competent to fulfill the request.[211] In this event, at least in the ordinary rogatory commissions that pass between tribunals, there will be no necessity for constituting a new tribunal. By the very request that has been received, the ordinary jurisdiction of the actual members of the tribunal will be prorogued so that they will have competence to exercise the desired act or acts.

Thus, the bishop, as well as the *officialis*, will be able to execute the rogatory commission. The bishop and the *officialis* constitute one tribunal, and it is the assistance of the tribunal that is requested. If an auditor has been permanently appointed in a tribunal, there is no reason why he cannot execute on commission, without a special delegation, those acts which are mentioned in his mandate as being within his ordinary sphere of power.

In the absence of a permanent auditor, the ordinary certainly can appoint one for this special task. Because of his being excluded from judicial matters, the Vicar General could not make such an appointment, unless he rules the diocese by reason of canon 429, § 1. The opinion is here offered that the *officialis* could delegate an auditor in individual instances to execute a rogatory commission. While it is true that he is not conducting a trial, as canon 1580, § 2, would seem to require as a necessary condition for a judge to appoint an auditor, nevertheless the work of executing a rogatory commission belongs to the *officialis* as much as a single trial does. In a diocese there is only one tribunal. Under the bishop, the *officialis* is the moderator of that tribunal. Whoever executes a rogatory commission, does a work that belongs principally to the *officialis,* unless the bishop has reserved it to himself. Inasmuch as

211 "Missis ad aliud tribunal litteris commendatis . . . Moderator tribunalis cui litterae rogatoriae diriguntur, postquam eas acceperit, per se vel per instructorem exsequendas curat."—Roberti, *De Processibus,* I, n. 89.

the execution of the rogatory commission belongs principally to the *officialis,* and inasmuch as the execution can be accomplished through another, it must be admitted that the *officialis* can appoint an auditor for the work. Canon 1580, § 2, does not intend to make a distinction between a judge's hearing of a trial and his conducting other work such as executing a rogatory commission, but it intends to distinguish between an ordinary's appointment of an auditor for all cases that arise and a judge's appointment of an auditor for the individual cases that pertain to him.

If, from the wording of the rogatory letter, it is evident that there was no intention on the part of the one issuing it to call upon the tribunal of the other diocese, but that there was the intention to make the request exclusively to the ordinary himself, but with the added authorization of delegating another,[212] then it seems that the ordinary must either execute the commission himself or delegate another for it. In this event the ordinary's tribunal would not be *ipso facto* competent, for competence depends on the commission as issued by the other tribunal. However, a tribunal has no right under the law to issue a rogatory commission of this type, for the Code solely grants the right to call upon another tribunal.

Unless the ordinary has made a special appointment of a notary, the *officialis* or the auditor can use any of the notaries of the curia who have been properly appointed for all cases that arise. If the execution of the rogatory commission requires the intervention of the defender of the bond or the promoter of justice, and these officials exist in the diocese as appointed for all cases that arise (*ad universalitatem causarum*), these will be cited without any special appointment. Otherwise they will have to be appointed for the particular work by the ordinary. The same will hold for the lesser members of the tribunal.

In the case of rogatory commissions issued by tribunals that have been delegated by the Holy See, a different procedure is followed. These are always sent directly to the ordinary. Since the local tribunals are absolutely incompetent in these cases, the local ordinary will have to subdelegate a special tribunal to execute the com-

[212] Cf. Doheny, *Practical Manual for Marriage Cases,* p. 175.

mission or do it himself.[213] The one whom the ordinary has subdelegated for the execution of the rogatory commission cannot further subdelegate it even for the purpose of obtaining the testimony of a person who is so distant from the court that he cannot make a personal appearance. Generally, in the instructions for processes of this type no express mention is made of the power of subdelegating.[214] The ordinary's subdelegate could, of course, request the appointment of another subdelegate in his place, and the ordinary could rightfully grant the request.

Regarding the judicial acts that are to be exercised in the executing of a rogatory commission, the fundamental principle is that the tribunal to which the request is made, like all tribunals other than the original tribunal of the case, is incompetent to act unless it is specifically requested to do so. This incompetence follows, as has been said, from the rulings contained in canons 1568 and 1725, 2°. Competence to exercise individual acts is, according to canon 1570, § 2, granted on the condition that the tribunal of the case makes a request for them; incompetence continues with reference to all acts other than those requested. The instructions contained in the letter of request must be carefully studied for the proper determination of the particular acts that have been requested and the corresponding authorization for the exercise of those acts. Pugliese arrives at this same conclusion by a different manner of argumentation.[215]

While it is true that there is no competence for exercising judiical acts in a trial that is being heard by another tribunal unless a request is received for these acts, it is also true, from the general principle of law, that a request for a particular act includes all the things that are necessary for the execution of this act. Thus, if a

[213] As regards the notary, the defender of the bond, and the promoter of justice, cf. canon 1607, § 2.

[214] Canon 199, § 5. Cf. S. C. de Sacramentis, *Regulae servandae in processibus super matrimonio rato et non consummato*, 7 maii 1923, n. 23—*AAS*, XV (1923), 396; S. C. de Sacramentis, *Regulae servandae in processibus super nullitate sacrae ordinationis vel onerum sacris ordinibus inhaerentium*, 9 maii 1931, n. 14—*AAS*, XXIII (1931), 461.

[215] "Le Rogatorie e i Poteri del Tribunale del Tribunale Delegato," *Salesianum*, VI (1944), 63.

tribunal is requested to hear the testimony of one of its own subjects, that request certainly also includes authorization for the citation of the witness. As implicitly requested must be considered also all of the specific requirements of law for the proper exercise of this act. Thus, the request for the testimony of a witness extends to the citation of the parties who have a right to be present at the taking of the oath by the witness; it extends also to the use of coercion on witnesses who, after they were properly cited, refused to appear or to answer in court. A judge executing a rogatory commission could punish witnesses who refused to appear or to answer in court, or who in giving testimony committed perjury. This presupposes that they were properly cited by their own authorities. The judge executing the rogatory commission would be competent by reason of the delict of perjury committed in his territory, if not also otherwise by reason of domicile, quasi-domicile, or also actual residence, if the latter must supplant the considerations of domicile or of quasi-domicile.

A commission to conduct the interrogation of the parties would not necessarily imply also the right to declare them contumacious. Consequently, if the defendant refuses to appear before a tribunal that had been commissioned to interrogate him, the documents concerning the valid citation and its proper delivery should be sent to the tribunal of the case, but a decree of contumacy should not be issued unless it has been explicitly asked for.

One of the greatest difficulties in the use of the rogatory commission turns about the factor of time. The Code does not offer any special rule regarding the duration of time in which a rogatory commission should be executed. Apparently canon 1627 does not apply to the executing of requests from other tribunals, for it speaks of the order in which complete trials are to be handled. However, it must be kept in mind that months may elapse between the time when a case is officially docketed by entrance into the protocol book of a particular court, and the time when the case actually comes up for a hearing. If a rogatory commission were for its execution placed at the bottom of the docket, so that it would receive its due attention only after the normal order of the court's own cases, a great deal of harm could ensue. Mutual courtesy and a common desire for justice should prompt tribunals to provide for the execution of rogatory commissions outside of the order of their own trials on the docket, that is, as soon as possible after they have been received.

As soon as the one to whom it pertains from the constitutions or from the practice of the tribunal to execute the request has taken up the work, he will cite the parties or their proxies unless he has been informed that the parties have relinquished their right. It belongs to the intrinsic or essential form of a judicial process that only those acts be considered judicial which are performed not only under the direction of the judicial authority but also with the opportunity for the contending parties to defend their rights.[216] The parties, therefore, have a right to be present at all of the sessions for the execution of a rogatory commission, unless in specific cases mention is made in law to the contrary.

The parties have a right to raise an exception of suspicion against the executor of the rogatory commission, or against any other member of the tribunal. This objection will have to be heard in accordance with the rules enacted in canon 1614. An objection against an auditor, even though he was appointed for all cases that arise, would be judged by the *officialis*. Unless the bishop has reserved to himself the work of executing rogatory commissions and has then committed it in a particular case to an auditor, the auditor would, in the work of executing a rogatory commission, depend on the *officialis*. The work that he does pertains primarily to the *officialis*, and the *officialis* would be understood whenever the Code speaks of a particular act as being exercised by the judge. The *officialis*, therefore, will judge an exception of suspicion against the auditor who works in his place, just as he will review an exception of suspicion when it is raised against the promoter of justice, the defender of the bond, or the notary.

In the execution of the rogatory commission all of the norms which are prescribed by law for the exercise of the particular judicial acts in question must be followed. Canon 1570, § 2, makes specific mention of this point. Consequently, if the nature of the trial demands it, the promoter of justice, or the defender of the

[216] Lega, *De Iudiciis Ecclesiasticis*, I, n. 391.

bond, or even both, will have to be cited to appear. If not cited and not given all of their usual rights, the acts will be invalid. No matter what be the nature of the particular act that must be executed, it will have to be carried out step by step just as if it were being exercised by the original tribunal of the case. Besides having all of the obligations which the Code imposes for the exercise of certain acts, the executor has also all of the rights. Thus, he can act *ex officio* when the law permits him to do so in the particular act that has been requested. This is especially important in the taking of testimony on commission in marriage cases when the law gives the judge the right and the duty to examine the witnesses *ex officio* in addition to examining them by means of the questions prepared by the defender. The defender of the bond has the right and the duty of proposing to the judge during the examination new questions to be asked of the witness.

In addition to the common law of the Code, the particular law of the place where the commission is to be executed must be followed.[217] This follows from the principle of law, *"locus regit actum,"* which has been held in an absolute fashion by civilists and canonists since the fourteenth century,[218] and which has been received into the Code even as obligatory on travelers outside of their own territory.[219] The particular laws through which are made applicable the universal law of procedure in ecclesiastical trials fall under this principle, for they determine the solemnity of acts.[220]

The obligation to follow the particular law of the place as regards the solemnity of acts can be particularly important when it differs between dioceses. In a matrimonial trial the collegiate tribunal may have reserved to itself the hearing of all of the witnesses,

217 "In executione vero singulorum actuum tenetur observare quae statuta sunt sive iure communi sive particulari, viget enim et hic principium quoslibet actus processuales lege tribunalis esse ordinandos."—Roberti, *De Processibus,* I, n. 89.

218 Onclin, *De territoriali vel personali legis indole* (Gemblaci: J. Duculot, 1938), p. 351.

219 Canon 14, § 1, 2°.

220 Hammill, *The Obligations of the Traveler according to Canon 14,* p. 135; Onclin, *op. cit.,* p. 352; Roberti, *De Processibus,* I, n. 36; Besté *Introductio in Codicem,* p. 74.

but the testimony of absent witnesses may have to be taken by a tribunal where, according to the constitutions, all testimony is to be taken by an auditor permanently appointed for this work. The tribunal issuing the rogatory commission could not force the other tribunal to take the testimony in the presence of three judges. The tribunal issuing the rogatory commission could request that certain formalities be observed in the executing of it, and the other tribunal can, if it so desires, accede to these wishes, provided that they are not contrary to its own particular law. If the observance of certain requested formalities, in addition to the provisions of the universal law, is contrary to the particular law of the place where the rogatory commission is to be executed, it cannot be carried out.[221] While the act is performed according to the solemnities of the locality where it is placed, its juridical value will have to be determined according to the standards of the tribunal before which the case is being tried.[222] Usually, however, in Canon Law, these standards, at least for the validity of the acts, are fairly uniform for the evident reason that the law of the Code is obligatory on all tribunals.

With the execution of the rogatory commission completed, the commissioned tribunal will recall that it is not allowable to exceed the issued request. Consequently, the acts are not to be published unless under particular instructions the tribunal was requested to do so. It simply remains for this tribunal to transmit the acts to the competent tribunal of the trial.

All of the acts that were executed by a tribunal on commission from another tribunal shall be drawn up in accordance with the rulings of canons 1642-1643. Before undertaking the work, the executor will see to it that in the acts mention is made of the request that had been received, and of the authority by which he undertook the execution of it. In the case of the ordinary or the *officialis,* their right to execute the commission will be evident from their very position. If the executor had to be delegated for the execution of the request, a copy of the delegation will be inserted in the acts. These formalities will neutralize the force of any later

221 Contuzzi, *Il Digesto Italiano,* s. v. *Commissione Rogatoria,* nn. 55-56.

222 Roberti, *De Processibus,* I, n. 36; Contuzzi, *loc. cit.*

possible objections with reference to the competence of the executor. The remainder of the acts will follow the prescriptions of the universal and applicable particular law. At the conclusion of the work the executor will opportunely decree that the commission has been executed and that all of the acts, either the acts themselves or an authentic copy of them, as he sees fit according to canon 1644, § 1, shall be sent to the tribunal that requested them. If the acts are to be sent to a country where a different language is used, the executor will order a translation into Latin of the acts which were recorded in the vernacular.[223] He will then add a note regarding the expenses that are owed for the execution of the rogatory commission. After the addition of the date and the notation of the place, the final document will be signed by the executor and the notary, and the seal of the tribunal will be affixed.

In accordance with the decree of the executor, the acts themselves or an authentic copy of them will be bound together and there will be added to them an index of the acts and the documents to be transmitted. Each page of the acts or of the authentic copy will be signed by the notary; they will also be numbered and will bear the seal of the tribunal. Finally, the notary or the chancellor will certify the completeness of the acts, the correspondence of the copy with the original, and, if necessary, the faithfulness of the translation.[224]

Before being sent to the original tribunal of the case, the acts of the rogatory commission will be closed and sealed. This is more important here than in the case of the transmission of acts from a court of one instance to a court of higher instance, since for the most part the acts taken on commission are not made public before being sent. The sealing of the acts should be meticulously observed. Thus, there will be forestalled the possible objection by the one party that the other party could have inspected them and thus could have gained an unfair advantage.

[223] The Code puts on the tribunal which drew up the acts the obligation to translate them into Latin. This is reasonable, for it is easier to make a translation from one's own tongue into Latin, than it would be for the other tribunal to translate from a foreign tongue into its own; cf. Canon 1644, § 2.

[224] Canon 1643; 1644.

ARTICLE 8. JUDICIAL EXPENSES FOR THE EXECUTION OF A ROGATORY COMMISSION

Judicial expenses can be conveniently classified under four headings:

(1) Fees for attorneys and proxies. While the law establishes certain qualifications for these positions, and provides for the setting of fees that can be demanded by them, the choice of an attorney or a proxy is generally left to the parties, and the parties usually can renounce the assistance of such professional service or representation.[225] The compensation for these services is to be taken care of privately. For the poor, special provision is made.[226]

(2) Compensations for the expenses of witnesses, and salaries and compensations for the expenses of experts. In these matters the amount is to be determined by the judge according as the individual instances may demand.[227]

(3) Notaries' fees for translations and copies of documents, for the examination and verification of documents, and for the copying of certificates or documents from the archives. These fees are to be set by a provincial council or by the bishops of a province in a joint meeting.[228]

(4) Court fees which go into the treasury of the tribunal and are used for the sustenance of its members. These fees should be specific for different judicial acts,[229] and are to be established by a provincial council, or by a meeting of the bishops of the province.[230] For these court fees, as for notaries' fees, there is no need for the approval of the Holy See.[231]

[225] Canons 1909, § 1; 1655.

[226] Canon 1916.

[227] Canons 1787, § § 1, 2; 1805.

[228] Canon 1909, § 1.

[229] S. C. de Sacramentis, instr. 15 aug. 1936, art. 233—*AAS*. XXVIII (1936), 359.

[230] Canon 1909, § 1.

[231] Vermeersch-Creusen, *Epitome Iuris Canonici*, II, n. 827; Noval, *De Iudiciis*, n. 688.

The question of the judicial expenses for the execution of a rogatory commission demands special attention, for the fees as established at the court issuing the rogatory commission may differ widely from the fees as established at the court where it is to be executed.

Mention has been made of the principle, *"locus regit actum,"* and it was stated that judicial acts are ruled by the particular law of the territory where they are to be placed. This principle also applies to the expenses that are attached to judicial acts.[232] Each tribunal is obliged to live up to its own particular legislation, just as it is obliged to follow the laws of the Code. But after attorneys' and proxies, fees, notaries' fees, and court fees have been properly established in a province, they are particular law for that province, and are binding on every tribunal of that province. Naturally, witnesses' and experts' expenses will have to be determined from the particular circumstances of the individual cases, and will, therefore, have to differ from place to place.

The consideration of justice likewise leads to the conclusion that the judicial expenses incurred in the executing of a rogatory commission are to be regulated by the law of the place where the execution is to be effected. Since living expenses differ, sometimes very greatly, from place to place, it is but just that the fees to be paid for the execution of judicial acts should be determined according to the locality where the acts are to be exercised.

One of the difficulties in assigning the court fees for the execution of a rogatory commission is that fees have usually been established for entire cases. It seems preferable that the provincial council or the bishops of a province in a joint meeting determine these fees as specified for the individual and separate acts of the trial, as the Instruction *Provida Mater Ecclesia* suggested for marriage cases.[233] However, if in a particular province such a listing of distinct fees for separate acts is not in effect, the amounts of the in-

[232] "Quapropter etiam expensae, lege tribunalis quod actus exsequitur, reguntur."—Roberti, *De Processibus,* I, n. 89; cf. also Roberti "De expensis iudicialibus pro exequendis litteris rogatoriis," *Apollinaris,* X (1937), 278.

[233] S. C. de Sacramentis, instr. 15 aug.° 1936, art. 233—*AAS,* XXVIII (1936), 359.

dividual fees could be figured out equitably from a consideration of the sum that has been established for the entire trial.[234]

If, because of poverty, the right of a gratuitous defense or of a diminution of judicial expenses has been accorded to one or both of the parties by the original tribunal of the case, then generally this same right would have to be recognized by another tribunal when called upon to assist in the case.[235] There is no particular ruling in the Code on this point. A norm, however, can be found in the general principles that regulate the granting of a gratuitous defense or the lessening of judicial expenses in a tribunal of second or further instance after it had been properly conceded in the tribunal of first instance.

As a general rule, when a gratuitous defense or a reduction of expenses has been granted in the tribunal of first instance, it must also be granted in tribunals which hear the case in further instance. The Code is silent in this matter, but the rule of the Roman Rota,[236] plainly reflecting the usage and practice of the Roman Curia, indicates the practical norm. Thus, when a party asks for a gratuitous defense or a reduction of expenses in second or further instance, and the judge of the first instance testifies to the poverty of the person and to the fact that a gratuitous defense or a reduction of expenses was granted at his court, the court of second or further instance institutes no process for establishing the poverty of the petitioner. The poverty is accepted as a notorious fact and therefore not calling for proof. Consequently, the petition must be granted.[237] What holds true for a tribunal of second or further instance in regard to a decision of the tribunal of the first instance

[234] Roberti, "De expensis iudicialibus pro exequendis litteris rogatoriis," *Apollinaris,* X (1937), 279.

[235] "At si tribunal apud quod agitur causa alterutri parti concesserit gratuitum patrocinium vel expensarum deminutionem, haec et tribunal cui litterae rogatoriae diriguntur, tenetur revereri."—Roberti, *loc. cit.*

[236] Normae S. R. Rotae Tribunalis, 29 iun. 1934, art. 179—*AAS,* XXVI (1934), 490.

[237] Coronata, *Institutiones Iuris Canonici,* III, n. 1435; Lega-Bartoccetti, *Commentarius in Iudicia Ecclesiastica,* III, 75; Wernz-Vidal, *Ius Canonicum,* VI, n. 652.

concerning expenses should also hold for a tribunal that executes a rogatory commission at the request of another tribunal.

After a judge has given a decision based on documentary proof as the law demands, and has admitted the request for a gratuitous defense or a reduction of expenses because of the poverty of the petitioner, and the promoter of justice, whose duty it was to be present and to protect the public interest in this matter,[238] could not raise a weighty objection to it, then the poverty should be regarded as a notorious fact,[239] and therefore not calling for proof before the tribunal that is requested to execute a rogatory commission in the same trial. Therefore, the testimony of the judge of the case in regard to the poverty of the party, and the fact that a gratuitous defense or a reduction of expenses has been conceded before his tribunal, should as a rule be sufficient for another tribunal to make the same concession in the execution of a rogatory commission.

The basis for the granting of a gratuitous defense or of a reduction of the expenses by a tribunal executing a rogatory commission on the testimony of the judge who issued the commission is the notoriety of the fact of poverty. The notoriety of the fact, however, depends upon the inability to raise any objection of value against that fact. But what the promoter of justice of the original tribunal of the case found unobjectionable may not prove equally such to the promoter of justice of the court executing the rogatory commission.[240] Consequently, in an individual case the tribunal executing a rogatory commission may feel dissuaded to accept the poverty of a petitioner as a notorious fact simply for the reason that the judge of the trial has testified to it and has reported that a gratuitous defense or a reduction of the expenses has been granted before his tribunal.

[238] Canon 1915, § 2; cf. Noval, *De Iudiciis,* n. 698.

[239] "Notorium notorietate facti ex iure Codicis haberi videtur si delicti tales habeantur iudiciales probationes ut nihil contra opponi possit."—Coronata, *Institutiones Iuris Canonici,* IV, n. 1647; cf. also Normae S. R. Rotae Tribunalis, 29 iun. 1934, art. 179—*AAS,* XXVI (1934), 490.

[240] "Si pars quae actus processuales petit, a proprio tribunali obtinuerit gratuitum patrocinium, valde expedit ut tribunal cui acta conficienda commissa sunt, rationem habeat huius concessionis; ad eam vero observandam, absolute loquendo, non videtur obligari."—Roberti, *De Processibus,* I, n. 89.

Poverty frequently is gauged in a relative fashion. The standards for measuring poverty could differ very widely from court to court. This is not very probable if both courts are of the same country, but frequently it will be true when the courts are of different countries whose standards of living differ widely, and when the rate of exchange for foreign currency may be particularly favorable to the one country. Of course, for these same reasons it can just as easily happen that a party who did not merit a gratuitous defense or a reduction of expenses in the court where the trial is being principally prosecuted may have a very good cause for receiving a favorable decision to the same petition in the court where one or the other of the acts of the case would have to be executed on commission.

Ordinarily, therefore, when a gratuitous defense or a reduction of expenses has been granted in the original tribunal of the case, the tribunal executing a rogatory commission in the same case will make the same concession, and to do so does not postulate any previous process for the gaining of proof. The testimony of the judge, to the effect that it had been granted in the first court, will suffice. If, however, a serious objection is raised against the poverty of the petitioner in the court which has been requested to execute a rogatory commission in the case, that court will have the right to judge the matter according to the particular law of its own constitutions. If no petition is filed for a gratuitous defense or a reduction of expenses, it is presumed that the ordinary expenses will be properly met. A petition can be filed in the court which is to execute the rogatory commission, even though no such petition had been made to the court of the trial. In this case the petitioner would have to prove his claim according to canon 1915, and the process outlined by the same canon would be followed.

In regard to judicial expenses, the judge can, if he sees fit, demand that a sum of money or a bond be deposited with the chancellor to cover these expenses.[241] If the money is for the compensation of witnesses, and it is not deposited in the time allotted by the judge, the parties are presumed to have renounced the calling of

[241] Canon 1909, § 2.

these witnesses.[242] If the money is for court expenses and it is not deposited, evidently there is no obligation for the judge to proceed with the case, unless it is a case in which a gratuitous defense is to be asked for and granted. The same demands can be made by a judge in executing a rogatory commission.

242 Canon 1788.

CHAPTER IV

THE USE OF THE ROGATORY COMMISSION IN INFORMAL CASES (CANONS 1990-1992)

ON December 6, 1943, the Commission for the interpretation of the Code gave the decision that the matrimonial process spoken of in canons 1990-1992, and frequently referred to as the informal case, was of the judicial order.[1] Previously many had considered it to be of an administrative nature.[2]

With this official declaration it became certain that the process mentioned in canons 1990-1992 was essentially the same as the judicial summary process that existed before the Code. From the wording of canon 1990, *"praetermissis solemnitatibus hucusque recensitis,"* the informal process is cut to the bare essentials demanded for the nature of a judicial procedure. That the essentials of a judicial process must be had is self-evident. But the pre-Code summary process, as established by Pope Clement V in the Council of Vienne (1311-1312),[3] also consisted exclusively of the solemnities essential to a judicial process. These essential solemnities included a petition, the citation of the parties, proofs, legitimate defense, and, of course, a sentence. The solemnities that could be omitted were: formalities surrounding the drawing up of the peti-

[1] P. C. I., 6 dec. 1943—*AAS, XXXVI* (1944), 94.

[2] Kennedy, *The Special Matrimonial Process in Cases of Evident Nullity,* The Catholic University of America Canon Law Studies, n. 93 (Washington, D. C.: The Catholic University of America, 1935), pp. 69-71; for lists of authors for and against the administrative nature of this process, cf. Kay, "Canon 1990 and the S. C. S. Instruction of 15 August, 1936, on Matrimonial Procedure"—*The Ecclesiastical Review* (from 1895: *The American Ecclesiastical Review,* Vols. I-XXXII, Philadelphia, 1895-1905; from 1905: *The Ecclesiastical Review,* Vols. XXXIII-CIX, Philadelphia, 1905-1943; from 1944: *The American Ecclesiastical Review,* Washington, D. C., Vol. CX, 1944—), XCVIII (1938), 262-270.

[3] C. 2, *de iudiciis,* II, 1, in Clem.; c. 2, *de verborum significatione,* V, 11, in Clem.

tion, the joinder of issues, the observance of legal holidays, the hearing of useless exceptions and appeals, the closing of the evidence, and the publication of the acts.[4]

Bouix (d. 1870), speaking with reference to marriage trials,[5] was of the opinion that the summary process of Clement V was set aside by the Apostolic Constitution *Dei miseratione* of Benedict XIV (1740-1758).[6] The more common opinion, however, even up to the time of the Code, was that the summary process could be used in marriage trials, provided that the formalities as delineated in the Constitution *Dei miseratione* were observed.[7]

In the Constitution *Dei miseratione,* Pope Benedict XIV provided for the intervention of a defender of the marriage bond in the first instance of a marriage trial, the necessary appeal by this defender from the first instance to the metropolitan court, the intervention of a similar defender in the court of second instance, and the permission to enter a new marriage only after a double concordant sentence of nullity had been rendered.[8]

These provisions were mitigated by the Holy Office on June 5, 1889, for the cases of marriages that were evidently null and void because of a previous impediment of disparity of cult, valid marriage, consanguinity, affinity, spiritual relationship or clandestinity. For these cases the Holy Office permitted the ordinary to give a declaration of nullity as long as the defender of the bond intervened in

[4] Reiffenstuel, Lib. II, tit. 1, nn. 41-44; Schmalzgrueber, Lib. II, tit. 1, n. 10; Santi, *Praelectiones Juris Canonici,* Lib. II, tit. 1, n. 12; De Angelis, *Praelectiones Iuris Canonici,* Lib. II, tit. 1, nn. 11-12; Sebastianelli, *De Iudiciis Civilibus,* n. 8; Lega, *De Iudiciis Ecclesiasticis,* I, nn. 48, 597; Wernz, *Ius Decretalium,* V, n. 78; Laurentius, *Institutiones Iuris Ecclesiastici* (Friburgi Brisgoviae, 1903), n. 341.

[5] *Tractatus de Judiciis Ecclesiasticis,* II, 445-446.

[6] Benedictus XIV, const. *Dei miseratione,* 3 nov. 1741—*Fontes,* n. 318.

[7] Santi, *Praelectiones Juris Canonici,* Lib. II, tit. 1, n. 13; Sebastianelli, *De Iudiciis Civilibus,* n. 9; Wernz, *Ius Decretalium,* V, n. 757; Lega, *De Iudiciis Ecclesiasticis,* IV, n. 420; Smith, *Elements of Ecclesiastical Law* (3 vols., Vol. II, *Ecclesiastical Trials,* 2. ed., New York, Cincinnati and Chicago, 1888), II, n. 1273; cf. also Johnson, "De natura processuum matrimonialium exceptorum" *Apollinaris,* IX (1936), 379-380.

[8] Benedictus XIV, const. *"Dei miseratione,"* 3 nov. 1741, § § 6, 7, 8, 10, 11—*Fontes,* n. 318.

the first instance; the other solemnities of the constitution *Dei miseratione* were not required: the defender was not obliged to appeal, and the parties could remarry even though a double concordant sentence had not been rendered.[9] If, however, the nullity of the marriage was not certain, the defender was obliged to appeal.[10]

Concerning the judicial nature of the process that was to be followed in the cases of evident nullity mentioned in the decree of the Holy Office of June 5, 1889, there can be no doubt. It was to be the summary judicial process.[11] With the omission of the erstwhile impediment of clandestinity and the addition of the impediments of Holy Orders and the solemn vow of chastity, canon 1990 is nothing other than a codification of the decree of June 5, 1889. In the Code, the words, "*praetermissis solemnitatibus hucusque recensitis,*" had to be used instead of "*praetermissis solemnitatibus in Constitutione Apostolica* Dei Miseratione *requisitis,*" in order to exclude the

[9] S. C. S. Off., decr. 5 iun. 1889: "Quando agitur de impedimento disparitatis cultus, et evidenter constat unam partem esse baptizatam, et alteram non fuisse baptizatam; quando agitur de impedimento ligaminis, et certo constat primum coniugem esse legitimum et adhuc vivere; quando denique agitur de consanguinitate aut affinitate ex copula licita, aut etiam de cognatione spirituali, vel de impedimento clandestinitatis in locis ubi decretum Triden. *Tametsi* publicatum est, vel uti tale diu observatur, dummodo ex certo et authentico documento, vel in huius defectu, ex certis argumentis evidenter constet de existentia huiusmodi impedimentorum super quibus Ecclesiae auctoritate dispensatum non fuerit; hisce in casibus praetermissis solemnitatibus in Constitutione Apostolica *Dei Miseratione* requisitis, matrimonium poterit ab Ordinariis declarari nullum, cum interventu tamen defensoris vinculi matrimonialis, quin opus sit secunda sententia."—*Fontes* n. 1118. This was a general decree, and was applicable throughout the universal Church; cf. S. C. S. Off., decr. 14 febr. 1894—*Fontes,* n. 1168.

[10] S. C. S. Off., decr. 27 mart. 1901: ". . . quae certitudo si desit, a defensore vinculi matrimonialis ad secundam instantiam procedendum erit."—*Fontes,* n. 1251.

[11] S. C. S. Off. (Albanen. in America), 10 iun. 1896: ". . . licet uti iam ab anno 1889 sub die 20 Martii, et iterum sub die 5 Iunii statuit haec ipsa S. Officii Congregatio, procedi possit praetermissis solemnitatibus in const. *Dei Miser.,* requisitis, modo summario et extraiudiciali; semper tamen forma iudicialis quoad substantialia servari debet, cum interventu defensoris vinculi matrimonialis . . . quod profecto praestari a nemine poterit, nisi prius habita speciali et regulari delegatione."—*Fontes,* n. 1180.

necessity of the ordinary solemnities of the positive law for formal trials, since the Code does not provide for a summary process as it existed in 1889.

The informal marriage procedure, therefore, as delineated in canons 1990-1992, must be considered as a process truly judicial with all the essential elements of a judicial process. In it there is required the intervention of the defender of the marriage bond, as canon 1990 specifically states. This intervention is to be ruled by canons 1968-1969, and these canons are to be carried out in their entirety, if and when occasion should arise.[12]

The Constitution *Dei miseratione* made no distinction between the part the defender of the bond was to play in summary processes and the part he was to have in solemn or ordinary processes. The decree of the Holy Office of June 5, 1889, was not considered as changing the part of the defender of the bond in the first instance of the trial, but only as freeing him from the necessity of lodging an appeal with a court of second instance, and as dispensing with the need of a double concordant sentence before the parties gained an acknowledged full status for marriage.[13]

Authors who wrote on the part of the defender of the marriage bond before the Code also made no distinction between his activity in solemn trials and his activity in summary processes.[14] From the

[12] Johnson, "De natura processuum matrimonialium exceptorum," *Apollinaris* IX (1936), 402; Doheny, Canonical Procedure in Matrimonial Cases (2 vols., Vol. II, *Informal Procedure,* Milwaukee: Bruce Publishing Company, 1944), II, 141; Blat, *Commentarium Textus Codicis Iuris Canonici,* IV, n. 551.

[13] "Dans tous ces cas, il est nécessaire que la nullité soit évidente; la principale des solennités dont on peut alors se dispenser, est l'appel d'office; enfin, la présence du défendeur du lien est toujours requise, et c'est a lui de voir si, en conscience, il peut regarder la nullité comme assez évidente pour pouvoir omettre l'appel"—*Le Canoniste Contemporain* (Paris, 1878-1922), XIII (1890), 224; cf. also Wernz, *Ius Decretalium,* IV, n. 728; Laurentius, *Institutiones Iuris Ecclesiastici,* n. 698; Wernz-Vidal, *Ius Canonicum,* V, n. 704; Lega, *De Iudiciis Ecclesiasticis,* IV, n. 420.

[14] Santi, *Praelectiones Juris Canonici,* Lib. II, tit. 1, n. 13; Sebastianelli, *De Rebus* (2. ed., Romae, 1905), nn. 178, 180; Smith, *The Marriage Process in the United States* (New York, Cincinnati and Chicago, 1893), nn. 399, 429; Laurentius, *Institutiones Iuris Ecclesiastici,* n. 698; Lega, *De Iudiciis Eccle-*

nature of a judicial process as an argumentation (*disceptatio*),[15] and from the fact that the defender of the bond has all the rights and obligations of a party to the trial with the special purpose of defending the marriage tie,[16] it follows that the defender has the right and the duty to intervene in an active manner during the entire course of the trial, i. e., from the citation of the defendant to the granting of the decision, and even to the lodging of a judicial appeal if this is considered necessary. An interested party does not intervene merely at the last moment to review the acts of the case,[17] but makes his legitimate defense, even by means of exceptions and appeals, during the entire trial. From the very beginning, the right to a legitimate defense was recognized in the summary process in exactly the same manner as it had been in the solemn process, although there was an attempt to do away with exceptions and appeals that were vain and trivial.[18] A defender of the marriage bond could not be said to have the opportunity of properly defending the marriage bond if, in all cases, he were called into the trial merely at the last moment before the pronouncement of the sentence.

The words of canon 1990, *"cum interventu tamen defensoris vinculi,"* are taken from the decree of June 5, 1889,[19] and, there-

siastics, IV, nn. 442-443; Gasparri, *Tractatus Canonicus de Matrimonio* (3. ed., 2 vols., Parisiis, 1904), II, nn. 1470-1471; Wernz, *Ius Decretalium,* IV, n. 730.

15 Canon 1552, § 1.

16 Cf. Roberti, *De Processibus,* I, n. 124; Coronata, *Institutiones Iuris Canonici,* III, n. 1484.

17 This against Bastnagel, "Testimony in Summary Cases," *The Jurist* (Washington, D. C., 1941—), V (1945), 445.

18 *Glossa Ordinaria* s. v. *dilatorias,* ad c. 2, *de verborum significatione,* V, 11, in Clem.; Zabarella, *Commentaria in Clementinarum Volumen,* Lib. V, tit. 11, c. 2; Panormitanus, *Commentaria in Clementinas,* Lib. V, tit. 11, c. 2, nn. 21, 37; Reiffenstuel, Lib. II, tit. 1, n. 44; *Schmalzgrueber,* Lib. II, tit. 1, n. 10; Laurentius, *Institutiones Iuris Ecclesiastici,* n. 341; Sebastianelli, *De Iudiciis Civilibus,* n. 8; Smith, *Elements of Ecclesiastical Law,* II, nn. 1270-1271; De Angelis, *Praelectiones Iuris Canonici,* Lib. II, tit. 1, n. 12; Wernz, *Ius Decretalium,* V, nn. 754-755; Lega, *De Iudiciis Ecclesiasticis,* I, n. 597. Lega, however, seemed to admit only three exceptions of nullity in a summary process, namely, for lack of jurisdiction or competence, for lack of a citation, and for lack of a mandate; cif. *De Iudiciis Ecclesiasticis,* II, n. 361; IV, n. 277.

19 Cf. *supra,* p. 140, footnote 9.

fore, must be interpreted in accordance with the pre-Code authors. In theInstruction *Provida,* the words *"voto etiam exquisito defensoris vinculi"* [20] do not fully describe the activity of the defender of the bond in these cases, but rather presuppose his inspection of the documents and, as is claimed, his active presence at any other judicial acts of this summary but judicial process.

The position is here taken that in these informal marriage processes of evident nullity a tribunal must be competent. This competence will be determined in accordance with the general norms given in the Code, namely, that competence belongs to that tribunal in whose territory the marriage was celebrated, or where the defendant or, if one of the parties is a non-Catholic, the Catholic party has a domicile or a quasi-domicile.[21] Canon 1990 permits the setting aside of procedural formalities, but competence is not a mere formality. It is something more fundamental, namely, the measure of judicial jurisdiction.

If, as some claim,[22] even the usual norms of competence are to be dispensed with in these informal cases, this would necessitate falling back on the general principle of jurisdiction as stated in canon 201.[23] The very purpose of a judicial sentence is that right may be declared by a public authority. But a public authority is only public in reference to a definite group of persons, namely, its subjects. Consequently, an ordinary could not give an effective declaration of nullity in the favor of travelers, since these are not subjects except in relation to the public order and the solemnity of acts.[24]

20 S. C. de Sacramentis, instr. 15 aug. 1936, art. 227, § 1—*AAS,* XXVIII (1936), 358.

21 Doheny, *Canonical Procedure in Matrimonial Cases,* II, 146-148; Johnson, "De natura processuum matrimonialium exceptorum," *Apollinaris,* IX (1936), 401-402; Cappello, *Tractatus Canonico-Moralis de Sacramentis* (3 vols. in 6, Vol. III, 4. ed., Taurinorum Augustae-Romae: Marietti, 1939), III, n. 891.

22 Kennedy, *The Special Matrimonial Process in Cases of Evident Nullity,* pp. 79-80; cf. also Doheny, *Canonical Procedure in Matrimonial Cases,* II, 148-150.

23 Doheny, *loc. cit.*

24 Cf. *supra,* pp. 57-58.

It is particularly in reference to travelers that there is the desire to extend the jurisdiction of the ordinary. But the defect inherent in his lack of jurisdiction over travelers would even be irremediable if the general laws regarding competence were disregarded, for it is these laws about competence which precisely demarcate the distinction between absolute and relative competence and, in the case of relative incompetence, supply jurisdiction under certain conditions when it is lacking.

A disregard of the usual norms of competence would restrict the power of the local bishop rather than enlarge it. It would necessitate the prosecution of this process in the territory where the defendant is a subject. Canon 1990 demands the citing of the parties. While one could suppose that the petitioner would be sufficiently interested to appear, and thus make a valid citation unnecessary, this would not always be so with the defendant. Even though a person is not subject to a particular judge by reason of domicile, quasi-domicile, or the lack of any fixed residence elsewhere, a legitimate title of competence created through his status of defendant in a trial makes him subject to that judge, so that the judge is able to cite him and constrain him to appear,[25] and even to punish him for contumacy.[26]

If the titles of competence and the canons connected with them do not bind in informal cases, an ordinary could, as is claimed,[27] exercise jurisdiction indirectly over a defendant by declaring invalid a marriage which took place in the ordinary's territory, and he thus could exercise jurisdiction by reason of the solemnities of the act,[28] but he could not exercise jurisdiction over the defendant directly by citing him, as canon 1990 demands, unless the latter were a subject of the ordinary according to the norm of the general law. Thus, if the ordinary rules of competence do not hold in informal cases, the process would always have to be conducted by the ordinary who has jurisdiction over the defendant, unless the defendant would willingly appear. Only an ordinary who has juris-

[25] Canons 1964; 1646.
[26] Canon 1845.
[27] Doheny, *loc. cit.*
[28] Canon 14, § 1, 2°.

diction over the defendant could give him an order to appear in court, i. e., could cite him.

Then, too, if the ordinary titles of competence were considered non-applicable in informal processes, it would not be legitimate to invoke canon 1567 to warrant the exercise of jurisdiction in declaring null and void a marriage between non-subjects by reason of jurisdiction over a third party who wishes to enter a marriage with one of them.[29] Canon 1567 likewise furnishes a title of judicial competence, and would, therefore, become non-applicable with the rest. It may be added that in the case here contemplated the connection between the subject and the non-subject results only at the time of the contracting of the marriage, and consequently there would be no possibility of exercising jurisdiction before the marriage by reason of that connection.

Another argument can be drawn from the doctrine of the pre-Code authors. The citation of the parties was considered an essential part of a judicial process, so that it could never be omitted even in a summary process.[30] But, without distinguishing between solemn and summary processes, authors held that, if a citation was given by a judge who was incompetent, the citation itself was null, and the defendant was not obliged to appear.[31] Lega specifically held that an exception of nullity could be brought against an incompetent judge in a summary process.[32]

It is claimed, therefore, that the laws governing competence apply for informal as well as for formal judicial processes. The ordinary requires competence in accordance with canon 1964 before he can cite parties to his tribunal and issue a sentence in the informal marriage procedure treated in canons 1990-1992. Competence, when once established, although generally relative in character, would then be exclusive. Once a tribunal has cited the defendant, all other

[29] Cf. Doheny, *ibidem,* p. 150.

[30] Cf. *supra,* p. 138.

[31] Reiffenstuel, Lib. II, tit. 2, n. 8; Schmalzgrueber, Lib. II, tit. 3, n. 28; Bouix, *Tractatus de Judiciis Ecclesiasticis,* I, 242; De Angelis *Praelectiones Iuris Canonici,* Lib. II, tit. 2, n. 7; Sebastianelli, *De Iudiciis Civilibus,* n. 98; Laurentius, *Institutiones Iuris Ecclesiastici,* n. 310; Lega, *De Iudiciis Ecclesiasticis,* I, n. 350; Wernz, *Ius Decretalium* V, n. 397.

[32] *De Iudiciis Ecclesiasticis,* II, n. 361; IV, n. 277.

tribunals, even though previously equally competent, would then be rendered incompetent.[33]

From what has been said, therefore, the informal marriage procedure outlined in canons 1990-1992 is a true judicial process. It must contain the essentials of a judicial process, namely, a petition, the citing and hearing of the parties, proofs, an opportunity for defense, and the sentence. While these essential parts of the process need not necessarily be clothed with all of the formalities mentioned in the Code, nevertheless their substantial nature must never be violated. To conduct the process, the ordinary must have competence. The defender of the bond must be cited for all of the judicial acts of the trial. With these points established, it will now be possible to outline the use of the rogatory commission in these cases.

As an administrative matter the informal cases falling under canons 1990-1992 would not have been vested with the rights accorded by canon 1570, § 2. With the authentic interpretation of December 6, 1943, it is now definitely certain that recourse can be made to canon 1570, § 2, as a basis for insisting on the assistance of other tribunals in the prosecution of informal cases. As these cases are judicial in character, they are to be handled by tribunals, and each tribunal has the right to call upon another tribunal for assistance in that sphere of activity that is proper to itself.

While it is now certain that the informal cases treated in canons 1990-1992 are of a judicial nature, it does not follow that every single aspect of them is judicial. As a matter of fact, they are particularly documentary processes. Apart from the judicial acts, all the documents are drawn up *extra iudicium*.[34] For the securing of these extra judicial documents a tribunal does not have the right to call upon another tribunal. The assistance of a tribunal is not required for the securing of birth, baptismal, confirmation, marriage, ordination, or religious profession certificates, or even of sworn

[33] Canons 1568; 1725, 2°; S. C. de Sacramentis, instr. 15 aug. 1936, art. 11—*AAS*, XXVIII (1936), 316; also Coronata, *Institutiones Iuris Canonici*, III, n. 1481; Cappello, *Tractatus Canonico-Moralis de Sacramentis*, III, 868.

[34] Canon 1813, § 1, 3°.

affidavits, civil or ecclesiastical. The certification by an ecclesiastical notary that a certain person made specific declarations under oath before him is not an act of a judicial character. In a specific case there may be desired the sworn statement of a person who lives in another diocese at too great a distance from the diocesan curia where the ecclesiastical notaries are usually available. In such a case a request could be made to a local ordinary to appoint a special notary before whom the declaration could be made and an oath taken, but such an appointment is merely an administrative matter, and is obligatory merely by analogy with canon 1570, § 2.

It is possible that at times, not only the securing of documents, but also the prosecution of these informal cases will be extrajudicial. This can occur when authentic extrajudicial documents evince the nullity of a marriage. While the essence of a judicial process must always be maintained, the manner of procedure may be extrajudicial. A response of the Holy Office of June 10, 1896, to the Bishop of Albany, New York, in explanation of the decree of June 5, 1889, specifically stated that extrajudicial procedure was permissible.[35]

Thus, the interrogation of the parties would not have to be judicially executed. In summary processes before the Code, the parties generally could be interrogated by the judge without the usual judicial formalities, even secretly.[36] They had to be judicially cited, for the citation of the parties belonged to the essence of the judicial process, and they had to be given a judicial hearing which allowed them every opportunity for protecting their rights, but the process would not have been substantially defective if the questioning of the parties had not been made part of the written acts of the case.[37] The same must also be true of the present summary process as outlined in canons 1990-1992. An affidavit given by the parties before

[35] S. C. S. Off. (Albanen. in America), 10 iun. 1896—*Fontes,* n. 1180; cf. *supra,* p. 140, footnote 11; also S. C. S. Off. (Ep. Wayne Castren.), 20 mart. 1889—*Fontes,* n. 1114.

[36] Ferrari, *Summa Institutionum Canonicarum* (7. ed., 2 vols., Genuae: Ex Tipographia Archiepiscopali, 1901), II, n. 905.

[37] S. R. R., *Impedimenti ad matrimonium et damnorum,* 31 aug. 1912, coram R. P. D. Aloisio Sincero, dec. XXXVII, n. 2—*S. Romanae Rotae Decisiones seu Sententiae* (Romae, 1912—), IV (1912), 431-432.

an ecclesiastical notary would suffice to satisfy the prescription that the ordinary must hear the parties. In this event a rogatory commission would not be necessary for the hearing of the parties in these cases.

It is not denied that the ordinary could demand that the parties appear in court and submit to judicial interrogation. Such a demand could also be made by the defender of the bond, and by either party as regards the adverse party. The judge could do this in the interest of the public good, and the parties or the defender of the bond, in pursuance of their right of defense. If a judicial interrogation of the parties were decided upon, another tribunal could be called upon to execute it in the event that the party or parties to be interrogated could not return and make a personal appearance in the courtroom of the trial. If this demand were made by the defender of the bond, he would have all the rights accorded him by the law of the Code as regards being present at the interrogation, proposing questions to the judge, and adding additional questions during the session.

It is not within the scope of this work to weigh the relative values of judicial testimonies and sworn affidavits. The testimony of witnesses can certainly be used in these informal processes.[38] If this testimony is taken extrajudicially, i. e., by means of sworn affidavits made before an ecclesiastical or civil notary, it will have adminicular force.[39] If it is desired to derive full proof from the testimony of two witnesses, and to take advantage of the presumption of law given in canon 1791, § 2, the procedure will have to be judicial. Consequently, it will have to be executed with all of the precautions which the universal and the particular law have established for the forestalling of error in the taking of judicial testimony. The rights of the parties and of the defender of the bond will have to be honored. Laws which have been made for the purpose of precluding error are not mere solemnities; they pertain to the search after

[38] P. C. I., 16 iun. 1931—*AAS,* XXIII (1931), 353-354.

[39] S. R. R., *Nullitatis matrimonii,* 5 iun. 1926, coram R. P. D. Iosepho Florczak, dec. XXIV, n. 7—*S. Romanae Rotae Decisiones seu Sententiae,* XVIII (1926), 105.

truth,[40] which is the primary purpose in the use of judicial power. Consequently, the taking of *judicial* testimony on commission will be executed in the informal cases similarly as in the formal cases.

In the use of the rogatory commission in informal cases there is one point in particular that is important to keep in mind. From the use of the word "*Ordinarius*" in canon 1990, it is clear that the local ordinary alone is competent to act in these cases. The *officialis* is incompetent without a special mandate.[41] Consequently, a petition for the execution on commission of any judicial acts that are reserved to the ordinary would have to emanate from the ordinary himself. If the ordinary had given a special mandate to his *officialis* or to any other qualified person, he also could commission another tribunal to exercise any of the judicial acts that are delineated in the mandate he received. Of course, the trial could not in its entirety be committed to another tribunal.

In committing to another tribunal those things that are reserved to the ordinary in these cases, the commission can be given to another ordinary, as he also is competent. The rogatory commission does not actually connote any delegating of the second ordinary, for the ordinary who conducts the trial is using his own ordinary power, and therefore cannot exercise or delegate it outside of his own territory. The ordinary who executes the rogatory commission also uses his own ordinary power, and he becomes competent in the case by reason of the letter of request that he has received. The ordinary who has received the request must either execute it himself or give a special mandate to his *officialis,* or to some other qualified person, to do so. The *officialis* of the place where the rogatory commission is to be executed is just as incompetent to effect the execution without a special mandate as is the *officialis* of the original tribunal of the case in regard to acts to be placed in his own territory. To be sure, an *officialis* or some other qualified person could be given a permanent mandate as an auditor in these cases.

The ordinary who has received the request could, but he would

[40] Lega, *De Iudiciis Ecclesiasticis,* IV, n. 420.

[41] S. C. de Sacramentis, instr. 15 aug. 1936, art. 228—*AAS,* XXVIII (1936), 358.

not be obliged to, appoint a special defender of the bond and a special notary for the execution of the rogatory commission. If he is not going to execute the commission personally, the one to whom he has given the special mandate would use the ordinary defender of the bond, one of the ordinary notaries, and, if necessary, the ordinary promoter of justice of the diocesan curia, unless the bishop had actually made special appointments for the work.[42]

Since there is no joinder of issue in these informal cases, their very nature demands that no *judicial* acts be attempted before the parties are cited and are accorded their natural right of the defense of their interests. This is also true of the defender of the marriage bond, and when the defender is mentioned here, the promoter of justice is also to be included if he should have to intervene in the case. Consequently, no rogatory commission will be issued until the parties and the defender of the bond have been given all of their rights that are recognized to them under the law. These rights include the offering of points about which the other party or the witnesses are to be questioned, the matter regarding the rejection of witnesses, the matter of being present at their taking of the oath, at the inspection of documents, or during judicial access, etc. Of course, a party can expressly relinquish such rights, and in the event of contumacy is presumed to have done so.[43] The defender of the bond, however, can make no such renunciation.

Since the informal cases outlined in canons 1990-1992 are especially documentary processes, the rogatory commission can be particularly helpful for the judicial inspection of documents. If a doubt should arise about the faithfulness of the transcript of a document, and the original document is in another territory and cannot be brought to the courtroom of the trial, the judge can petition the ordinary of that territory to examine and compare the original with the transcript. The parties have the right to be present at this examination,[44] and the defender of the bond must also be cited.[45]

[42] Canon 1607, § 2.

[43] Coronata, *Institutiones Iuris Canonici,* III, n. 1373.

[44] Canon 1821, §§ 1, 2.

[45] Canons 1587, §§ 1, 2; 1968, 2°; cf. Lega-Bartoccetti, *Commentarius in Iudicia Ecclesiastica,* II, 809.

Another use of the rogatory commission could consist in its compelling a third party, who was not under the jurisdiction of the judge of the trial, to produce the necessary documents. This right is given as regards documents that are common property or in which there is a common interest.[46] When these documents are in the possession of one of the parties of the original trial, the judge can directly insist that they be produced. However, when they are in the possession of a third party who is not under his jurisdiction, he will hear the petition and be competent to do so by reason of the connection between the minor and the major issue of the case.[47]

If, by an interlocutory sentence, he decides that the desired document must be exhibited, he will send a letter of request to the ordinary who has jurisdiction over the third party who has the document in his possession. This particular rogatory letter has the special name *"litterae compulsoriales."* [48] While this is an interlocutory sentence as far as the original point at issue is concerned, it is a definitive sentence in regard to the third party. Consequently, the execution will be effected by the ordinary in accordance with canon 1920, § 1; to effect the execution he will use warnings and precepts, and even spiritual punishments and censures, if these should become necessary.[49]

This action to secure documents can also become a matter of necessity when in another diocese documents cannot be removed from certain registers, or when transcripts cannot be made of them without a court order.[50]

The foregoing discussion is not regarded as furnishing an exhaustive list of the uses of the rogatory commission in informal cases. In general, there applies the same principle as in formal cases, namely, that any judicial art can be committed to another tribunal except the final sentence. In informal trials there is no formal joinder of issue, no closing of the evidence, no publication of the acts. But any of the judicial acts that are exercisable in informal

[46] Canon 1822.
[47] Canon 1567.
[48] Lega-Bartoccetti, *Commentarius in Iudicia Ecclesiastica,* I, 105.
[49] Canon 1924.
[50] Wernz-Vidal, *Ius Canonicum,* VI, n. 512.

cases can be committed to other tribunals under the ordinary conditions.

The committing of acts to other tribunals in informal cases will proceed under the same conditions as in formal cases: the tribunal making the request must be competent; the acts requested must be of a judicial and legitimate nature, and must fall under the jurisdiction of the ordinary to whom the request is made; and there is postulated a reason of necessity for demanding the assistance. Conflicts will be settled and expenses will be determined in the same manner as in formal trials.

CONCLUSIONS

1. Without exception, jurisdiction can never be directly exercised over non-subjects. Judicial acts, other than those provided for by the exceptions mentioned in canon 201, § 2, are invalid if they are placed outside of the territory of the judge. Probably the incompetence of the judge outside of his territory is absolute.

2. A local tribunal uses its own ordinary jurisdiction to execute a rogatory commission which it has received from another local tribunal. The issuing of the rogatory commission has the juridical force of making a tribunal *competent* to place acts in a trial that is being prosecuted by another tribunal. Tribunals delegated by the Holy See must subdelegate other ordinaries to execute rogatory commissions.

3. The right to request another tribunal to exercise acts in a trial, and the corresponding obligation to fulfill that request, come from positive ecclesiastical law. Every competent ecclesiastical tribunal without exception has the right to call upon other tribunals for assistance in conducting trials. A tribunal which is absolutely incompetent has no such right, but rarely could this assistance be refused to a tribunal because of its relative incompetence. The request must be necessary and must relate to a judicial and legitimate act that falls under the jurisdiction of the court that is called upon to execute it. In the case of conflict, a judicial appeal cannot be used, but a recourse can be invoked with the Holy See.

4. The entire trial, the pronouncement of the final sentence, and such acts which must be exercised in the territory where the trial is being conducted, or which purport to coerce those who are subjects exclusively of that territory, cannot be committed to other tribunals. All acts other than those mentioned can be committed to other tribunals.

5. Testimony is to be taken on commission only when the witnesses, even though they be of another jurisdiction, cannot without serious inconvenience come to the diocese and appear at the scene of the trial. Witnesses who are not under the jurisdiction of the judge

of the trial must be cited by their own tribunals, even though they will give their testimony before the original tribunal of the case.

6. Other ordinaries can be called upon to execute final decisions, and, if called upon, are obliged to assist. This, however, is not a judicial, but an administrative matter.

7. Whoever has the power to exercise certain acts in a trial can call upon other tribunals for assistance in exercising these acts when necessity arises. Thus, even an auditor can issue a rogatory commission for any of the acts that for his competence are specified in his mandate.

8. The decree committing acts to another tribunal should be included in the written records of the case, since it furnishes the title of competence for the other tribunal in its fulfillment of the request. In ordinary trials it should be clear that it is the assistance of the *tribunal* that is desired, and not the personal attention of the ordinary. If the tribunal is called upon for assistance, it can execute the request apart from the need of any special appointments.

9. In informal marriage cases (canons 1990-1992), the same rules of competence apply as for formal trials; however, there will be little use for a rogatory commission, since most of the acts of these cases are executed in an extrajudicial manner. But, inasmuch as these processes are truly judicial in character, an ordinary has the right to call upon other ordinaries for such judicial acts as he may deem necessary. If the taken testimony is to have the full value of judicial testimony, it must be obtained in exactly the same manner in which judicial testimony is obtained in formal trials.

BIBLIOGRAPHY

Sources

Acta Apostolicae Sedis, Commentarium Officiale, Romae, 1909—

Bruns, H., *Canones Apostolorum et Conciliorum Saeculorum IV-VII,* 2 vols., Berolini, 1839.

Codex Iuris Canonici Pii X Pontificis Maximi iussu digestus, Benedicti Papae XV auctoritate promulgatus, Romae: Typis Polyglottis Vaticanis, 1917. Reimpressio, 1933.

Codicis Iuris Canonici Fontes cura Emi Petri Gasparri editi, 9 vols., Romae (postea Civitate Vaticana): Typis Polyglottis Vaticanis, 1923-1939. (Vols. VII-IX. ed. cura et studio Emi Iustiniani Serédi.)

Corpus Iuris Canonici, Editio Lipsiensis II (E. Richter-E. Friedberg), 2 vols., Lipsiae, 1879-1881.

Corpus Iuris Civilis, 5 vols., Lugduni, 1553-1557.

Corpus Iuris Civilis, 3 vols., Berolini, 1928-1929. *Institutiones,* quas recognovit P. Kreuger, ed. stereotypa 15., 1928; *Digesta* quae recognovit T. Mommsen et retractavit P. Kreuger, ed. stereotypa 15., 1928; *Codex Iustinianus,* quem recognovit et retractavit P. Kreuger, ed. stereotypa 10., 1929; *Novellae,* quas recognovit R. Schoell, et absolvit G. Kroll, ed. stereotypa 5., 1928.

Decretales D. Gregorii Papae, una cum glossis restitutae, 2 vols., Romae, 1582.

Decretum Gratiani emendatum et notationibus illustratum una cum glossis, 2 vols., Romae, 1582.

Denziger, H.-Bannwart, C.-Umberg, J. B., *Enchiridion Symbolorum, Definitionum, et Declarationum de Rebus Fidei et Morum,* 21.-23. ed., Friburgi Brisgoviae: Herder & Co., 1937.

Hardouin, J., *Acta Conciliorum et Epistolae Decretales ac Constitutiones Summorum Pontificum,* 12 vols., Parisiis, 1714-1715.

Hinschius, P., *Decretales Pseudo-Isidorianae et Capitula Angilramni,* Lipsiae, 1863.

Jaffé, P., *Regesta Pontificum Romanorum ab condita ecclesia ad annum post Christum natum MCXCVIII,* 2. ed. (F. Kaltenbrunner, P. Ewald, S. Loewenfeld), 2 vols. in 1, Lipsiae, 1885-1888.

Liber Sextus Decretalium D. Bonifatii Papae VIII suae integritati una cum Clementinis et Extravagantibus earumque Glossis restitutus, Romae, 1582.

Mansi, J. D., *Sacrorum Conciliorum Nova et Amplissima Collectio,* 53 vols. in 60, Parisiis, 1901-1927.

Potthast, A., *Regesta Pontificum Romanorum inde ab anno post Christum natum MCXCVIII ad annum MCCCIV,* 2 vols., Berolini, 1874-1875.

Schroeder, H. J., *Canons and Decrees of the Council of Trent: Original Text with English Translation,* St. Louis and London: B. Herder Book Co., 1941.

S. Romanae Rotae Decisiones seu Sententiae, Romae, 1912—

Turner, C., *Ecclesiae Orientalis Monumenta Iuris Antiquissima: Canonum et Conciliorum Grecorum Interpretationes Latinae,* 2 vols. in 7 parts, Oxonii: E Typographeo Clarendoniano, 1899-1939.

Authors

Aichner, S., *Compendium Juris Ecclesiastici,* 6. ed., Brixinae, 1887.

Altimarus, B., *Tractatus de Nullitatibus,* 2 vols., Neapoli, 1678-1682.

Augustine, Charles, *A Commentary on the New Code of Canon Law,* 2 vols., Vol. VII, St. Louis and London: B. Herder Book Co., 1921.

Augustini Hippoensis Episcopi, Sancti Aurelii, Opera, opera et studio Monachorum Ordinis S. Benedicti et Congregationis S. Mauri, 18 vols., Venetiis, 1756-1769.

Barbosa, A., *Collectanea Doctorum tam Veterum quam Recentiorum,* 5 vols., Lugduni, 1656.

Bartolus a Saxoferrato, *In Digestum Commentaria,* 6 vols., Venetiis, 1585.

Begnudelli Basso, F., *Bibliotheca Juris Canonico-Civilis Practica,* ed. novissima, 4 vols., Mutinae, 1757-1758.

Bertachini, I., *Repertorium,* 5 vols., Venetiis, 1570.

Berutti, C., *Institutiones Iuris Canonici,* 5 vols., Taurini-Romae: Marietti, 1936-1943.

Besté, U., *Introductio in Codicem,* 3. ed., Collegeville, Minn.: St. John's Abbey Press, 1946.

Billecard, M., Les Commissions Rogatoires en Droit International Privé, Paris: V. Giard e E. Brière, 1902.

Blat, A., *Commentarium Textus Codicis Iuris Canonici,* 5 vols. in 6, Vol. II, 2. ed., 1921; Vol. IV, 1927, Romae: Libraria del Collegio "Angelico."

Boich, H., *In Quinque Decretalium Libros Commentaria,* Venetiis, 1576.

Bouix, D., *Tractatus de Judiciis Ecclesiasticis,* 3. ed., 2 vols., Parisiis, 1883.

Cappello, F., *Summa Iuris Canonici,* 3 vols., Vols. I, II, 4. ed., 1945; Vol. III, 2. ed., 1940, Romae: Apud Aedes Universitatis Gregorianae.

Cappello, F., *Summa Iuris Publici Ecclesiastici,* 4. ed., Romae: Apud Aedes Universitatis Gregorianae, 1936.

Cappello, F., *Tractatus Canonico-Moralis de Sacramentis,* 3 vols. in 6, Vol. III, 4. ed., Taurinorum Augustae-Romae: Marietti, 1939.

Catholic Encyclopedia, The, 15 vols., Index and 2 Supplements, New York, 1907-1922.

Cavagnis, F., *Institutiones Iuris Publici Ecclesiastici,* 2 vols., Romae, 1882-1883.

Chelodi, I., *Ius de Personis,* 3. ed., curavit P. Ciprotti, Trento: Libraria Moderna Editrice, 1942.

Chokier, Erasmus a, *Tractatus de Jurisdictione Ordinarii in Exemptos*, Coloniae Agrippinae, 1629.

Cicognani, A., *Canon Law*, 2. ed., authorized English version by J. O'Hara and F. Brennan, Philadelphia: The Dolphin Press, 1935.

Cocchi, G., *Commentarium in Codicem Iuris Canonici*, 8 vols. in 5, Vol. II, 4. ed., 1937; Vol. VII, 3. ed., 1940, Taurinorum Augustae: Marietti.

Coronata, Matthaeus Conte a, *Institutiones Iuris Canonici*, 2. ed., 5 vols., Taurini: Marietti, 1939-1947.

Craisson, D., *Manuale Totius Juris Canonici*, 5. ed., 4 vols., Pictavii, 1877.

De Angelis, P., *Praelectiones Iuris Canonici*, 5 vols. in 9, Romae, 1877-1891.

De Luca, I., *Theatrum Veritatis et Justitiae*, 16 vols. in 9, Coloniae, 1706.

De Meester, A., *Juris Canonici et Juris Canonico-Civilis Compendium*, nova editio, 3 vols. in 4, Brugis: Sumptibus et Typis Societatis Sancti Augustini, 1921-1928.

De Smet, A., *Tractatus Theologico-Canonicus de Sponsalibus et Matrimonio*, 4. ed., Brugis: Car. Beyaert, 1927.

Devoti, I., *Ius Canonicum Universum Publicum et Privatum*, 3 vols., Romae, 1837.

Digesto Italiano, Il, 24 vols. in 49, Torino: Unione Tip. Editrice Torinese, 1884-1921.

Doheny, W., *Canonical Procedure in Marriage Cases*, 2 vols., Vol. II, Milwaukee: Bruce Publishing Co., 1944.

Doheny, W., *Practical Manual for Marriage Cases*, New York, Milwaukee and Chicago: The Bruce Publishing Co., 1938.

Durantis, G., *Speculum Iuris*, 4 vols. in 3, Venetiis, 1577.

Eichmann, E., *Lehrbuch des Kirchenrechts auf Grund des Codex Iuris Canonici*, 2. ed., Paderborn: Verlag Ferdinand Schöningh, 1926.

Enciclopedia Italiana di Scienze, Lettere ed Arti, 36 vols. and Appendice, Roma: Istituto Giovanni Treccani, 1929-1939.

Engel, L., *Collegium Universi Iuris Canonici*, 9. ed.; post omnes alias recognita et locupleta; cui nunc primum adjectae sunt annotationes Caspari Barthel, 1760.

Fabricius, J., *Bibliotheca Latina Mediae et Infimae Aetatis*, 3 vols., Florentiae, 1858.

Fagnanus, P., *Commentaria super Quinque Libros Decretalium*, 5 vols., Romae, 1661.

Farinacius, P., *Tractatus de Testibus*, Venetiis, 1609.

Fermosinus, N., *Opera Omnia Canonica Civilia et Criminalia*, 2. ed., 14 vols., Coloniae Allobrogum, 1741.

Ferrari, I., *Summa Institutionum Canonicarum*, 7. ed., 2 vols., Genuae: Ex Tipographia Archiepiscopali, 1901.

Ferraris, L., *Prompta Bibliotheca Canonica, Iuridica, Moralis, Theologica, necnon Ascetica, Polemica, Rubricistica, Historica*, ed., noviss., 8 vols., Parisiis, 1852-1857.

Ferreres, J., *Institutiones Canonicae,* 2. ed., 2 vols., Barcinone: Eugenius Subirana, 1920.

Forcellinus, A., *Lexicon Totius Latinitatis,* 3. ed., 6 vols., curaverunt F. Corradini et I. Perin, Patavii: Typis Seminarii, 1940.

Gasparri, P., *Tractatus Canonicus de Matrimonio,* 3. ed., 2 vols., Parisiis, 1904.

Gothofredus, D., *Corpus Iuris Civilis cum notis integris,* Coloniae Allobrogum, 1781.

Grandeclaude, E., *Jus Canonicum iuxta Ordinem Decretalium,* 3 vols., Parisiis, 1882-1883.

Guido de Bayso, *In Decretorum Volumen Commentaria,* Venetiis, 1577.

Hammill, J., *The Obligations of the Traveler according to Canon 14,* The Catholic University of America Canon Law Studies, n. 160, Washington, D. C.: The Catholic University of America Press, 1942.

Hostiensis, Cardinalis (Henricus de Segusia), *Commentaria in Quinque Libros Decretalium,* 5 vols. in 3, Venetiis, 1581.

Icard, H., *Praelectiones Juris Canonici,* 3 vols., Lutetiae Parisiorum, 1859.

Innocentius IV (Sinibaldus Fliscus), *Apparatus super Libros Decretalium,* Argentorati, 1478.

Ioannes Andreae, *Commentaria Novella,* Venetiis: Ioannes et Gregorius de Gregoriis de Forlivio, 1489.

Ioannes Andreae, *Commentaria Novella,* 5 vols. in 4, Venetiis, 1505.

Kennedy, E., *The Special Matrimonial Process in Cases of Evident Nullity,* The Catholic University of America Canon Law Studies, n. 93, Washington, D. C.: The Catholic University of America, 1935.

Laurentius, I., *Institutiones Iuris Ecclesiastici,* Friburgi Brisgoviae, 1903.

Lega, M., *Praelectiones in Textum Iuris Canonici: De Iudiciis Ecclesiasticis,* 4 vols., Romae, 1896-1901.

Lega, M.-Bartoccetti, V., *Commentarius in Iudicia Ecclesiastica iuxta Codicem Iuris Canonici,* 3 vols., Romae: Anonima Libraria Cattolica Italiana, 1938-1941.

Leurenius, P., *Forum Ecclesiasticum . . . Jus Canonicum Universum,* 5 vols. in 4, Venetiis, 1729.

Lombardi, C., *Iuris Canonici Privati Institutiones,* 2. ed., 3 vols., Romae, 1901.

McClunn, J., *Administrative Recourse,* The Catholic University of America Canon Law Studies, n. 240, Washington, D. C.: The Catholic University of America Press, 1946.

Maschat a S. Erasmo, R., *Institutiones Canonicae,* 4 vols., Florentiae, 1854.

Michiels, G., *Normae Generales Juris Canonici,* 2 vols., Lublin: Universitas Catholica, 1929.

Mocchegiani, P., *Jurisprudentia Ecclesiastica,* 3 vols., Friburgi Brigoviae, 1904-1905.

Moriarty, E., *Oaths in Ecclesiastical Courts,* The Catholic University of America Canon Law Studies, n. 110, Washington, D. C.: The Catholic University of America, 1937.

Muñiz, T., *Procedimientos Eclesiásticos,* 2. ed., 3 vols., Sevilla: Imp. y Lib. De Sobrino de Izquierdo, 1925-1926.

Noval, J., *Commentarium Codicis Iuris Canonici,* Liber IV, *De Processibus,* Pars I, *De Iudiciis,* Augustae Taurinorum-Romae: Marietti, 1920.

Oesterle, G., *Praelectiones Iuris Canonici,* Vol. I, Romae: In Collegio S. Anselmi, 1931.

Oliva e Souza, Felicianus de, *Tractatus de Foro Ecclesiae,* 3 vols. in 1, Coloniae Allobrogum, 1733.

Onclin, G., *De territoriali vel personali legis indole,* Gemblaci: J. Duculot, 1938.

Ottaviani, A., *Institutiones Iuris Publici Ecclesiastici,* 2 vols., Vol. I, 3. ed., Civitas Vaticana: Typis Polyglottis Vaticanis, 1947.

Panormitanus, Abbas (Nicolaus de Tudeschis) *Commentaria in Quinque Libros Decretalium,* 5 vols. in 7, Venetiis, 1588.

Pellegrini, C., *Praxis Vicariorum,* Venetiis, 1706.

Piasecus, P., *Praxis Episcopalis,* Coloniae Agrippinae, 1620.

Pichler, V., *Ius Canonicum secundum Quinque Decretalium Titulos Explicatum,* 2 vols., Venetiis-Ravennae, 1741.

Pirhing, E., *Jus Canonicum in V Libros Decretalium,* 5 vols. in 4, Dilingiae, 1722.

Popek, A., *The Rights and Obligations of Metropolitans,* The Catholic University of America Canon Law Studies, n. 260, Washington, D. C.: The Catholic University of America Press, 1947.

Prümmer, D., *Manuale Iuris Canonici,* 3. ed., Friburgi Brisgoviae: Herder & Co., 1922.

Regatillo, E., *Institutiones Iuris Canonici,* 2 vols., Vol. I, 2. ed., 1946; Vol. II, 1942, Santander: Sal Terrae.

Reiffenstuel, A., *Ius Canonicum Universum,* 5 vols. in 6, Romae, 1831-1834.

Roberti, F., *De Processibus,* 2 vols., Vol. I, 2. ed., Romae: Apud Custodiam Librariam Pontificii Instituti Utriusque Iuris, 1941; Vol. II, Romae: Apud Aedes Facultatis Iuridicae ad S. Apollinaris, 1926.

Romani, S., *Institutiones Juris Canonici,* 2 vols. in 3, Romae: Editrice "Iustitia," 1941-1945.

Ryan, G., *Principles of Episcopal Jurisdiction,* The Catholic University of America Canon Law Studies, n. 120, Washington, D. C.: The Catholic University of America Press, 1939.

Sanguineti, S., *Iuris Ecclesiastici Institutiones,* 3. ed., Romae, 1896.

Santi, F., *Praelectiones Juris Canonici,* 5 vols. in 2, Ratisbonae, Neo-Eboraci et Cincinnati, 1886.

Scaccia, S., *De Iudiciis,* 2 vols., Venetiis, 1663.

Schaefer, T., *De Religiosis,* 3. ed., Romae: S. A. L. E. R., 1940.

Schmalzgrueber, F., *Ius Ecclesiasticum Universum,* 5 vols. in 12, Romae, 1843-1845.

Schmier, F., *Jurisprudentia Canonico-civilis* seu *Jus Canonicum Universum*, 2 vols., Venetiis, 1754.
Sebastianelli, G., *De Iudiciis Ecclesiasticis*, Pars Prima (*De Iudiciis Civilibus*), 2. ed., Ratisbonae, Neo-Eboraci, Cincinnati, 1905-1906.
Sebastianelli, G., *De Rebus*, 2. ed., Ratisbonae, Neo-Eboraci, Cincinnati, 1905.
Sipos, S., *Enchiridion Iuris Canonici*, 3. ed., Pécs: Ex Typographia "Haladás R.T.," 1936.
Smith, S., *Elements of Ecclesiastical Law*, 3 vols., Vol. II, *Ecclesiastical Trials*, 2. ed., New York, Cincinnati and Chicago, 1888.
Smith, S., *The Marriage Process in the United States*, New York, Cincinnati, and Chicago, 1893.
Taparelli, L., *Saggio Teoretico di Dritto Naturale*, 2 vols., Romae, 1855.
Torre, J., *Processus Matrimonialis*, 2. ed., Neapoli: M. D'Auria, 1947.
Toso, A., *Ad Codicem Juris Canonici . . . Commentaria Minora*, 5 vols. in 2, Taurini-Romae: Marietti, 1920-1927.
Tuschus, D., *Practicae Conclusiones Iuris in Omni Foro Frequentiores*, 8 vols., Lugduni, 1634; *Additiones*, Vol. IX, Lugduni, 1670.
Ubertus, G., *De Citationibus*, Romae, 1680.
Ventriglia, I., *Praxis Rerum Notabilium*, 2 vols. in 1, Venetiis, 1694.
Van Hove, A., *Commentarium Lovaniense in Codicem Iuris Canonici*, Vol. I, tom. 1, *Prolegomena ad Codicem Iuris Canonici*, 2. ed., 1945; Vol. I, tom. 5, *De Privilegiis-De Dispensationibus*, 1939, Mechliniae-Romae: H. Dessain.
Vermeersch, A.-Creusen, J., *Epitome Iuris Canonici*, 3 vols., Vol. I, 6. ed., 1937; Vol. II, 6. ed., 1940; Vol. III, 6. ed., 1946, Mechliniae-Romae: H. Dessain.
Wenger, L., *Institutes of the Roman Law of Civil Procedure*, revised ed., translation by Otis Harrison Fisk, New York: Veritas Press, 1940.
Wernz, F. X., *Ius Decretalium*, 2. ed., 6 vols., Romae et Prati, 1906-1913.
Wernz, F. X.-Vidal, P., *Ius Canonicum*, 7 vols. in 8, Vol. II, 3. ed., a P. Aguirre recognita, 1943; Vol. V, 3. ed., a P. Aquirre recognita, 1946; Vol. VI, 1928, Romae: Apud Aedes Universitatis Gregorianae.
Woywod, S.-Smith, C., *A Practical Commentary on the Code of Canon Law*, revised and enlarged edition, 2 vols., New York: John F. Wagner, 1948.
Zabarella, F., *Commentaria in Clementinarum Volumen*, Venetiis, 1504.

Articles

Bastnagel, C., "Testimony in Summary Cases," *The Jurist*, V (1945), 441-447.
Haring, J., "Delegation eines Eheprozesses," *Theologisch-praktische Quartalschrift*, LXXXIII (1930), 140-142.
Hilling, N., "Über den Gebrauch des Ausdrucks *Iurisdictio* im kanonischen Recht während der ersten Hälfte des Mittelalters," *Archiv für katholisches Kirchenrecht*, CXVIII (1938), 165-170.
Kuttner, S.-Smalley, B., "The 'Glossa Ordinaria' to the Gregorian Decretals," *The English Historical Review*, LX (1945), 97-105.

Kay, T., "Canon 1990 and the S. C. S. Instruction of 15 August, 1936, on Matrimonial Procedure," *The Ecclesiastical Review,* XCVIII (1938), 262-270.

Pugliese, A., "Le Rogatorie e i Poteri del Tribunale Delegato," *Salesianum,* VI (1944), 51-78.

Ramos, D., "De Conditione Saecularium in Domibus Religiosorum," *Commentarium pro Religiosis,* VI (1925), 28-33; 82-85; 136-140; 324-329; 479-483.

Roberti, F., "De expensis iudicialibus pro exequendis litteris rogatoriis," *Apollinaris,* X (1937), 278-279.

Van de Kerckhove, M., "De Notione Jurisdictionis in Jure Romano," *Jus Pontificium,* XVI (1936), 49-65.

———, "De Notione Jurisdictionis apud Decretistas et priores Decretalistas," *Jus Pontificium,* XVIII (1938), 10-14.

Periodicals

American Ecclesiastical Review, The, Vols. I-XXXII, Philadelphia, 1895-1905; from 1905: *The Ecclesiastical Review,* Vols. XXXIII-CIX, Philadelphia, 1905-1943; from 1944: *The American Ecclesiastical Review,* Washington, D. C., Vol. CX, 1944—

Analecta Iuris Pontificii, Romae, 1855-1869; Parisiis, 1872-1891.

Apollinaris, Romae, 1928—

Archiv für katholisches Kirchenrecht, Insbruck, 1857-1861; Mainz, 1862—

Canoniste Contemporain, Le, Paris, 1878-1922; ab anno 1924-1926, *Le Canoniste.*

Commentarium pro Religiosis, Romae, 1920-1934; ab anno 1935: *Commentarium pro Religiosis et Missionariis.*

English Historical Review, The, London, 1886—

Jurist, The, Washington, D. C., 1941—

Jus Pontificium, Romae, 1921-1940.

Salesianum, Torino, 1939—

Theologisch-praktische Quartalschrift, Linz, 1848—

Abbreviations

AAS—Acta Apostolicae Sedis.

Bruns—*Canones Apostolorum et Conciliorum saec. IV-VII,* ed. Bruns.

C.—*Codex Iustinianus* or Causa.

c.—canon or caput.

D.—*Digestum Iustinianum* or Distinctio.

Fontes—Codicis Iuris Canonici Fontes . . . cura Gasparri editi.

Hardouin—*Acta Conciliorum, etc.*

Hinschius—*Decretales Pseudo-Isidorinaae et Capitula Angilramni.*

JE—Jaffé, *Regesta Pontificum Romanorum* (edited by P. Ewald; for the years 590-882).
JK—Jaffé, *op. cit.* (edited by F. Kaltenbrunner; to the year 590).
JL—Jaffé, *op. cit.* (edited by S. Loewenfeld; for the year 882-1198).
Jus Pont.—*Jus Pontificium.*
Mansi—*Sacrorum Conciliorum Nova et Amplissima Collectio.*
Nov.—*Novellae Iustinianae.*
P. C. I.—*Pontificia Commissio ad Codicis Canones Authentice Interpretandos.*
Potthast—*Regesta Pontificum Romanorum, etc.*
Q.—Quaestio.
S. C. de Prop. Fide—Sacra Congregatio de Propaganda Fide.
S. C. de Sacramentis—Sacra Congregatio de Disciplina Sacramentorum.
S. C. Ep. et Reg.—Sacra Congregatio Episcoporum et Regularium.
S. C. S. Off.—Sacra Congregatio Sancti Officii.
S. R. R.—Sacra Romana Rota.

ALPHABETICAL INDEX

BIOGRAPHICAL NOTE

MARION JUSTIN REINHARDT was born September 21, 1915, in Hicksville, Long Island, and there attended St. Ignatius Parochial School. He attended also the Brooklyn Diocesan Minor Seminary and completed his philosophical studies at Immaculate Conception Seminary, Huntington, Long Island. In October, 1937, he was sent to *Almo Collegio Capranica,* Rome, Italy, to make his theological studies at the Pontifical Gregorian University, where he received the Baccalaureate degree in Theology in 1939. Because of international hostilities, he returned to the United States in June, 1940, and completed his theological studies at the above-mentioned Immaculate Conception Seminary, Huntington, Long Island. He was ordained to the priesthood on June 7, 1941. In the fall of 1946 he entered upon a course of studies in the School of Canon Law at the Catholic University of America, Washington, D. C., where he received the Baccalaureate degree in Canon Law in June, 1947, and the Licentiate degree in Canon Law in June, 1948.

CANON LAW STUDIES *

1. FRERIKS, REV. CELESTINE A., C.PP.S., J.C.D., Religious Congregations in Their External Relations, 121 pp., 1916.
2. GALLIHER, REV. DANIEL M., O.P., J.C.D., Canonical Elections, 117 pp., 1917.
3. BORKOWSKI, REV. AURELIUS L., O.F.M., J.C.D., De Confraternitatibus Ecclesiasticis, 136 pp., 1918.
4. CASTILLO, REV. CAYO, J.C.D., Disertacion Historico-Canonica sobre la Potestad del Cabildo en Sede Vacante o Impedida del Vicario Capitular, 99 pp., 1919 (1918).
5. KUBELBECK, REV. WILLIAM J., S.T.B., J.C.D., The Sacred Penitentiaria and Its Relation to Faculties of Ordinaries and Priests, 129 pp., 1918.
6. PETROVITS, REV. JOSEPH, J.C., S.T.D., J.C.D., The New Church Law on Matrimony, X-461 pp., 1919.
7. HICKEY, REV. JOHN J., S.T.B., J.C.D., Irregularities and Simple Impediments in the New Code of Canon Law, 100 pp., 1920.
8. KLEKOTKA, REV. PETER J., S.T.B., J.C.D., Diocesan Consultors, 179 pp., 1920.
9. WANENMACHER, REV. FRANCIS, J.C.D., The Evidence in Ecclesiastical Procedure Affecting the Marriage Bond, 1920 (Printed 1935).
10. GOLDEN, REV. HENRY FRANCIS, J.C.D., Parochial Benefices in the New Code, IV-119 pp., 1921 (Printed 1925).
11. KOUDELKA, REV. CHARLES J., J.C.D., Pastors, Their Rights and Duties According to the New Code of Canon Law, 211 pp., 1921.
12. MELO, REV. ANTONIUS, O.F.M., J.C.D., De Exemptione Regularium, X-188 pp., 1921.
13. SCHAAF, REV. VALENTINE THEODORE, O.F.M., S.T.B., J.C.D., The Cloister, X-180 pp., 1921.
14. BURKE, REV. THOMAS JOSEPH, S.T.D., J.C.D., Competence in Ecclesiastical Tribunals, IV-117 pp., 1922.
15. LEECH, REV. GEORGE LEO, J.C.D., A Comparative Study of the Constitution "Apostolicae Sedis" and the "Codex Juris Canonici," 179 pp., 1922.
16. MOTRY, REV. HUBERT LOUIS, S.T.D., J.C.D., Diocesan Faculties According to the Code of Canon Law, II-167 pp., 1922.
17. MURPHY, REV. GEORGE LAWRENCE, J.C.D., Delinquencies and Penalties in the Administration and the Reception of the Sacraments, IV-121 pp., 1923.
18. O'REILLY, REV. JOHN ANTHONY, S.T.B., J.C.D., Ecclesiastical Sepulture in the New Code of Canon Law, II-129 pp., 1923.

* All published numbers are available from the Catholic University of America Press, 620 Michigan Avenue, N.E., Washington 17, D. C., except the following: Nos. 1-114 inclusive, 115, 118, 120, 122, 123, 136, 153, 162, 182 and 198. But the following numbers, now reissuel, are obtainable from *The Jurist*, The Catholic University of America, Washington 17, D. C., namely: Nos. 5, 7, 11, 17, 18, 19, 26, 28, 30, 31, 34, 42, 44, 51, 52 and 61.

19. Michalicka, Rev.- Wenceslas Cyrill, O.S.B., J.C.D., Judicial Procedure in Dismissal of Clerical Exempt Religious, 107 pp., 1923.
20. Dargin, Rev. Edward Vincent, S.T.B., J.C.D., Reserved Cases According to the Code of Canon Law, IV-103 pp., 1924.
21. Godfrey, Rev. John A., S.T.B., J.C.D., The Right of Patronage According to the Code of Canon Law, 153 pp., 1924.
22. Hagedorn, Rev. Francis Edward, J.C.D., General Legislation on Indulgences, II-154 pp., 1924.
23. King, Rev. James Ignatius, J.C.D., The Administration of the Sacraments to Dying Non-Catholics, V-141 pp., 1924.
24. Winslow, Rev. Francis Joseph, O.F.M., J.C.D., Vicars and Prefects Apostolic, IV-149 pp., 1924.
25. Correa, Rev. Jose Servelion, S.T.L., J.C.D., La Potestad Legislativa de la Iglesia Catolica, IV-127 pp., 1925.
26. Dugan, Rev. Henry Francis, A.M., J.C.D., The Judiciary Department of the Diocesan Curia, 87 pp., 1925.
27. Keller, Rev. Charles Frederick, S.T.B., J.C.D., Mass Stipends, 167 pp., 1925.
28. Paschang, Rev. John Linus, J.C.D., The Sacramentals According to the Code of Canon Law, 129 pp., 1925.
29. Piontek, Rev. Cyrillus, O.F.M., S.T.B., J.C.D., De Indulto Exclaustrationis necnon Saecularizationis, XIII-289 pp., 1925.
30. Kearney, Rev. Richard Joseph, S.T.B., J.C.D., Sponsors at Baptism According to the Code of Canon Law, IV-127 pp., 1925.
31. Bartlett, Rev. Chester Joseph, A.M., LL.B., J.C.D., The Tenure of Parochial Property in the United States of America, V-108 pp., 1926.
32. Kilker, Rev. Adrian Jerome, J.C.D., Extreme Unction, V-425 pp., 1926.
33. McCormick, Rev. Robert Emmett, J.C.D., Confessors of Religious, VIII-266 pp., 1926.
34. Miller, Rev. Newton Thomas, J.C.D., Founded Masses According to the Code of Canon Law, VII-93 pp., 1926.
35. Roelker, Rev. Edward G., S.T.D., J.C.D., Principles of Privilege According to the Code of Canon Law, XI-166 pp., 1926.
36. Bakalarczyk, Rev. Richardus, M.I.C., J.U.D., De Novitiatu, VIII-208 pp., 1927.
37. Pizzuti, Rev. Lawrence, O.F.M., J.U.L., De Parochis Religiosis, 1927. (Not Printed.)
38. Bliley, Rev. Nicholas Martin, O.S.B., J.C.D., Altars According to the Code of Canon Law, XIX-132 pp., 1927.
39. Brown, Mr. Brendan Francis, A.B., LL.M., J.U.D., The Canonical Juristic Personality with Special Reference to its Status in the United States of America, V-212 pp., 1927.
40. Cavanaugh, Rev. William Thomas, C.P., J.U.D., The Reservation of the Blessed Sacrament, VIII-101 pp., 1927.

41. DOHENY, REV. WILLIAM J., C.S.C., A.B., J.C.D., Church Property: Modes of Acquisition, X-118 pp., 1927.
42. FELDHAUS, REV. ALOYSIUS H., C.PP.S., J.C.D., Oratories, IX-141 pp., 1927
43. KELLY, REV. JAMES PATRICK, A.B., J.C.D., The Jurisdiction of the Simple Confessor, X-208 pp., 1927.
44. NEUBERGER, REV. NICHOLAS J., J.C.D., Canon 6 or the Relation of the Codex Juris Canonici to the Preceding Legislation, V-95 pp., 1927.
45. O'KEEFE, REV. GERALD MICHAEL, J.C.D., Matrimonial Dispensations, Powers of Bishops, Priests, and Confessors, VIII-232 pp., 1927.
46. QUIGLEY, REV. JOSEPH A. M., A.B., J.C.D., Condemned Societies, 139 pp. 1927.
47. ZAPLOTNIK, REV. JOHANNES LEO, J.C.D., De Vicariis Foraneis, X-142 pp. 1927.
48. DUSKIE, REV. JOHN ALOYSIUS, A.B., J.C.D., The Canonical Status of the Orientals in the United States, VIII-196 pp., 1928.
49. HYLAND, REV. FRANCIS EDWARD, J.C.D., Excommunication, Its Nature, Historical Development and Effects, VIII-181 pp., 1928.
50. REINMANN, REV. GERALD JOSEPH, O.M.C., J.C.D., The Third Order Secular of Saint Francis, 201 pp., 1928.
51. SCHENK, REV. FRANCIS J., J.C.D., The Matrimonial Impediments of Mixed Religion and Disparity of Cult, XVI-318 pp., 1929.
52. COADY, REV. JOHN JOSEPH, S.T.D., J.U.D., A.M., The Appointment of Pastors, VIII-150 pp., 1929.
53. KAY, REV. THOMAS HENRY, J.C.D., Competence in Matrimonial Procedure, VIII-164 pp., 1929.
54. TURNER, REV. SIDNEY JOSEPH, C.P., J.U.D., The Vow of Poverty, XLIX-217 pp., 1929.
55. KEARNEY, REV. RAYMOND A., A.B., S.T.D., J.C.D., The Principles of Delegation, VII-149 pp., 1929.
56. CONRAN, REV. EDWARD JAMES, A.B., J.C.D., The Interdict, V-163 pp., 1930.
57. O'NEILL, REV. WILLIAM H., J.C.D., Papal Rescripts of Favor, VII-218 pp., 1930.
58. BASTNAGEL, REV. CLEMENT VINCENT, J.U.D., The Appointment of Parochial Adjutants and Assistants, XV-257 pp., 1930.
59. FERRY, REV. WILLIAM A., A.B., J.C.D., Stole Fees, V-136 pp., 1930.
60. COSTELLO, REV. JOHN MICHAEL, A.B., J.C.D., Domicile and Quasi-Domicile, VII-201 pp., 1930.
61. KREMER, REV. MICHAEL NICHOLAS, A.B., S.T.B., J.C.D., Church Support in the United States, VI-136 pp., 1930.
62. ANGULO, REV. LUIS, C.M., J.C.D., Legislation de la Iglesia sobre la intencion en la application de la Santa Misa, VII-104 pp., 1931.
63. FREY, REV. WOLFGANG NORBERT, O.S.B., A.B., J.C.D., The Act of Religious Profession, VIII-174 pp., 1931.

64. ROBERTS, REV. JAMES BRENDAN, A.B., J.C.D., The Banns of Marriage, XIV-140 pp., 1931.
65. RYDER, REV. RAYMOND ALOYSIUS, A.B., J.C.D., Simony, IX-151 pp., 1931.
66. CAMPAGNA, REV. ANGELO, PH.D., J.U.D., Il Vicario Generale del Vescovo, VII-205 pp., 1931.
67. COX, REV. JOSEPH GODFREY, A.B., J.C.D., The Administration of Seminaries, VI-124 pp., 1931.
68. GREGORY, REV. DONALD J., J.U.D., The Pauline Privilege, XV-165 pp., 1931.
69. DONOHUE, REV. JOHN F., J.C.D., The Impediment of Crime, VII-110 pp., 1931.
70. DOOLEY, REV. EUGENE A., O.M.I., J.C.D., Church Law on Sacred Relics, IX-143 pp., 1931.
71. ORTH, REV. CLEMENT RAYMOND, O.M.C., J.C.D., The Approbation of Religious Institutes, 171 pp., 1931.
72. PERNICONE, REV. JOSEPH M., A.B., J.C.D., The Ecclesiastical Prohibition of Books, XII-267 pp., 1932.
73. CLINTON, REV. CONNELL, A.B., J.C.D., The Paschal Precept, IX-108 pp., 1932.
74. DONNELLY, REV. FRANCIS B., A.M., S.T.L., J.C.D., The Diocesan Synod, VIII-125 pp., 1932.
75. TORRENTE, REV. CAMILO, C.M.F., J.C.D., Las Procesiones Sagradas, V-145 pp., 1932.
76. MURPHY, REV. EDWIN J., C.PP.S., J.C.D., Suspension Ex Informata Conscientia, XI-122 pp., 1932.
77. MACKENZIE, REV. ERIC F., A.M., S.T.L., J.C.D., The Delict of Heresy in its Commission, Penalization, Absolution, VII-124 pp., 1932.
78. LYONS, REV. AVITUS E., S.T.B., J.C.D., The Collegiate Tribunal of First Instance, XI-147 pp., 1932.
79. CONNOLLY, REV. THOMAS A., J.C.D., Appeals, XI-195, pp., 1932.
80. SANGMEISTER, REV. JOSEPH V., A.B., J.C.D., Force and Fear as Precluding Matrimonial Consent, V-211 pp., 1932.
81. JAEGER, REV. LEO A., A.B., J.C.D., The Administration of Vacant and Quasi-Vacant Episcopal Sees in the United States, IX-229 pp., 1932.
82. RIMLINGER, REV. HERBERT T., J.C.D., Error Invalidating Matrimonial Consent, VII-79 pp., 1932.
83. BARRETT, REV. JOHN D. M., S.S., J.C.D., A Comparative Study of the Councils of Baltimore and the Code of Canon Law, IX-223 pp., 1932.
84. CARBERRY, REV. JOHN J., PH.D., S.T.D., J.C.D., The Juridical Form of Marriage, X-177 pp., 1934.
85. DOLAN, REV. JOHN L., A.B., J.C.D., The Defensor Vinculi, XII-157 pp., 1934.
86. HANNAN, REV. JEROME D., A.M., S.T.D., LL.B., J.C.D., The Canon Law of Wills, IX-517 pp., 1934.

87. Lemieux, Rev. Delise A., A.M., J.C.D., The Sentence in Ecclesiastical Procedure, IX-131 pp., 1934.
88. O'Rourke, Rev. James J., A.B., J.C.D., Parish Registers, VII-109 pp., 1934.
89. Timlin, Rev. Bartholomew, O.F.M., A.M., J.C.D., Conditional Matrimonial Consent, X-381 pp., 1934.
90. Wahl, Rev. Francis X., A.B., J.C.D., The Matrimonial Impediments of Consanguinity and Affinity, VI-125 pp., 1934.
91. White, Rev. Robert J., A.B., LL.B., S.T.B., J.C.D., Canonical Ante-Nuptial Promises and the Civil Law, VI-152 pp., 1934.
92. Herrera, Rev. Antonio Parra, O.C.D., J.C.D., Legislacion Ecclesiastica sobra el Ayuno y la Abstinencia, XI-191 pp., 1935.
93. Kennedy, Rev. Edwin J., J.C.D., The Special Matrimonial Process in Cases of Evident Nullity, X-165 pp., 1935.
94. Manning, Rev. John J., A.B., J.C.D., Presumption of Law in Matrimonial Procedure, XI-111 pp., 1935.
95. Moeder, Rev. John M., J.C.D., The Proper Bishop for Ordination and Dismissorial Letters, VII-135 pp., 1935.
96. O'Mara, Rev. William A., A.B., J.C.D., Canonical Causes for Matrimonial Dispensations, IX-155 pp., 1935.
97. Reilly, Rev. Peter, J.C.D., Residence of Pastors, IX-81 pp., 1935.
98. Smith, Rev. Mariner T., O.P., S.T.Lr., J.C.D., The Penal Law for Religious, VIII-169 pp., 1935.
99. Whalen, Rev. Donald W., A.M., J.C.D., The Value of Testimonial Evidence in Matrimonial Procedure, XIII-297 pp., 1935.
100. Cleary, Rev. Joseph F., J.C.D., Canonical Limitations on the Alienation of Church Property, VIII-141 pp., 1936.
101. Glynn, Rev. John C., J.C.D., The Promoter of Justice, XX-337 pp., 1936.
102. Brennan, Rev. James H., S.S., M.A., S.T.B., J.C.D., The Simple Convalidation of Marriage, VI-135 pp., 1937.
103. Brunini, Rev. Joseph Bernard, J.C.D., The Clerical Obligations of Canons 139 and 142, X-121 pp., 1937.
104. Connor, Rev. Maurice, A.B., J.C.D., The Administrative Removal of Pastors, VIII-159 pp., 1937.
105. Guilfoyle, Rev. Merlin Joseph, J.C.D., Custom, XI-144 pp., 1937.
106. Hughes, Rev. James Austin, A.B., A.M., J.C.D., Witnesses in Criminal Trials of Clerics, IX-140 pp., 1937.
107. Jansen, Rev. Raymond J., A.B., S.T.L., J.C.D., Canonical Provisions for Catechetical Instruction, VII-153 pp., 1937.
108. Kealy, Rev. John James, A.B., J.C.D., The Introductory Libellus in Church Court Procedure, XI-121 pp., 1937.
109. McManus, Rev. James Edward, C.SS.R., J.C.D., The Administration of Temporal Goods in Religious Institutes, XVI-196 pp., 1937.

110. Moriarty, Rev. Eugene James, J.C.D., Oaths in Ecclesiastical Courts, X-115 pp., 1937.
111. Rainer, Rev. Eligius George, C.SS.R., J.C.D., Suspension of Clerics, XVII-249 pp., 1937.
112. Reilly, Rev. Thomas F., C.SS.R., J.C.D., Visitation of Religious, VI-195 pp., 1938.
113. Moriarty, Rev. Francis E., C.SS.R., J.C.D., The Extraordinary Absolution from Censures, XV-334 pp., 1938.
114. Connolly, Rev. Nicholas P., J.C.D., The Canonical Erection of Parishes, X-132 pp., 1938.
115. Donovan, Rev. James Joseph, J.C.D., The Pastor's Obligation in Prenuptial Investigation, XII-322 pp., 1938.
116. Harrigan, Rev. Robert J., M.A., S.T.B., J.C.D., The Radical Sanation of Invalid Marriages, VIII-208 pp., 1938.
117. Boffa, Rev. Conrad Humbert, J.C.D., Canonical Provisions for Catholic Schools, VII-211 pp., 1939.
118. Parsons, Rev. Anscar John, O.M.Cap., J.C.D., Canonical Elections, XII-236 pp., 1939.
119. Reilly, Rev. Edward Michael, A.B., J.C.D., The General Norms of Dispensation, XII-156 pp., 1939.
120. Ryan, Rev. Gerald Aloysius, A.B., J.C.D., Principles of Episcopal Jurisdiction, XII-172 pp., 1939.
121. Burton, Rev. Francis James, C.S.C., A.B., J.C.D., A Commentary on Canon 1125, X-222 pp., 1940.
122. Miaskiewicz, Rev. Francis Sigismund, J.C.D., Supplied Jurisdiction According to Canon 209, XII-340 pp., 1940.
123. Rice, Rev. Patrick William, A.B., J.C.D., Proof of Death in Prenuptial Investigation, VIII-156 pp., 1940.
124. Anglin, Rev. Thomas Francis, M.S., J.C.D., The Eucharistic Fast, VIII-183 pp., 1941.
125. Coleman, Rev. John Jerome, J.C.D., The Minister of Confirmation, VI-153 pp., 1941.
126. Downs, Rev. John Emmanuel, A.B., J.C.D., The Concept of Clerical Immunity, XI-163 pp., 1941.
127. Esswein, Rev. Anthony Albert, J.C.D., Extrajudicial Penal Powers of Ecclesiastical Superiors, X-144 pp., 1941.
128. Farrell, Rev. Benjamin Francis, M.A., S.T.L., J.C.D., The Rights and Duties of the Local Ordinary Regarding Congregations of Women Religious of Pontifical Approval, V-195 pp., 1941.
129. Feeney, Rev. Thomas John, A.B., S.T.L., J.C.D., Restitutio in Integrum, VI-169 pp., 1941.
130. Findlay, Rev. Stephen William, O.S.B., A.B., J.C.D., Canonical Norms Governing the Deposition and Degradation of Clerics, XVII-279 pp., 1941.

131. GOODWINE, REV. JOHN, A.B., S.T.L., J.C.D., The Right of the Church to Acquire Property, VIII-119 pp., 1941.
132. HESTON, REV. EDWARD LOUIS, C.S.C., Ph.D., S.T.D., J.C.D., The Alienation of Church Property in the United States, XII-222 pp., 1941.
133. HOGAN, REV. JAMES JOHN, A.B., S.T.L., J.C.D., Judicial Advocates and Procurators, XIII-200 pp., 1941.
134. KEALY, REV. THOMAS M., A.B., Litt.B., J.C.D., Dowry of Women Religious, IX-152 pp., 1941.
135. KEENE, REV. MICHAEL JAMES, O.S.B., J.C.D., Religious Ordinaries and Canon 198, V-164 pp., 1941 (printed 1942).
136. KERIN, REV. CHARLES A., S.S., M.A., S.T.B., J.C.D., The Privation of Christian Burial, XVI-279 pp., 1941.
137. LOUIS, REV. WILLIAM FRANCIS, M.A., J.C.D., Diocesan Archives, X-101 pp., 1941.
138. MCDEVITT, REV. GILBERT JOSEPH, A.B., J.C.D., Legitimacy and Legitimation, X-247 pp., 1941.
139. MCDONOUGH, REV. THOMAS JOSEPH, A.B., J.C.D., Apostolic Administrators, X-217 pp., 1941.
140. MEIER, REV. CARL ANTHONY, A.B., J.C.D., Penal Administrative Procedure Against Negligent Pastors, XI-240 pp., 1941.
141. SCHMIDT, REV. JOHN ROGG, A.B., J.C.D., The Principles of Authentic Interpretation in Canon 17 of the Code of Canon Law, XII-331 pp., 1941.
142. SLAFKOSKY, REV. ANDREW LEONARD, A.B., J.C.D., The Canonical Episcopal Visitation of the Diocese, X-197 pp., 1941.
143. SWOBODA, REV. INNOCENT ROBERT, O.F.M., J.C.D., Ignorance in Relation to the Imputability of Delicts, IX-271 pp., 1941.
144. DUBÉ, REV. ARTHUR JOSEPH, A.B., J.C.D., The General Principles for the Reckoning of Time in Canon Law, VIII-299 pp., 1941.
145. MCBRIDE, REV. JAMES T., A.B., J.C.D., Incardination and Excardination of Seculars, XX-585 pp., 1941.
146. KRÓL, REV. JOHN T., J.C.D., The Defendant in Ecclesiastical Trials, XII-207 pp., 1942.
147. COMYNS, REV. JOSEPH J., C.SS.R., A.B., J.C.D., Papal and Episcopal Administration of Church Property, XIV-155 pp., 1942.
148. BARRY, REV. GARRETT FRANCIS, O.M.I., J.C.D., Violation of the Cloister, XII-260 pp., 1942.
149. BOLDUC, REV. GATIEN, C.S.V., A.B., S.T.L., J.C.D., Les Études dans les Religions Cléricales, VIII-155 pp., 1942.
150. BOYLE, REV. DAVID JOHN, M.A., J.C.D., The Juridic Effects of Moral Certitude on Pre-Nuptial Guarantees, XII-188 pp., 1942.
151. CANAVAN, REV. WALTER JOSEPH, M.A., Litt.D., J.C.D., The Profession of Faith, XII-143 pp., 1942.
152. DESROCHERS, REV. BRUNO, A.B., Ph.L., S.T.B., J.C.D., Le Premier Concile Plénier de Québec et le Code de Droit Canonique, XIV-186 pp., 1942.

153. Dillon, Rev. Robert Edward, A.B., J.C.D., Common Law Marriage, X-148 pp., 1942.
154. Dodwell, Rev. Edward John, Ph.D., S.T.B., J.C.D., The Time and Place for the Celebration of Marriage, X-156 pp., 1942.
155. Donnellan, Rev. Thomas Andrew, A.B., J.C.D., The Obligation of the Missa pro Populo, VII-131 pp., 1942.
156. Eltz, Rev. Louis Anthony, A.B., J.C.D., Cooperation in Crime, XII-208 pp., 1942.
157. Gass, Rev. Sylvester Francis, M.A., J.C.D., Ecclesiastical Pensions, XI-206 pp., 1942.
158. Guiniven, Rev. John Joseph, C.SS.R., J.C.D., The Precept of Hearing Mass, XIV-188 pp., 1942.
159. Gulczynski, Rev. John Theophilus, J.C.D., The Desecration and Violation of Churches, X-126 pp., 1942.
160. Hammill, Rev. John Leo, M.A., J.C.D., The Obligations of the Traveler According to Canon 14, VIII-204 pp., 1942.
161. Haydt, Rev. John Joseph, A.B., J.C.D., Reserved Benefices, XI-148 pp., 1942.
162. Huser, Rev. Roger John, O.F.M., A.B., J.C.D., The Crime of Abortion in Canon Law, XII-187 pp., 1942.
163. Kearney, Rev. Francis Patrick, A.B., S.T.L., J.C.D., The Principles of Canon 1127, X-162 pp., 1942.
164. Linahen, Rev. Leo James, S.T.L., J.C.D., De Absolutione Complicis in Peccato Turpi, V-114 pp., 1942.
165. McCloskey, Rev. Joseph Aloysius, A.B., J.C.D., The Subject of Ecclesiastical Law According to Canon 12, XVII-246 pp., 1942 (printed 1943).
166. O'Neill, Rev. Francis Joseph, C.SS.R., J.C.D., The Dismissal of Religious in Temporary Vows, XIII-220 pp., 1942.
167. Prince, Rev. John Edward, A.B., S.T.B., J.C.D., The Diocesan Chancellor, X-136 pp., 1942.
168. Riesner, Rev. Albert Joseph, C.SS.R., J.C.D., Apostates and Fugitives from Religious Institutes, IX-168 pp., 1942.
169. Stenger, Rev. Joseph Bernard, J.C.D., The Mortgaging of Church Property, 186 pp., 1942.
170. Waldron, Rev. Joseph Francis, A.B., J.C.D., The Minister of Baptism, XII-197 pp., 1942.
171. Willett, Rev. Robert Albert, J.C.D., The Probative Value of Documents in Ecclesiastical Trials, X-124 pp., 1942.
172. Woeber, Rev. Edward Martin, M.A., J.C.D., The Interpellations, XII-161 pp., 1942.
173. Benko, Rev. Matthew Aloysius, O.S.B., M.A., J.C.D., The Abbot *Nullius*, XVI-148 pp., 1943.

174. Christ, Rev. Joseph James, M.A., S.T.L., J.C.D., Dispensation from Vindicative Penalties, XIV-285 pp., 1943.

175. Clancy, Rev. Patrick M. J., O.P., A.B., S.T.Lr., J.C.D., The Local Religious Superior, X-229 pp., 1943.

176. Clarke, Rev. Thomas James, J.C.D., Parish Societies, XII-147 pp., 1943.

177. Connolly, Rev. John Patrick, S.T.L., J.C.D., Synodal Examiners and Parish Priest Consultors, X-223 pp., 1943.

178. Drumm, Rev. William Martin, A.B., J.C.D., Hospital Chaplains, XII-175 pp., 1943.

179. Flanagan, Rev. Bernard Joseph, A.B., S.T.L., J.C.D., The Canonical Erection of Religious Houses, X-147 pp., 1943.

180. Kelleher, Rev. Stephen Joseph, A.B., S.T.B., J.C.D., Discussions with Non-Catholics: Canonical Legislation, X-93 pp., 1943.

181. Lewis, Rev. Gordian, C.P., J.C.D., Chapters in Religious Institutes, XII-169 pp., 1943.

182. Marx, Rev. Adolph, J.C.D., The Declaration of Nullity of Marriages Contracted Outside the Church, X-151 pp., 1943.

183. Matulenas, Rev. Raymond Anthony, O.S.B., A.B., J.C.D., Communication, a Source of Privileges, XII-225 pp., 1943.

184. O'Leary, Rev. Charles Gerard, C.SS.R., J.C.D., Religious Dismissed After Perpetual Profession, X-213 pp., 1943.

185. Power, Rev. Cornelius Michael, J.C.D., The Blessing of Cemeteries, XII-231 pp., 1943.

186. Shuhler, Rev. Ralph Vincent, O.S.A., J.C.D., Privileges of Religious to Absolve and Dispense, XII-195 pp., 1943.

187. Ziolkowski, Rev. Thaddeus Stanislaus, A.B., J.C.D., The Consecration and Blessing of Churches, XII-151 pp., 1943.

188. Heneghan, Rev. John Joseph, S.T.D., J.C.D., The Marriages of Unworthy Catholics: Canons 1065 and 1066, XVI-213 pp., 1944.

189. Carroll, Rev. Coleman Francis, M.A., S.T.L., J.C.L., Charitable Institutions.

190. Ciesluk, Rev. Joseph Edward, Ph.B., S.T.L., J.C.D., National Parishes in the United States, VI-178 pp., 1944.

191. Coburn, Rev. Vincent Paul, A.B., J.C.D., Marriages of Conscience, XII-172 pp., 1944.

192. Connors, Rev. Charles Paul, C.S.Sp., A.B., J.C.D., Extra-Judicial Procurators in the Code of Canon Law, X-94 pp., 1944.

193. Coyle, Rev. Paul Raymond, A.B., J.C.D., Judicial Exceptions, X-142 pp., 1944.

194. Fair, Rev. Bartholomew Francis, A.B., S.T.L., J.C.D., The Impediment of Abduction, XII-122 pp., 1944.

195. Gallagher, Rev. Thomas Raphael, O.P., A.B., S.T.Lr., J.C.D., The Examination of the Qualities of the Ordinand, X-166 pp., 1944.

196. Gannon, Rev. John Mark, S.T.L., J.C.D., The Interstices Required for the Promotion to Orders, XII-100 pp., 1944.
197. Goldsmith, Rev. J. William, B.C.S., S.T.L., J.C.D., The Competence of Church and State Over Marriages—Disputed Points, X-128 pp., 1944.
198. Goodwine, Rev. Joseph Gerard, A.B., S.T.B., J.C.D., The Reception of Converts, XIV-326 pp., 1944.
199. Kowalski, Rev. Romuald Eugene, O.F.M., A.B., J.C.D., Sustenance of Religious Houses of Regulars, X-174 pp., 1944.
200. McCoy, Rev. Alan Edward, O.F.M., J.C.D., Force and Fear in Relation to Delictual Imputability and Penal Responsibility, XII-160 pp., 1944.
201. McDevitt, Rev. Vincent John, Ph.B., S.T.L., J.C.L., Perjury.
202. Martin, Rev. Thomas Owen, Ph.D., S.T.D., J.C.D., Adverse Possession, Prescription and Limitation of Actions: The Canonical "Praescriptio," XX-208 pp., 1944.
203. Miklosovic, Rev. Paul John, A.B., J.C.L., Attempted Marriages and Their Consequent Juridic Effects.
204. Mundy, Rev. Thomas Maurice, A.B., S.T.L., J.C.D., The Union of Parishes, X-164 pp., 1944.
205. O'Dea, Rev. John Coyle, A.B., J.C.D., The Matrimonial Impediment of Nonage, VIII-126 pp., 1944.
206. Olalia, Rev. Alexander Ayson, S.T.L., J.C.D., A Comparative Study of the Christian Constitution of States and the Constitution of the Philippine Commonwealth, XII-136 pp., 1944.
207. Poisson, Rev. Pierre-Marie, C.S.C., A.B., Ph.L., Th.L., J.C.L., Droits Patrimoniaux des Maisons et des Eglises Religieuses.
208. Stadalnikas, Rev. Casimir Joseph, M.I.C., J.C.D., Reservation of Censures, X-141 pp., 1944.
209. Sullivan, Rev. Eugene Henry, S.T.L., J.C.D., Proof of the Reception of the Sacraments, X-165 pp., 1944.
210. Vaughan, Rev. William Edward, J.C.D., Constitutions for Diocesan Courts, X-210 pp., 1944.
211. Paro, Rev. Gino, S.T.D., J.C.D., The Right of Papal Legation, X-221 pp., 1944 (printed 1947).
212. Balzer, Rev. Ralph Francis, C.P., J.C.D., The Computation of Time in a Canonical Novitiate, X-227 pp., 1945.
213. Dougherty, Rev. John Whelan, A.B., S.T.L., J.C.D., De Inquisitione Speciali, XII-195 pp., 1945.
214. Dziob, Rev. Michael Walter, J.C.D., The Sacred Congregation for the Oriental Church, XII-181 pp., 1945.
215. Eidenschink, Rev. John Albert, O.S.B., B.A., J.C.D., The Election of Bishops in the Letters of Pope Gregory the Great, VIII-200 pp., 1945.
216. Gill, Rev. Nicholas, C.P., J.C.D., The Spiritual Prefect in Clerical Religious Houses of Study, X-140 pp., 1945.

217. Hynes, Rev. Harry Gerard, S.T.L., J.C.D., The Privileges of Cardinals, XII-183 pp., 1945.
218. McDevitt, Rev. Gerald Vincent, S.T.L., J.C.D., The Renunciation of an Ecclesiastical Office, XIV-179 pp., 1945.
219. Manning, Rev. Joseph Leroy, J.C.D., The Free Conferral of Offices, VII-116 pp., 1945.
220. Meyer, Rev. Louis G., O.S.B., A.B., S.T.B., J.C.D., Alms-gathering by Religious, XII-163 pp., 1945.
221. O'Donnell, Rev. Cletus Francis, M.A., J.C.D., The Marriage of Minors, XII-268 pp., 1945.
222. Prunskis, Rev. Joseph, J.C.D., Comparative Law, Ecclesiastical and Civil, in Lithuanian Concordat, X-161 pp., 1945.
223. Sweeney, Rev. Francis Patrick, C.SS.R., J.C.D., The Reduction of Clerics to the Lay State, X-199 pp., 1945.
224. Vogelpohl, Rev. Henry John, J.C.D., The Simple Impediments to Holy Orders, XVI-190 pp., 1945.
225. Brockhaus, Rev. Thomas Aquinas, O.S.B., J.C.D., Religious who are known as *Conversi*, X-127 pp., 1945.
226. Griese, Rev. Orville Nicholas, S.T.D., J.C.D., The Marriage Contract and the Procreation of Offspring, XVI-224 pp., 1946.
227. Boudreaux, Rev. Warren Louis, J.C.D., The *"ab acatholicis nati"* of Canon 1099, § 2, XII-110 pp., 1946.
228. Bowe, Rev. Thomas Joseph, A.B., J.C.D., Religious Superioresses, VIII-206 pp., 1946.
229. Diederichs, Rev. Michael Ferdinand, S.C.J., J.C.D., The Jurisdiction of the Latin Ordinaries over their Oriental Subjects, XIV-153 pp., 1946.
230. Dingman, Rev. Maurice John, A.B., S.T.L., J.C.L., The Plaintiff in Contentious Trials.
231. Frison, Rev. Basil, C.M.F., M.Mus., J.C.D., The Retroactivity of Law, X-221 pp., 1946.
232. Galvin, Rev. William Anthony, M.A., J.C.D., The Administrative Transfer of Pastors, XII-288 pp., 1946.
233. Goracy, Rev. Joseph C., J.C.L., The Diriment Matrimonial Impediment of Major Orders.
234. Hale, Rev. Joseph Francis, M.A., S.T.L., J.C.D., The Pastor of Burial, X-247 pp., 1946 (printed 1949).
235. Henry, Rev. Joseph Arthur, A.B., J.C.D., The Mass and Holy Communion: Interritual Law, XII-138 pp., 1946.
236. Linenberger, Rev. Herbert, C.PP.S., J.C.D., The False Denunciation of an Innocent Confessor, VIII-205 pp., 1946 (1949).
237. Lowry, Rev. James Martin, A.B., J.C.D., Dispensation from Private Vows, XII-266 pp., 1946.
238. Lynch, Rev. George Edward, A.B., S.T.L., J.C.D., Coadjutors and Auxiliaries of Bishops, X-107 pp., 1946 (printed 1947).

239. Lynch, Rev. Timothy, M.S.SS.T., J.C.D., Contracts between Bishops and Religious Congregations, XIII-232 pp., 1946.
240. McClunn, Rev. Justin David, A.B., S.T.L., J.C.D., Administrative Recourse, VII-142 pp., 1946.
241. Lohmuller, Rev. Martin Nicholas, A.B., J.C.D., The Promulgation of Law, XII-140 pp., 1947.
242. McGrath, Rev. James, A.B., J.C.D., The Privilege of the Canon, XII-156 pp., 1946.
243. Marbach, Rev. Joseph Francis, A.B., J.C.D., Marriage Legislation for the Catholics of the Oriental Rites in the United States and Canada, XIV-314 pp., 1946.
244. Shimkus, Rev. Bernard Aloysius, A.B., J.C.L., The Determination and Transfer of Rite.
245. Smith, Rev. Vincent Michael, A.B., S.T.L., J.C.L., Ignorance Affecting Matrimonial Consent.
246. Wachtrle, Rev. Paul Anthony, A.B., J.C.L., The Baptism of the Children of Non-Catholics.
247. Crotty, Rev. Matthew Michael, J.C.D., The Recipient of First Holy Communion, X-142 pp., 1947.
248. Eagleton, Rev. George, J.C.D., The Quinquennial Faculties, Formula IV, XIV-199 pp., 1947 (printed 1948).
249. Gibbons, Rev. Marion Leo, C.M., J.C.L., Domicile of the Wife Unlawfully Separated from Her Husband, XIV-171 pp., 1947.
250. Kelly, Rev. Bernard M., S.T.L., J.C.D., The Functions Reserved to Pastors, XII-141 pp., 1947.
251. Kilcullen, Rev. Thomas J., LL.M., J.C.D., The Collegiate Moral Person as Party Litigant, X-150 pp., 1947.
252. Lafontaine, Rev. Germaine Joseph, W.F., J.C.D., Relations Canoniques entre le Missionaire et Ses Superieurs, X-117 pp., 1947.
253. Lane, Rev. Loras Thomas, A.B., S.T.L., J.C.D., Matrimonial Procedure in the Ordinary Court of Second Instance, XVI-184 pp., 1947.
254. Lover, Rev. James Francis, C.Ss.R., J.C.D., The Master of Novices, X-168 pp., 1947.
255. McNicholas, Rev. Timothy Joseph, J.C.L., The *Septimae Manus* Witness.
256. Marositz, Rev. Joseph John, M.S.C., J.C.D., Obligations and Privileges of Religious Promoted to the Episcopal or Cardinalitial Dignities, XII-180 pp., 1947.
257. Murphy, Rev. Francis Joseph, J.C.D., Legislative Powers of the Provincial Council, XII-158 pp., 1947.
258. O'Brien, Rev. Romaeus William, O.Carm., J.C.D., The Provincial Superior in Religious Orders of Men, X-294 pp., 1947.
259. Pfaller, Rev. Benedict Anthony, O.S.B., J.C.D., *The ipso facto* Effected Dismissal of Religious, XII-225 pp., 1947.

260. POPEK, REV. ALPHONSE SYLVESTER, J.C.D., The Rights and Obligations of Metropolitans, XX-460 pp., 1947.
261. RISTUCCIA, REV. BERNARD JOSEPH, C.M., J.C.D., Quasi-Religious, XVI-318 pp., 1947 (printed 1949).
262. SONNTAG, REV. NATHANIEL LOUIS, O.F.M.Cap., J.C.D., Censorship of Special Classes of Books, XII-147 pp., 1947.
263. STADLER, REV. JOSEPH NICHOLAS, J.C.D., Frequent Holy Communion, X-158 pp., 1947.
264. SZAL, REV. IGNATIUS JOSEPH, J.C.D., The Communication of Catholics with Schismatics, XII-217 pp., 1947.
265. WAGNER, REV. URBAN S., O.F.M. Conv., J.C.D., Parochial Substitute Vicars and Supplying Priests, IX-126 pp., 1947.
266. QUINN, REV. JOSEPH, M.A., J.C.D., Documents Required for the Reception of Orders, XIV-207 pp., 1948.
267. BENNINGTON, REV. JAMES CLEMENT, A.B., J.C.L., The Recipient of Confirmation.
268. BLAHER, REV. DAMIAN JOSEPH, O.F.M., A.B., J.C.L., The Ordinary Processes in Causes of Beatification and Canonization.
269. CLUNE, REV. ROBERT BELL, B.A., J.C.L., The Judicial Interrogation of the Parties.
270. COURTEMANCHE, REV. BASIL F., B.A., J.C.L., The Total Simulation of Matrimonial Consent.
271. DLOUHY, REV. MAUR JOHN, O.S.B., A.B., J.C.L., The Ordination of Exempt Religious.
272. DONOVAN, REV. JOHN THOMAS, PH.B., S.T.L., J.C.D., The Clerical Obligation of Canons 138 and 140, XII-209 pp., 1948.
273. FREKING, REV. FREDERICK W., A.B., S.T.B., J.C.L., The Canonical Installation of Pastors.
274. FULTON, REV. THOMAS B., J.C.L., Prenuptial Investigation.
275. GODLEY, REV. JAMES P., J.C.L., Time and Place for the Celebration of Mass.
276. KANE, REV. THOMAS A., A.B., B.S., J.C.D., Jurisdiction of the Patriarchs of the Major Sees, XII-153 pp., 1948 (printed 1949).
277. KENNEDY, REV. ANDREW A., J.C.L., The Annual Pastoral Report to the Local Ordinary.
278. KONRAD, REV. JOSEPH GEORGE, J.C.L., Transfer of Religious.
279. KRESS, REV. ALPHONSE, J.C.L., Contumacy in Ecclesiastical Trials.
280. MCCARTNEY, REV. MARCELLUS ANTHONY, O.F.M., M.A., J.C.L., Faculties of Regular Confessors.
281. MCCASLIN, REV. EDWARD PATRICK, M.A., S.T.L., J.C.L., The Division of Parishes.
282. MCELROY, REV. FRANCIS J., A.B., J.C.L., The Privileges of Bishops.

283. QUINN, REV. STEPHEN, M.S.SS.T., J.C.D., Relation Between the Local Ordinary and Religious of Diocesan Approval, XII-153 pp., 1948 (printed 1949).
284. SCHNEIDER, REV. EDELHARD LOUIS, S.D.S., B.A., J.C.L., The Status of Secularized Ex-Religious Clerics, X-155 pp., 1948.
285. THOMPSON, CHESTER J., A.B., J.C.L., The Simple Removal from Office.
286. O'BRIEN, REV. KENNETH R., A.B., J.C.D., The Nature of Support of Diocesan Priests in the United States, XVI-162 pp., 1949.
287. METZ, REV. JOHN E., S.T.L., J.C.D., The Recording Judge in the Ecclesiastical Collegiate Tribunal, X-130 pp., 1949.
288. REINHARDT, REV. MARION J., S.T.L., J.C.L., The Rogatory Commission.
289. ORTEGA UHIUK, REV. JUAN, S.J., J.C.L., De Delicto Sollicitationis.
290. CASEY, REV. JAMES V., J.C.L., A Study of Canon 2222 § 1.
291. ALLGEIER, REV. JOSEPH L., J.C.L., The Canonical Obligation of Preaching in Parish Churches.
292. CAHILL, REV. DANIEL R., J.C.L., The Custody of the Holy Eucharist.
293. CARR, REV. AIDEN, O.F.M. Carm., S.T.D., J.C.L., Vocation to the Priesthood: Its Canonical Concept.
294. KNOPKE, REV. ROCH F., O.F.M., J.C.L., Reverential Fear in Matrimonial Cases in Asiatic Countries: Rota Cases.
295. LAVELLE, REV. HOWARD D., J.C.L., The Obligation of Holding Sacred Missions in Parishes.
296. MICKELLS, REV. ANTHONY B., J.C.L., The Constitutive Elements of Parishes.
297. NOONE, REV. JOHN J., J.C.L., Nullity in Judicial Acts.
298. SHEEHAN, REV. DANIEL E., J.C.L., The Minister of Holy Communion.
299. STATKUS, REV. FRANCIS J., J.C.L., The Minister of the Last Sacraments.
300. COOK, REV. JOHN P., J.C.L., Ecclesiastical Communities and Their Ability to Induce Legal Customs.
301. FAZZALARO, REV. FRANCIS J., J.C.L., The Place for the Hearing of Confessions.
302. HANNAN, REV. PHILIP M., J.C.L., The Canonical Concept of *congrua sustentatio* for the Secular Clergy.
303. QUINN, REV. HUGH G., S.T.L., J.C.L., The Particular Penal Precept.
304. GALLAGHER, REV. JOHN F., J.C.L., The Matrimonial Impediment of Public Propriety.
305. WELSH, REV. THOMAS J., J.C.L., The Use of the Portable Altar.

www.ingramcontent.com/pod-product-compliance
Lightning Source LLC
LaVergne TN
LVHW050234080826
844660LV00012B/530

* 9 7 8 0 8 1 3 2 2 4 6 4 0 *